THE LEBANESE CIVIL WAR

Marius Deeb

THE LEBANESE CIVIL WAR

Foreword by Charles Issawi

PRAEGER

PRAEGER SPECIAL STUDIES • PRAEGER SCIENTIFIC

Library of Congress Cataloging in Publication Data

Deeb, Marius.
    The Lebanese civil war.

    Bibliography: p.
    Includes index.
    1. Lebanon--History--Civil War, 1975-
I. Title.
DS87.5.D43   1980   956.92'04   79-19833
ISBN 0-03-039701-4

Published in 1980 by Praeger Publishers
CBS Educational and Professional Publishing
A Division of CBS, Inc.
521 Fifth Avenue, New York, New York 10017 U.S.A.

© 1980 by Praeger Publishers

0123456789   038   987654321

Printed in the United States of America

To my parents
who went through the ordeal of the Civil War,
to my wife
who as always shares my work and my ideas,
and to our son, Hadi.

FOREWORD
by Charles Issawi

Few conflicts have as tangled roots as the Civil War in Lebanon. One can view it as a communal struggle between Christians (more precisely Maronites) and Muslims, and a continuation of the clashes of 1845, 1860, and 1958. It is also a class conflict, pitting the poor—particularly the slumdwellers of Beirut and the refugees from the war-torn South—against those who have been so greatly enriched by the wealth flowing from Arab oil. It is moreover a political battle between leaders like Shamun, Franjie, the late Kamal Junblatt, Salam and others. These men were driven mostly by personal ambitions but also fought over questions of constitutional reform, in particular the power of the Presidency and the basis of Parliamentary elections. They differed in their economic and social philosophy, their emphasis on the role of the state, and their desire to control the private sector. In addition, there was a fundamental opposition between those who stressed Lebanon's "Arabness" and those who saw it as essentially a Mediterranean country, that is, culturally, economically, and politically oriented toward the West. To make matters worse, the lines of cleavage did not cut across each other—as did those between Protestants and Catholics, Germans and French, rich and poor in Switzerland during the Sonderbund and the Civil War of 1847—but to a large extent coincided and therefore widened the social fissures.

Nevertheless, Lebanon managed to cope with these tensions for some 30 years after its independence in 1943. In the process, it became the freest, most highly educated, and most tolerant and hospitable of the Arab countries. It was also the one in which the mass of the people enjoyed the greatest well-being and dignity. It might have continued to do so and even to carry out some reforms in its obsolete political and administrative institutions, but for the burden imposed by the unresolved Arab-Israeli conflict and the presence of the Palestinian refugees. Their increasing guerrilla raids into Israel, and the indiscriminate Israeli retaliations, not only created unrest and caused much loss of life and property, but polarized the Lebanese. One faction felt they owed the Palestinians the greatest possible measure of support while the other saw in them an armed state more powerful than and a threat to the very existence of Lebanon.

The Palestinian problem merged into the broader question of inter-Arab relations and great power rivalries. Nearly 20 years ago I wrote, "Lebanon is too conspicuous and successful an example of political democracy and economic liberalism to be tolerated in a region that has turned its back on both systems." There is no doubt that sheer envy, and dislike of an uncongenial, disturbing, and fundamentally alien phenomenon helped to determine some Arab states' attitude toward Lebanon in 1975, as had happened in 1958. But other issues were also at stake, including conflicting ambitions and ideologies.

Marius Deeb has provided a factual, well-documented, analytical, and remarkably objective account of the circumstances that led to the Civil War and the events thereafter. All who are interested in understanding the tragic conflict in Lebanon—a country which has played, and is still playing, a leading role in the cultural life of the Arab world—can read this scholarly book with great profit.

Charles Issawi

PREFACE

Lebanon came into being, in its present political form, in 1943, with its struggle for independence and the National Pact. The Civil War of 1958, however, uncovered some of the National Pact's fundamental weaknesses and foreshadowed the events which were to come almost two decades later. Under the Shihabist era, a successful attempt was made to reaffirm the National Pact, both domestically and on the Arab level, in a manner which suited the times, and in effect stabilized the political system.

The Civil War of 1975-76, nevertheless, demonstrated again how precarious the foundations of the Lebanese political community still were. Thus the questions which had seemed satisfactorily answered by the National Pact of 1943, have been raised once again: What kind of a political system is Lebanon now to have? What are the changes, both political and socioeconomic, that are necessary for the viability of Lebanon as a political community?

A mere recounting of the major events, alliances, and battles of the Civil War would appear, at best, confusing to the reader unfamiliar with the complexities of Lebanese and inter-Arab politics. I have therefore attempted in this study to explain the events of the Civil War of 1975-76 from the perspective of each of the major participants involved. I have examined the attitudes, political stands, and objectives of the parties, organizations, groups, and prominent politicians. It is only by understanding what each was fighting for that a comprehensive picture of the Civil War can emerge.

This study of the Civil War of 1975-76 was also sketched against a background of inter-Arab politics. Lebanon has always been a microcosm of the Arab world because it reflects the rivalries and squabbles of the Arab powers. One could even say that the interplay of Arab powers on the Lebanese stage, during the Civil War of 1975-76, was an enactment of inter-Arab politics in the Arab world today.

The study of the Civil War was divided on the basis of two criteria. The first is an ordering of the principal events themselves, in seven stages, each marked by major turning points affecting the relations of the participants to each other and leading to new developments in the Civil War itself. Although these events affected each group in different ways, they were chosen for their overall significance to the Lebanese crisis as a whole. The second criterion was the categorization of the major participants in the Civil War. A great many organizations, parties, groups, and so on, were involved. We have attempted to classify them into five broad categories: first, the conservative Lebanese parties and organizations, which were predominantly Maronite, and included the Phalangist Party, Sham'un's Party, Franjiya, and the Lebanese Maronite orders of monks, and several other minor organizations. The word "conservative" is used in this study in the economic sense, meaning strongly anti-Communist parties believing in a free enterprise economic system. Some of these elements were politically closer to social democrats, and still others were more the left on the issue of secularism than their Muslim counterparts. The second group was the traditional Muslim leaders, both Sunni and Shi'ite, who also tended to be conservative-centrists on socioeconomic matters, but had Arab nationalist leanings. The third group comprised the parties and organizations of the National Movement, which included Marxist-Leninists, social democrats, and nationalists, whether Arab or Syrian, with reformist tendencies. The fourth group was composed of the organizations of the Palestinian Resistance Movement, with its moderate and radical components. And, finally, the fifth actor in the Civil War was Syria, with its Lebanese and Palestinian allies and supporters. Thus, the Civil War of 1975-76 will be analyzed in terms of the interplay of these major forces, their leadership struggles, conflicts, and alliances, in a roughly chronological sequence based on the seven stages mentioned above.

The sources on which this work is based are almost entirely primary. I have used the speeches, statements, manifestos, interviews, and documents of all the major groups concerned, as they appeared in the daily newspapers, periodicals, or separately published pamphlets or leaflets. The free press of Lebanon became even freer in the anarchy of the Civil War, and the reports on the activities of the parties were covered quite objectively by those newspapers that were nonpartisan. The memoirs and diaries of prominent leaders also proved to be very enlightening, especially those of Kamal Junblat and Camille Sham'un. I also conducted key interviews with major observers of and participants in the Civil War.

ACKNOWLEDGMENTS

This book owes much to many friends and colleagues, some of whom read and commented on the manuscript and others who shared with me their insights on the Civil War in Lebanon.

I cannot thank all and everyone here, so I just wish to express my very special gratitude to Professor Robert L. Tignor, Chairman of the History Department, and to Professor John Marks and the members of the Near East Studies Department at Princeton, who made it possible for me to spend a most exciting and stimulating year as Visiting Fellow of the Near East Department, where I was able to write most of the manuscript for this book. I am most grateful to Professor Charles Issawi for having read my manuscript and written the forward to it, and for all his kindness and his help throughout my stay in Princeton. I also wish to thank Professor L. Carl Brown for reading my manuscript and expressing a continued interest in my work. I owe an intellectual debt to Professor Albert Hourani of Oxford University, whose writings have been a source of inspiration to me and who was kind enough to read and comment on my manuscript. Professor Michael C. Hudson, of the Center for Contemporary Arab Studies at Georgetown University, made many invaluable comments concerning my work, for which I am deeply grateful. I also wish to thank Professor Walid Khalidi, of the American University of Beirut, who gave willingly of his time to discuss with me many aspects of the Civil War, and L. Dean Brown, President of the Middle East Institute, who deepened my understanding of the U.S. role in the Lebanese conflict. Last but not least I want to express my thanks to Ghassan Tuwaini, Lebanese Ambassador to the United Nations, for the fruitful and stimulating discussions we had on the Lebanese situation.

CONTENTS

LIST OF ACTIVE ORGANIZATIONS
DURING THE CIVIL WAR, 1975–76

The Conservative Lebanese Front, also known as the Kufur Front and the Front for Freedom and Man in Lebanon (FFML)

Phalangist Party: led by Pierre Jumayil; its militia led by Bashir Jumayil
National Liberal Party: led by Camille Sham'un; its militia, al-Numur, led by Nihad Shalhat
Al Tanzim: led by Fu'ad Shamali
Guardians of the Cedars: led by Etienne Saqr
Zghartan Liberation Army (Marada Brigade): led by Toni Franjiya
The Permanent Congress of the Lebanese Orders of Monks: led by Sharbal Qassis

Parties, Organizations, and Militias Allied to the Conservative Lebanese Front

Zahla Bloc: led by Ilyas al-Harawi
Lebanon's Army: led by Major Fu'ad Malik
Mountain Brigade: led by Henri Sfair
'Akkar Brigade: led by army officers from 'Akkar
Al-Muqaddamin Brigade: led by local leaders from Bsharri
Lebanese Youth Movement: led by Marun al-Khuri
Fayadiya army units: led by Colonel Antoine Barakat

The National Movement (led by Kamal Junblat)

Progressive Socialist Party: led by Kamal Junblat
Independent Nasirites' Movement: led by Ibrahim Qulailat; its militia was *al-Murabitun*
Lebanese Communist Party: led by Niqula al-Shawi
Arab Socialist Ba'th Party: led by 'Abd al-Majid al-Rafi'i
Organization of Communist Action: led by Muhsin Ibrahim
Arab Socialist Action Party: led by George Habash
Syrian Social Nationalist Party: led by In'am Ra'd
Arab Socialist Union in Lebanon: led by Khalid Shihab and Kamal Yunis
Union of the Forces of the Working People—Corrective Movement: led by 'Isam al-'Arab; its militia was *Quwwat Nasir*

The 24th of October Democratic Socialist Movement: led by Faruq al-Muqaddam
National Christians' Front
Populist Nasirite Organization: led by Mustafa Sa'd
(Allied to the NM was Lebanon's Arab Army, led by Ahmad al-Khatib.)

Organizations in which Traditional Muslim Leaders Participated

Muslim Bloc
National Union Front
National Muslim Front

The Nationalist Front (pro-Syrian during the Civil War)

Organization of the Ba'th Party: led by 'Asim Qansu
Union of the Forces of the Working People: led by Kamal Shatila
Syrian Social Nationalist Party: a faction led by Ilyas Qanaizah
The Movement of the Disinherited: led by Imam Musa al-Sadr; its militia was
    Amal
The Progressive Vanguards: led by Muhammad Zakariya 'Itani
(Kamal al-As'ad and his parliamentary Democratic Socialist Party were only
    allied to the Nationalist Front and not part of it.)

The Palestinian Resistance Movement during the Civil War

Fath: led by Yasir 'Arafat
Popular Democratic Front for the Liberation of Palestine: led by Nayif Hawatima
Popular Front for the Liberation of Palestine: led by George Habash
Popular Front for the Liberation of Palestine—General Command: led by Ahmad
    Jabril
Sa'iqa Organization: led by Zuhair Muhsin
Arab Liberation Front: led by 'Abd al-Wahhab al-Kayyali
Populist Struggle Front: led by Bahjat Abu Gharbiya

LIST OF ABBREVIATIONS

ADF	Arab Deterrent Force
AFSPR	Arab Front in Support of the Palestinian Revolution
ALF	Arab Liberation Front
ANM	Arab Nationalist Movement
ASAP	Arab Socialist Action Party
ASBP	Arab Socialist Ba'th Party
ASUL	Arab Socialist Union in Lebanon
CLF	Conservative Lebanese Front (or simply Lebanese Front; same as FFML or the Kufur Front)
CPC	Central Political Council (of National Movement)
FFML	The Front of Freedom and Man in Lebanon (same as the CLF or the Kufur Front)
FNPPF	Front of National and Progressive Parties and Forces (same as the National Movement)
FPPOP	Front of Progressive Parties, Organizations, and Personalities
HCC	High Coordination Committee (sometimes HMCC)
HMC	High Military Committee (or Tripartite HMC)
INM	Independent Nasirites' Movement
LAA	Lebanon's Arab Army
LCP	Lebanese Communist Party
NDC	National Dialogue Committee
NLP	National Liberal Party
NM	The National Movement (better known than its original name, FNPPF)
NUF	National Union Front
OBP	Organization of the Ba'th Party
OCA	Organization of Communist Action
OLS	Organization of Lebanese Socialists
PDFLP	Popular Democratic Front for the Liberation of Palestine
PFLP	Popular Front for the Liberation of Palestine
PFLP-GC	Popular Front for the Liberation of Palestine—General Command
PLA	Palestine Liberation Army
PLO	Palestine Liberation Organization
PNO	Populist Nasirite Organization
PRM	Palestinian Resistance Movement
PSP	Progressive Socialist Party
SSNP	Syrian Social Nationalist Party
UFWP	Union of the Forces of the Working People
UFWP-CM	Union of the Forces of the Working People—The Corrective Movement

1

THE SEVEN PHASES OF
THE CIVIL WAR IN LEBANON:
AN APERÇU

THE FIRST PHASE: APRIL 13–JUNE 30, 1975

This phase was characterized by fighting between the Palestinians and the Phalangist Party, which resulted in a cabinet crisis and in turn was transformed into a conflict among the Lebanese themselves. It ended with the formation of the six-member "Salvation Cabinet" of Karami.

The civil war can be divided into seven phases. The first phase began on April 13, 1975, when a bus with mostly Palestinian, as well as some Lebanese, passengers was ambushed by a group of armed Phalangists at 'Ain al-Rummanah suburb of Beirut. It was coming from a political rally and was on its way to Tal al-Za'tar. Twenty-seven passengers were killed and 20 others were wounded. This incident triggered heavy fighting between the Phalangists and the Palestinian Resistance Movement (PRM). Prime Minister Rashid al-Sulh, who was backed by Kamal Junblat and his leftist allies, was forced to resign on May 15, 1975 after the resignation of the Phalangist and National Liberal cabinet members and their allies. Their resignation was in protest to Junblat's attempt to boycott and isolate politically, in both Lebanon and the Arab world, the Phalangist Party, which Junblat believed was responsible for the bus ambush. Junblat and his leftist and Palestinian allies accused the Phalangists of seeking a confrontation with the Palestinian Resistance Movement. Outgoing Prime Minister Rashid al-Sulh concurred with this view and said so in his statement explaining the reasons for his resignation. This incurred the wrath of the Phalangists, and the fighting resumed.

Rashid al-Sulh's resignation demonstrated the precariousness and weakness of the prime minister as compared with the president of the republic. Rashid Karami, an ex-prime minister and prominent Sunni leader, reiterated his intention of running in the next presidential elections and maintained that the position of the prime minister in Lebanon had become ineffective and devoid of any real power in decision making. Since the resignation of the prominent Sunni leader, Sa'ib Salam, in April 1973, over the issue of whether General Iskandar Ghanim, commander in chief of the army, was to be dismissed because of his passive role when Israelis raided Beirut and assassinated three major leaders of the Palestinian Resistance Movement on April 11, 1973, President Franjiya had begun appointing a series of relatively weak prime ministers. Amin Hafiz, one of the newly appointed prime ministers, was a deputy from Tripoli, who won his seat on Rashid Karami's list, and had no significant power of his own. Taqiy al-Din al-Sulh, an ex-deputy, was another of President Franjiya's choices, who belonged to the distinguished al-Sulh family, but did not have a powerful popular base. And lastly, Rashid al-Sulh owed his seat partly to Junblat's support and was backed in his cabinet by Junblat himself and his allies, but was regarded by the Sunni establishment as a novice, and therefore not strong enough to withstand the formidable powers of the president.

This process of the weakening of the premiership culminated in the decision taken by the president to form a completely military cabinet (except for one civilian), on May 23, 1975, headed by Nur al-Din al-Rifa'i. This was an unprecedented act. The immediate reaction of the Sunni establishment was to ask al-Rifa'i to resign. Fighting and clashes between the Phalangists and their allies on the one hand, and the National Movement and their Palestinian allies, on the other, immediately followed the announcement of the military cabinet. This prompted Syria to send its Minister of Foreign Affairs 'Abd al-Halim Khaddam and Vice-Minister of Defense General Naji Jamil to mediate.

Rifa'i's military cabinet lasted only three days. It was forced to resign on May 21, 1975, and Rashid Karami was asked to form a new cabinet. He was chosen by the Sunni leadership as the sole candidate for the post, and was imposed upon the president himself with some decisive pressure from Syria on his behalf.

Rashid Karami's task was not an easy one. Fighting continued uninterruptedly throughout the month of June 1975. Karami, faced with Junblat's position of boycotting and isolating the Phalangists, had to rely on Syrian mediation and help to form a new cabinet. After two crucial visits to Lebanon by Syrian Foreign Minister Khaddam, on June 16 and June 29, a six-man cabinet was formed on June 30, 1975. Prime Minister Rashid Karami also became minister of defense, and ex-President Camille Sham'un, the leader of the National Liberal Party, and close ally of the Phalangist Party, held the important post of minister of the interior. The formation of the *Inqadh* or Salvation Cabinet was announced on July 1, 1975, and ended the first phase of the Lebanese Civil War.

THE SECOND PHASE: JULY 1–SEPTEMBER 24, 1975

This phase was characterized by a temporary halt in the fighting, which lasted until early September 1975 when large scale fighting broke out and resulted in the destruction of the downtown commercial area of Beirut. This phase ended with the formation of a twenty-member National Dialogue Committee.

The second phase of the Civil War began with fighting which broke out in late August and early September 1975, after almost two months without any incident. It began in Zahla, a city in al-Biqa' Valley, and then spread to the North, especially between Zgharta (President Franjiya's town) and Tripoli (Prime Minister Rashid Karami's city). At the same time, Israeli forces conducted four separate raids by land, sea, and air against Palestinian bases and refugee camps in Southern Lebanon.

The Karami cabinet and President Franjiya could not agree on whether to send the army to separate the combatants between Zgharta and Tripoli. The source of disagreement stemmed from the accusation made by Junblat and his front of Progressive and National Parties and Organizations, later known as the National Movement, and by the Palestinian Resistance Movement, that the army was dominated by pro-Phalangist and Sham'unist officers, and, in particular, that it was headed by General Iskandar Ghanim, the Commander-in-Chief of the Army, whose partisan views were well known. As a compromise, Ghanim was removed from his post on September 10, 1975, and Brigadier Hanna Sa'id was appointed in his place.

After the fighting subsided in the North, except for one serious incident in 'Akkar, fighting resumed this time in Beirut, and part of the commercial downtown area was bombed and set on fire. The Syrian Foreign Minister Khaddam came back to Beirut on September 19, and, due to his efforts, a National Dialogue Committee (NDC), or *Lajnat al-Hiwar al-Watani*, was formed on September 24, 1975. It was composed of 20 members, equally divided between Muslim and Christian sects. Some of the most prominent politicians were represented, such as: Kamal Junblat, the Druze chieftain, and the leader of the National Movement; the distinguished Sunni politicians Sa'ib Salam, 'Abdallah al-Yafi, and Rashid Karami; the Shi'ite traditional leader and president of the Chamber of Deputies, Kamil al-As'ad; the Secretary-General of the pro-Syrian Organization of the Ba'thist Party, 'Asim Qansu; and finally the Phalangist leader Pierre Jumayil, ex-president Camille Sham'un, and Raymond Iddi, the leader of the National Bloc Party.

ر ب ش ر ر ب

THE THIRD PHASE:
SEPTEMBER 25, 1975–FEBRUARY 13, 1976

This phase was characterized by the continued efforts to reach an agreement on political reforms. The fighting was no longer on fixed fronts as successful attempts were made by the Lebanese Front and the NM and the PRM to overrun each other's strongholds. In January the conflict took on a Lebanese-Palestinian character. By the end of this phase agreement on reforms was reached through the crucial mediation of top Syrian officials.

The third phase began with the discussion about the major issues in the NDC. Two problems loomed large on the agenda, namely, the issue of territorial sovereignty put forward by the Phalangists and their allies, and political reform including secularism advocated by the National Movement and their allies.

There were differences between Prime Minister Karami and President Franjiya concerning political reform, and when a compromise was reached to reinterpret rather than amend the Constitution on these matters, this created some friction between Karami and his allies, especially Junblat and the National Movement.

Another incident which had repercussions on the working of the cabinet was the discovery of a ship unloading arms in Junya on November 11, 1975. Karami and Sham'un were at loggerheads concerning the manner in which to prevent the import of arms into Lebanon by the various factions.

The third phase was characterized by violent clashes and fighting in most of the regions in the North, in Zahla, in Damur, and especially in Beirut itself. The fighting was no longer centered around fixed fronts. There were some successful attempts to overrun certain areas: the Ghawarina quarter in Antilyas and the Sibnay village in the Ba'abda area were attacked in November 1975, which led to the migration of their residents. More significantly, the Phalangists and the National Liberals occupied, after stiff resistance, the Christian Palestinian camp of Dubay on December 14, 1975. In reprisal, the Palestinians attacked Damur, a Sham'unist stronghold, but did not overrun it until January 20, 1976, after the Phalangists and the National Liberals destroyed the slum areas of the Karantina and al-Maslakh after evicting their residents on January 18–19, 1976. Camille Sham'un himself had to flee by helicopter from his residential palace in al-Sa'diyyat near Damur.

The issue of whether to use the army to stop the fighting led to more disagreement between Karami, the minister of defense, and Sham'un, the minister of interior. Accusations had already been made by the National Movement that the army was fighting side by side with the Phalangists and the National Liberals, as well as with the local militias in Zahla against those who were attacking the city.

Karami submitted his resignation on January 18, 1976, which was symbolic of the ineffectiveness of the cabinet. This occurred in the midst of the fighting in the Karantina and al-Maslakh areas. It was only with Syrian mediation, by their delegation composed of Khaddam, Naji Jamil, and Hikmat Shihabi, that a tripartite High Military Committee (HMC) was formed to supervise the keeping of order and security, and enforce a cease-fire. It was made up of Lebanese, Syrian, and Palestinian officers. The High Military Committee in turn formed 23 subcommittees to implement the cease-fire. As a result, Karami took back his resignation on January 24, after Franjiya refused to accept it.

Syria and the PLO Step In

The third phase witnessed an increase in the role of the Syrians as well as the PLO, in implementing and enforcing agreements for a cease-fire and the return to normal.

With the formation of the tripartite High Military Committee, the Syrian mediators managed to convince President Franjiya to accept certain changes in the political system, a process which was concluded when Franjiya visited Damascus on February 7, 1976. A declaration was made by Franjiya on February 14, concerning what became known as *al-Wathiqa al-Dusturiya*, the Constitutional Document, hailed by the Syrians as the most important event in the history of Lebanon since the National Pact of 1943.

The National Pact

The National Pact was the unwritten agreement between President Bishara al-Khuri and his Prime Minister Riyad al-Sulh, that Lebanon was neither to seek union with Syria or with Arab countries east of Lebanon nor seek to ally itself with any European colonial power. Lebanon was to be an independent sovereign state with an Arab character.* Moreover, the major political positions in the country would be divided among the major religious sects. The president of the republic was to be a Maronite Christian; the president of the Chamber of Deputies, a Shi'ite Muslim; the prime minister a Sunni Muslim. The Greek Orthodox were to have the vice-prime minister and the vice-president of the Chamber of Deputies. The National Pact of 1943 was thus a halfway house between the visions of the Lebanese nationalists who sought an independent Lebanon based on the concept that Lebanon had existed as a separate entity since the time of the Phoenicians, and was tied to the West and, in particular, to France, and the desires of the Lebanese who wanted it to merge with Arab countries east of

---

*Arab character refers to the "UN visage Arabe" expression.

Lebanon and in particular with Syria. Among the important provisions of this unwritten pact of 1943 was the principle that the Chamber of Deputies should have six Christian deputies for every five Muslim deputies, or a ratio of six to five. Thus, since independence in 1943, all Lebanese parliaments had been multiples of 11.

The Constitutional Document

The Constitutional Document introduced some changes in this National Pact of 1943. On the one hand it reasserted the custom of reserving major political posts to specific religious sects. On the other hand, however, it wanted parliament to be divided equally between Christians and Muslims. Moreover, it strengthened the position of the prime minister by stipulating that he was to be chosen by a majority vote of the members of the Chamber of Deputies, and not designated by the president as had been the case.

Whatever the merits or the weaknesses of the Constitutional Document, it could be regarded as an important landmark. It was an attempt by the Syrians and some traditional leaders to reach a compromise acceptable to both sides. In fact however, neither Junblat's National Movement nor the Phalangist Party was happy with the document.

Special Envoys

The third phase was also characterized by the arrival of special envoys from various countries, to help find solutions to Lebanon's problems. Msgr. Bertoli, the papal envoy, arrived on November 9, 1975, and the French Couve de Murville arrived on the 19th of the same month. Later, on December 26, Tariq 'Aziz, the Iraqi envoy, visited Beirut as well. They were unable to mediate however, although they did meet with most of the leaders of both the conservative Lebanese parties and the National Movement, and the traditional Muslim leaders. Similarly, the attempts made by some Arab countries (other than Syria) to mediate or find some solutions for Lebanon's plight, all met with the same fate, being completely unsuccessful. Syria made known her disapproval of such attempts.

THE FOURTH PHASE: FEBRUARY 14–MARCH 11, 1976

This phase was marked by a declaration of the Constitutional Document and the crowning of the Syrian mediation efforts to find a solution to the conflict. Two problems, however, remained: the inability to form a national reconciliation cabinet, and the continued disintegration of the Lebanese Army. This phase ended with Ahdab's coup: a desperate attempt to reunite the Lebanese Army.

The fourth phase of the Civil War, the shortest in duration, was nonetheless a very crucial period. It began with the proclamation of the Constitutional Document by President Franjiya on February 14, and ended with the coup d'état, which was neither intended nor in fact an actual coup d'état, by Brigadier 'Aziz al-Ahdab on March 11, 1976.

The Constitutional Document hailed by President Franjiya and the Syrians as a real achievement received mixed reactions from the various groups. The Phalangist Party ended up supporting it, as did most of the conservative Lebanese political groups. The National Movement however, tended to criticize the ambiguity of some of the 17 major parts of the document. Perhaps this document might have served as a first step in reaching an accord between the various groups.

However, two important elements changed the situation. First, the gradual disintegration of the army began in late January and reached its peak with the establishment of the Lebanon's Arab Army (LAA) headed by First Lieutenant Ahmad al-Khatib, who managed to get supporters from most of the army units all over the country, and especially from the South, Biqa', the North, and Beirut. The only exception was the Fayadiya military barracks, which were under the command of Colonel Antoine Barakat, a staunch supporter of the conservative parties, and of the Lebanese Air Force, whose commander, Colonel George Ghurayib, remained neutral throughout the Civil War. The majority of the soldiers and lower ranks of officers joined Ahmad al-Khatib's Lebanon's Arab Army but a sizable minority fought with the Phalangists, National Liberals, and Franjiya's militia. The fears that were expressed earlier by many politicians, that the army was going to be divided if it was ordered to intervene, were fully justified. In fact, the divisions that took place in the Lebanese army led to the attempted coup d'état by Brigadier 'Aziz al-Ahdab. His objective was to stop the disintegration of the army and attempt to reunite it. He wished to do so by blaming Franjiya for pursuing, since his ascendancy to the presidency, a policy of purging the army of its Shihabist officers, and appointing a commander in chief of the army who was close to the Phalangists and their allies, and allowing high-ranking officers in the army to maintain their ties with proconservative and rightist elements. The effect of Ahdab's coup was to shift the basic issue from how to reconcile the various parties on the basis of the Constitutional Document, to the resignation of Franjiya from the presidency and the election of a new president. However, Ahdab's coup was not able to force the president out of office, as Ahdab controlled only the army garrison of the Beirut headquarters.

Ahdab's action was the final blow to the attempt to form a new cabinet reconciling the various groups and parties, which was already floundering by early March 1976, due to a basic disagreement among the National Movement, the traditional Muslim leaders (who supported the Constitutional Document with some minor reservations) and the conservative front. Therefore, we maintain that the disintegration of the army, the inability to form a new cabinet or add new members to the old one, and the mixed reactions to the Constitutional Document, as well as Ahdab's demand for the resignation of the president, factors which characterized this fourth phase of the Civil War, prevented the various factions from reaching an agreement.

THE FIFTH PHASE: MARCH 12–MAY 31, 1976

Ahdab's coup ushered in a new phase as his demand for the resignation of President Franjiya changed the political situation. However, neither the Army was reunited nor did Franjiya resign, but a new president, Sarkis, was elected. Concomitantly, Junblat launched his military campaign in Mount Lebanon against the Lebanese Front, and consequently the rift between the NM and Syria became unbridgeable.

The fifth phase of the Civil War extended from March 12, 1976, to the end of May 1976, that is, from Ahdab's coup until the Syrian military intervention on June 1, 1976. Ahdab's coup was unsuccessful in forcing President Franjiya to resign, but it did lead to the amendment of Article 73 of the Constitution, to allow for the election of a new president no earlier than six months before the expiration of the term of the incumbent president (instead of two months earlier as stipulated in Article 73). The Parliament convened on April 10, and unanimously approved the amendment and, on April 24, 1976, President Franjiya countersigned the amended article.

Meanwhile, the National Movement, under the leadership of Junblat, went on the offensive in Mount Lebanon in part as a response to the Phalangist and National Liberal attacks on the Lebanese Communist Party (LCP) and the Syrian Social Nationalist Party (SSNP) strongholds in northern Matn province. The offensive was also made to strengthen the National Movement's position in the bargaining process, first, to change the Constitutional Document, bringing it closer to the National Movement's own program of reform, and second, to have a new president who would be its own candidate, such as Raymond Iddi. The Syrians, however, found a compromise to Ahdab's demands for the resignation of President Franjiya and the election of a new president, by keeping Franjiya in power till the end of his term, but agreeing to the election of a new president. Consequently, Parliament convened on May 8, 1976, and elected Ilyás Sarkis, the only candidate, as the new president. As an old Shihabi, Sarkis got the support of Rashid Karami, the prime minister, and was also Syria's candidate as well as that of the Conservative Front, now known as the Kufur front (Kufur referring to the new residence of President Franjiya after his presidential palace at Ba'abda was directly hit and he had to flee, in late March 1976). Junblat's

National Movement feared Sarkis's policies, since Sarkis was Syria's candidate (Syria had put tremendous pressure on the deputies to elect Sarkis).

Syria's role in Lebanese affairs during that phase increased tremendously. Pro-Syrian parties openly criticized Junblat and the leadership of the Palestinian Resistance Movement. King Husain of Jordan, during his visit to the United States, in early April 1976, maintained that only Syria would be able to put an end to the strife in Lebanon, and lobbied for Syrian military intervention in Lebanon. The U.S. envoy, L. Dean Brown, described Syria's role as constructive, and he remained in the area from April 1 until after the election of President Sarkis, on May 8, 1976. France tried to play the role of mediator, and President Giscard d'Estaing proposed on May 22, to send troops to Lebanon if this were acceptable to all parties concerned. This proposal was strongly rejected by both the National Movement and the traditional Muslim leaders. Only Pierre Jumayil, the leader of the Phalangist Party, welcomed the idea. This French proposal hastened the decision of Syria to intervene militarily in Lebanon.

The fifth phase of the Civil War had the signs of an imminent Syrian intervention. Two important incidents prepared the atmosphere for this intervention. First, the murder of Linda Junblat, Kamal Junblat's sister, on May 27, increased the tension and intensified the fighting between the National Movement and the Kufur Front. As she resided in the eastern part of Beirut, which was controlled by the Kufur's militias, it was assumed that they had been responsible for her death. Second, the Lebanon's Arab Army in the north, under the command of Ahmad al-Mi'mari, attacked without apparent reason two towns in the 'Akkar region, al-Qibbiyat and 'Andaqt. The people of these towns asked for help from Syrian President Asad, and he obliged by sending troops on June 1, 1976, to both the 'Akkar and Zahla (the central Biqa' valley) regions.

Prior to the Syrian military intervention, the National Movement had demanded, after the election of Sarkis as president, round table talks to discuss the issues that divided the various parties. This brought some reluctant support from Sham'un, ex-President and leader of the NLP, who feared the imminent Syrian intervention, and demanded UN or non-Arab troops to put an end to the fighting. However, when fighting intensified again, on almost all fronts, the chances for holding talks for a political solution became almost nil. Another factor that stood in the way of a political dialogue was the insistence of President Franjiya that he remain in power till the end of his term—September 22, 1976—despite the fact that a new president had already been elected. Franjiya's decision was backed by his allies, the Phalangists, and Sham'un, as well as by President Asad of Syria.

THE SIXTH PHASE: JUNE 1–SEPTEMBER 22, 1976

This phase began with the Syrian military intervention against the PRM and the NM. It led to a limited involvement of the Arab League in the conflict, and the sending of a token Arab Security Force to separate the combatants. This phase witnessed also the fall of the Palestinian Tal al-Za'tar camp in the hands of the Lebanese Front forces, an important landmark in the Civil War. This phase ended with the expiration of President Franjiya's term in office.

The sixth phase of the Civil War began with the Syrian military intervention on June 1, 1976. Syria had convinced the United States, through King Husain and the U.S. Ambassador in Damascus, Richard Murphy, that its role would be to reinstate security and put an end to civil strife in Lebanon, and that its projected military presence would not constitute a threat to Israel in its size or in its geographical distribution. President Asad feared, apart from Israeli intervention and U.S. objections to the Syrian role in Lebanon, the reaction of France (which always had a special relationship with Lebanon, since its independence), as well as of the Soviet Union. As for the latter, President Asad timed his intervention with Premier Kosygin's visit to Syria, embarrassing the Soviet Union into silence, and forcing it, if not into agreeing, at least into not going against Syrian military intervention. The Soviet Union, which had recently lost its influence in Egypt, wanted to keep its influence over Syria. To allay the fears of France, President Asad sent Syrian Minister for Foreign Affairs 'Abd al-Halim Khaddam, to Paris on June 2, 1976. The communiqué issued after he met his French counterpart included an endorsement of the Syrian role by the French, as well as an agreement to safeguard the sovereignty and territorial integrity of Lebanon.

Thus, the Syrian military intervention received the support of all the major countries that had any interest in Lebanon. Countries, however, that had supported the National Movement and the Palestinian Resistance were concerned about the rift between them and Syria. Foremost among these were Libya, and, to a lesser extent, Algeria. Iraq, with its rival Ba'th ruling party, exploited the differences between Syria on the one hand, and the National Movement and the Palestinian Resistance Movement on the other, to accuse Syria of betraying the Palestinian cause and cooperating with the United States and Israel. Libya feared that the rift between Syria and Syria's former allies in Lebanon would weaken Syria's stand against Egypt on the issue of the signing of the Second Sinai Disengagement Agreement on September 1, 1975. The Prime Minister of Libya, 'Abd al-Salam Jallud, came to Beirut and Damascus to bridge the gap between Syria, the National Movement, and the Palestinian Resistance, on the very day, June 8, that an emergency session of foreign ministers of the member countries of the Arab League met in Cairo, to discuss the Lebanese crisis. The Palestinian Resistance Movement, under the leadership of Yasir 'Arafat, had called the meeting, with Egyptian support, to put pressure on Syria to restrain its actions. The conference of Arab Ministers for Foreign Affairs offered partial endorsement of the Syrian role in Lebanon. While demanding an immediate cease-fire and the establishment of an Arab security force to eventually replace the Syrian troops, they agreed to have Syrian troops included in the Arab Security Force. The projected size of the force, however, of between

6,000 and 10,000 men, was hardly enough to enforce a cease-fire, let alone keep law and order.

The partial Arabization (the involvement of the Arab world via the Arab League in Lebanon) of the Civil War in Lebanon was welcomed by the National Movement and the Palestinian Resistance Movement, to counterbalance the Syrian military intervention. The conference of prime ministers of Syria, Egypt, Saudi Arabia, and Kuwait, held in Riyadh on June 23, 1976, endorsed the decisions of the Arab League concerning Lebanon. This meeting's concern was the reconciliation of Egypt and Syria, an important step toward a future consensus as to how to end the Civil War in Lebanon.

Syria's reluctant agreement to the partial Arabization of the Lebanese situation was the price it had to pay in order to continue playing a dominant role in Lebanon. The Kufur Front insisted on Syrian military intervention only because Syria prevented it from losing ground in many areas, and weakened its adversaries by fighting the National Movement as well as the Palestinian forces. By accepting the decisions of the Arab League, Syria gained time and hoped that eventually Syrian troops would constitute the backbone of the Arab Security Force.

Syria hastened to get international support for its actions. President Asad visited France on June 17, and the communiqué issued at the end of the talks with President Giscard d'Estaing was an endorsement by the French of the Syrian role in Lebanon, and the establishment of law and order to create an atmosphere favorable for political dialogue and settlement of the Lebanese Civil War. After leaving France, Syrian President Asad visited Yugoslavia and Rumania—the first to allay the fears of the nonaligned countries, and the second to give assurances to Israeli leaders of its nonbelligerent intentions toward Israel, as Rumania is the only Communist country with diplomatic relations with Israel. On July 3, 1976, the Syrian minister for foreign affairs was dispatched to Moscow for a five-day official visit to explain the Syrian point of view to the Russians.

The Soviet Union was basically in support of both the Syrians, on one side, and the National Movement and the Palestinian Resistance Movement, on the other. Junblat and 'Arafat thought that the Soviet Union would put decisive pressure on the Syrians to withdraw their troops from Lebanon, but nothing of the sort happened. The National Movement repeatedly called for a clearer Soviet stand on the Lebanese Civil War. The Soviet Union gave moral support and some medical and food supplies for blockaded West Beirut during June 1976.

'Abd al-Salam Jallud spent his time shuttling between Damascus and Beirut, in order to reconcile Syria with its former Palestinian allies, and criticized the Soviet Union for concerning itself more with détente than with giving support to liberation movements. However, the Libyan attitude was in effect rather similar to that of the Soviet Union. On the one hand, Libya expressed its nonacceptance of the military presence of Syria in Lebanon, while Jallud praised Syria, on June 21, for its role in the Civil War. Jallud was successful in obtaining the release of some of the leaders and members of pro-Syrian organizations, who had been arrested by the National Movement and the Palestinians, on June 23, 1976. Jallud also managed to get a partial Syrian withdrawal, beginning with the Beirut International Airport, on June 22. The Syrian troops were replaced by troops from the Arab Security Force, half of which was Syrian and the other half Libyan. Jallud described his position as neutral on the eve of the agreement reached between Syria and its former allies through his mediation.

The National Liberal Party, the Phalangist Party, and the allies of both parties, besieged and attacked the Palestinian camps of Jisr al-Basha and Tal-al-Za'tar on June 22, the eve of the meeting of the prime ministers of Syria, Egypt, Saudi Arabia, and Kuwait in Riyadh, and the same day as the beginning of the withdrawal of the Syrian troops from Beirut International Airport. This started the battle over the Palestinian camps, which lasted till August 12, 1976, with the fall of the Tal-Za'tar camp. The timing of these attacks was not coincidental, as the Kufur Front sent a statement to the meeting of prime ministers in Riyadh, attacking the Palestinian-Communist alliance and demanding an end to the Palestinian interference in Lebanese affairs, as well as threatening to ask for help from non-Arab friendly nations.

Junblat's call for intervention by other Arab countries, such as Saudi Arabia, Egypt, Iraq, and Algeria, produced no tangible results. A tripartite summit meeting held in Jedda on July 17, with the leaders of Saudi Arabia, Egypt, and Sudan, issued a statement calling for an immediate cease-fire, endorsing the decision taken by the Arab League in its previous meeting, and advocating round table talks to reconcile the parties to the conflict in Lebanon.

Only Jallud's indefatigable efforts throughout July harvested a modicum of success, when, on July 21, a delegation representing the major Palestinian guerrilla organizations accompanied him to Damascus to begin talks with the Syrian government.

Syria was in a strong position as it began to comply with the decisions of the Arab League. It kept its pressure on the Palestinians and the National Movement through the Kufur Front's militia attacks on Palestinian camps and received the Kufur's public support for their initiative in Lebanon. President Asad justified his actions by reminding the Palestinian Resistance Movement and the National Movement of the material and moral support they had received from Syria since the beginning of the Civil War. He also reminded the National Movement of their weakness in January 1976, and their fears that West Beirut was endangered by Phalangist and National Liberal occupation of the Maslakh and Karantina areas, and how he had allowed a unit of the Palestine Liberation Army to enter Lebanon and bolster up their positions, which resulted in the formation of the Tripartite High Military Committee, in late January 1976.

President Asad finally added that the Palestinian armed presence in Lebanon was greater than was needed for fighting Israel from the Lebanese borders.

Syrian-Palestinian Agreement

An important landmark of this sixth phase of the Civil War was the Syrian-Palestinian agreement of July 29, 1976, which stipulated the end of the fighting, and the Palestinian armed presence in accordance with the Cairo Agreement and its appendices, as well as with the Constitutional Document of February 14, 1976. Both sides agreed also to encourage the parties in the conflict to start a dialogue under the chairmanship of the President-elect, Ilyas Sarkis, and on the basis of the Constitutional Document.

Immediately after the signing of the Syrian-Palestinian Agreement, the National Movement established a new political body on July 22, 1976, the Central Political Council, which was headed by Junblat. On August 6, a Higher Organization for Civil Administration was also formed. The aim of both institutions was to run the former government services in West Beirut and in the towns and provinces which were under the military control of the National Movement and the PRM.

The conservative parties were not pleased with the agreement and played it down, claiming that due to the unorganized nature of the armed presence of the Palestinians in Lebanon such an agreement would not hold. Furthermore Pierre Jumayil, on the eve of the signing of the agreement, demanded the distribution of the Palestinians of Lebanon all over the Arab world, and threatened the Arab League that the Kufur Front would seek to "internationalize" the conflict.

The fighting over Tal al-Za'tar continued unabated, and as a result, it became impossible to conduct a political dialogue. The agreement also stipulated the formation of a committee representing Lebanon, Syria, and the PLO, to be headed by Arab League officials. However, Hasan Sabri al-Khuli, the Arab League envoy, failed to convene a conference in Sofar in Mount Lebanon, because the conservatives, and Sham'un in particular, wanted to keep a wide rift between Syria and the Palestinians and the National Movement. On August 4, the eve of the Sofar Conference, the conservative parties launched a successful attack on the Nab'a suburb of Beirut and forced its residents to flee.

The Fall of Tal al-Za'tar

With the fall of Tal al-Za'tar on August 13, the position of the National Movement and the PRM hardened. On the same day, the National Movement announced the formation of the Popular Liberation Forces and a committee to coordinate with Lebanon's Arab Army.

The conservative parties, on the other hand, bypassed the National Movement and insisted on a political dialogue with the traditional Muslim leaders, as Pierre Jumayil himself declared. Organizations, other than the Phalangist Party, insisted on continuing the fighting to control the whole of Lebanon. The leader of the extremist right-wing group, the Guardians of the Cedars, called for the expulsion and liquidation of every single Palestinian in Lebanon. And finally on August 30, the conservative parties formed a unified military command for all the Lebanese forces on their side, headed by Bashir Jumayil, the son of Pierre Jumayil.

Toward the end of that phase of the Civil War, Junblat began forming a broad and all-inclusive front: of traditional Muslim leaders, moderate Christian leaders, and the National Movement. He sent messages to the Arab leaders, urging them to attempt to convene an emergency summit conference. Abu Iyad (Salah Khalaf), a prominent leader of the PRM, complained of the inactivity as well as the reticence displayed by Arab countries, and demanded from all friendly non-Arab countries a clear statement of their stand in the Lebanese Civil War. The Soviet Union responded to the PRM by informing its leaders that pressure was being exerted in their favor. Moreover, on August 26, the Soviet Union issued a statement demanding the withdrawal of Syrian forces from Lebanon, and giving strong support to the National Movement and the PRM. This position however, underwent some changes when the Soviet Union attacked both the extreme Right and the extreme Left on September 8. Nevertheless, the impression was that the Soviet Union would eventually assist the National Movement and the PRM, in case of defeat. Junblat hoped that the Soviet Union would exert greater pressure on Syria, and faced with Sham'un and others who did not want to begin the dialogue, called for a long war in Mount Lebanon. He mobilized his forces, which included his own militias as well as those of other parties and groups, to put up a fight rather than withdraw from territories they had taken over in Mount Lebanon in the spring of 1976.

A few weeks before the end of the sixth phase of the Lebanese Civil War, Junblat reiterated his position on the need for reform of the political system and criticized the Constitutional Document for keeping the president of the republic the dominant political figure, while the prime minister continued to be a much weaker figure. The polemics between Junblat and the traditional Muslim leaders, especially Sa'ib Salam, concerning in part at least the merits of the Constitutional Document, reached a peak, and made the task of forming a broad front to face the Kufur Front very difficult. Divisions and in-fighting between Junblat's National Movement and Ahmad al-Khatib's Lebanon's Arab Army, became more frequent. Compounding his problems, Junblat criticized the PRM indirectly, by asking them to keep their forces under more control by forming a temporary governing body to run their affairs.

On the Palestinian side, the leaders of Fath, as well as of the Popular Democratic Front for the Liberation of Palestine (PDFLP), maintained that there could be no military solution to the conflict in Lebanon. On the other hand, the Rejection Front, whose spokesman was George Habash, demanded that "popular authority" be established, rejected reconciliation, and advocated a liberated Lebanon, which as he described it, would become an "Arab Hanoi." The leaders of Fath, the PDFLP, and other Palestinian groups, were not willing to budge from their positions in Mount Lebanon, except as part of a complete and comprehensive political solution to the Lebanese Civil War—a position identical to that of Junblat and his National Movement. Traditional Muslim leaders, like Salam, Karami, and Hasan Khalid, the Mufti of Lebanon, were more interested in political dialogue, especially with the President-elect, Ilyas Sarkis, as well as with the conservative front through Syrian mediation.

Two meetings held in Shtura on September 17 and 19, a few days before President Sarkis took office, between Syrian General Naji Jamil, President-elect Sarkis, Yasir 'Arafat, and the Arab League special envoy, Sabri al-Khuli, to reach a settlement about the issue of the withdrawal of the National Movement and the PRM forces from Mount Lebanon, produced no result.

THE SEVENTH PHASE:
SEPTEMBER 23–DECEMBER 9, 1976

This phase began with President Sarkis taking office. The Syrians immediately launched a second military offensive against the NM and the PRM forces. The Riyadh six-leader Conference of October 16, 1976 was instrumental in putting an end to the Lebanese conflict. It established the Arab Deterrent Force (ADF), mostly Syrian, to keep law and order. The deployment of the ADF forces in Lebanese territory and the formation of a new cabinet by Al-Huss marked the end of the Civil War.

The seventh phase of the Civil War began in Shtura on September 23, 1976 with the swearing in of Ilyas Sarkis as the sixth president of Lebanon since its independence. Neither the Prime Minister Rashid Karami, nor Junblat, the leader of the National Movement, attended the ceremony in the Chamber of Deputies. Sarkis, in his speech after the ceremony, tried to depict his role as that of a middle-of-the-road statesman. On the one hand, he stressed the unity of the Lebanese people and of their country, and therefore took a stand against those who believed in the partition of Lebanon; on the other hand, he emphasized the importance of safeguarding the sovereignty and territorial integrity of Lebanon, an indirect criticism of the armed presence of the Palestinians in Lebanon, and lack of organized control of the Palestinians' militias. He stressed that the Palestinians had to abide by the pacts and agreements that had been reached between the Palestinians and the Lebanese authorities. To placate the National Movement and those calling for reform, Sarkis, a believer in the reformist ideology of Shihabism (he had been the right-hand man of the late President

Fu'ad Shihab, who ruled Lebanon in the post-1958 Civil War to 1964), emphasized the need for changes and reforms. Changes had to take place first in the
political sphere, and then in the social and economic spheres as well. Greater
equality was needed, for instance, as well as more social justice among the
various sectors of the Lebanese population. Greater equality referred to equality
of sects within the political community, while social justice meant the redistri-
bution of wealth in terms of classes. Sarkis believed in a liberal economic system,
in which the government plays a greater role. In his speech, he also emphasized
the Arab role of Lebanon and its Arab identity, as well as the responsibility it
had in sharing the problems of its Arab world. These statements appealed to the
National Movement and the PRM, as they appeared to put more emphasis on
Lebanon's Arab character and its role in Arab affairs, than had the formulation
of the National Pact of 1943. Finally, Sarkis praised the role of the Syrians, and
stated that the presence of the Syrian troops was absolutely necessary for keeping law and order, and that they were to stay until the Lebanese Government
decided otherwise.

Despite the conciliatory, middle-of-the-road stand taken by President
Sarkis, it was not possible to bring together all the parties concerned to enforce
a cease-fire, and withdraw the militias and troops from the various regions. There
were two major reasons for Sarkis's failure to achieve these things after he took
over power. First, there were elements, such as Sham'un and his party, who
wanted to escalate the Civil War to push the Syrians further away from the
National Movement and the PRM. Sham'un attacked the Arab Security Force
and tried to fight them in the museum area, which divided eastern Beirut from
western Beirut. There were also extreme rightists, such as the Guardians of the
Cedars group, led by Etienne Saqr, who wanted to expel all the Palestinians from
Lebanon. These groups belonged to the conservative Kufur Front, in which the
Phalangist Party was the strongest militarily, and had been the first to take the
initiative and develop cordial relations with the Syrians.

Second, the National Movement, headed by Junblat, which had managed
through the Arab League, and later through Libya's mediation, to stop the
Syrian military campaign of June and July 1976 (the Syrian-Palestinian agreement was the outcome) hoped to continue exploiting the conflicts and rivalries
among the major Arab countries and thus prevent Syrian troops from remaining
in Lebanon much longer. The PRM, and in particular 'Arafat and his colleagues,
believed that a Syrian offensive was unlikely because Iraq, Libya, Algeria, Egypt,
even Kuwait, and Saudi Arabia—all the major Arab powers, would exert pressure
and prevent such a military offensive. Both Junblat and 'Arafat insisted that the
Arab Security Force be increased in size, and that more Arab countries send
troops in order to render it an effective deterrent force. They also hoped that
the Soviet Union would prevent a repetition of the Syrian military offensive
which had begun in June 1976.

The longer the PRM kept its troops under the Allied Command (as the forces of the National Movement [NM] and the PRM were called), the easier it was for Sham'un and Jumayil to point to the Palestinian intervention in Lebanon's internal affairs. The objective of the PRM was not only to help its ally, the NM, but also to safeguard its independence and its freedom of decision making vis-a-vis the Syrian Government.

Syria's Second Offensive

On September 28, 1976, the Syrians began their second offensive, after a lull of almost two months in their military activities in Lebanon, and after they failed to remove the PRM and the NM from Mount Lebanon through peaceful negotiations. Syrian troops advanced to the North and South Matn and the 'Alay province using both infantry and armored cars. Junblat, who was in Egypt at the time, began to tour the Arab countries, including Saudi Arabia and Iraq, so that they would exert pressure on Syria to stop its military offensive. At the same time, Junblat and the NM decided to fight the Syrians and put up a stiff resistance in the mountain areas. The Syrians were indirectly assisted by the troops of the conservative Kufur Front in fighting the NM and the PRM in Mount Lebanon.

While the Syrians were conducting their military offensive in the central and southern parts of Mount Lebanon, the NM and the PRM called for help from the "progressive" Arab countries and from the Soviet Union. Junblat arrived in Paris on October 3, and tried to convince the French Government to intervene and counterbalance the Syrians. France responded by calling for a round table conference of all the parties concerned and sent messages to President Sarkis, as well as to Egypt and Syria. While the Central Political Council of the NM was expecting a French initiative, it continued to mobilize the population and resist Syrian intervention. On October 9 and 11, meetings were held in Shtura between Lebanese army officers, representing Sarkis, and Syrian army officers, and representatives of the PRM. However, they were unsuccessful in reaching an agreement.

Meanwhile, the major Arab countries became more concerned about Syria's military intervention in Lebanon. Saudi Arabia pulled out its troops, which had been stationed in Syria since 1973. President Sadat of Egypt called for a six nation summit and appears to have threatened to send Egyptian troops to Lebanon. On October 15, while the fighting continued in Bhamdun, Sofar, and Jizzin, the Saudi Arabian king invited the six Arab leaders for an emergency summit conference to be held in Riyadh the next day. These leaders were President Asad of Syria, President Sarkis of Lebanon, Prince Sabah, the ruler of Kuwait, President Sadat of Egypt, Yasir 'Arafat, the leader of the PLO, and King Khalid of Saudi Arabia.

The conservative Kufur Front were elated by the second Syrian military offensive. Sham'un refused to participate at the round table talks which had been suggested by France, before Palestinian troops withdrew to their refugee camps. Pierre Jumayil, the leader of the Phalangist Party, criticized the Cairo Agreement as serving the interests of Israel. His son, Bashir Jumayil, who headed the Unified Military Command of the Kufur Front, spoke of the need to "liberate" Mount Lebanon, and the extreme rightist organization of the Guardians of the Cedars called for the expulsion of the Palestinians from Lebanon.

The Arab Summit Meeting in Riyadh

For a period of time, while the fighting was going on, the interests of Syria and those of the conservative Kufur Front were similar. 'Asim Qansu, the leader of the pro-Syrian Organization of the Ba'th Party (OBP) criticized the PRM, the NM, and the Arab Lebanese Army in a speech he made in eastern Beirut. President Asad tried unsuccessfully to get King Husain to the summit meeting in Riyad to further weaken 'Arafat's leadership. Qansu put Syria's position very clearly by stating that it would continue to pursue a military solution and would refuse any external interference. The Saudi decision to call the summit meeting forced Syria and the other parties to accept a cease-fire. The immediate reaction of the conservative Kufur Front was to reject the decisions made by the summit meeting, hoping that Syria would continue its military campaign against the PRM and the NM.

The decisions of the six leaders at the Arab summit of Riyadh safeguarded the sovereignty and territorial integrity of the Lebanese Republic, and reiterated that the PLO was the only representative and spokesman of the Palestinian people. It stipulated that an Arab Deterrent Force (ADF) of around 30,000 men under President Sarkis would enforce the cease-fire, and that the Lebanese authorities and the PLO would strictly adhere to the Cairo Agreement. The ADF would also collect the heavy weapons from all the various militias. The Arab countries would also guarantee the implementation of their decisions, and would form a committee representing Saudi Arabia, Egypt, Syria, and Kuwait, which would coordinate its activities with the Lebanese president to implement its decisions.

The reaction of the Kufur Front was mixed. Sham'un objected to 'Arafat's participation in the summit and accused Saudi Arabia and Kuwait of arming the PRM. The Phalangist Party was unhappy about the adherence by all parties to the Cairo Agreement, which meant the continued military presence of the Palestinians in southern Lebanon. Because of that decision, Israel began to be more actively involved in the Civil War, supporting the rightist forces in the South, and trying to prevent the return of the Palestinian guerrillas to that area.

Although Sarkis assured the conservative leaders that two-thirds of the Arab Deterrent Force (ADF) would be Syrian, Sham'un objected to the force entering eastern Beirut, as well as other areas under the command of the Kufur Front. The front threatened to ask for the military assistance of other non-Arab countries, and simultaneously Sham'un further developed his already existing ties with Israel.

Reluctantly, the Kufur Front accepted the decisions reached at the Riyad summit of October 1976, which were then endorsed in an all-Arab summit conference in Cairo, later that month. The Phalangist Party unwillingly agreed to the Arab Deterrent Force entering its areas. In fact, there were two major factions within the Phalangist Party: Pierre Jumayil, the leader, his son Amin Jumayil, and Karim Baqraduni, a member of the Phalangist politburo, were ready to accept the presence of the ADF; the second faction, led by Pierre Jumayil's second son, Bashir, was closer to the militant stand taken by Sham'un and Etienne Saqr, the leader of the Guardians of the Cedars. The Bashir Jumayil faction and Saqr tended to be strongly anti-Palestinian and more rightist in their outlook than the mainstream of the Phalangist Party. In fact, clashes did take place between them and the ADF troops in both Jizzin and Junya.

The leaders of the conservative Kufur Front had apprehensions about the restriction of the Palestinian guerrilla bases in southern Lebanon. They shared a common objective with Israel, as both wished to prevent the Palestinian guerrillas from returning to southern Lebanon. In fact, Israel, in alliance with local rightist militias, took the initiative in late October to forestall the return of the Palestinian guerrillas to the South. The Civil War had stopped by early November 1976, but was replaced by a mini-civil war in southern Lebanon. Sham'un and, to a lesser extent, the Phalangist Party, were using Israel to counterbalance the dominant position of Syria in Lebanon.

The Israeli military and logistic support for the rightist militias in the South immediately changed the relationship between Syria and the PRM. 'Arafat visited Damascus on October 22 to discuss the situation in the South. The pro-Syrian OBP, on November 1, 1976, called for fighting on the side of the PRM and the NM in southern Lebanon. The organ of the PRM, *Falastin al-Thawra*, hailed the end of the Syrian-Palestinian conflict and the Syrian prime minister declared publicly that Syria was giving its support to the PRM.

The NM was slower in accepting the facts, although its leaders spoke of a new page in Syrian and NM relations. Junblat started to use an intermediary to deal with Sarkis and the Lebanese commander of the ADF, Ahmad al-Hajj, and gradually accepted the new president, Ilyas Sarkis, reserving his frequent polemics for the Kufur Front.

The End of the Civil War

After the establishment of law and order in the country, except for the South, the Civil War came to an end, although the mini-war in the South reminded the Lebanese of the explosive potential of the situation. However, the basic contradictions and divisions remained. It was with this realization that President Sarkis formed a new cabinet of "technocrats" led by Dr. Salim al-Huss, a former professor of business administration at the American University of Beirut. Except for Fu'ad Butros, the minister of foreign affairs and defense, who was an old Shihabist politician, the rest of the eight member cabinet were nonpoliticians. The dialogue among the major parties and groups on the issues that still divided them was postponed. Lebanon had just managed to survive the Civil War, but major changes were still to take place.

2

THE CONSERVATIVE
LEBANESE FRONT

THE PHALANGIST PARTY

The most important single party, of what was to be called the Conservative Lebanese Front (which was formally organized as the FFML [The Front of Freedom and Man in Lebanon] on January 31, 1976), was the Lebanese Phalangist Party *(Hizb al-Kata'ib al-Lubnaniya)*. It was founded on November 21, 1936, and was concerned, at first, with youth and athletics, rather than with politics. It appealed to Christian youth and especially to the Maronite community. Pierre Jumayil, one of the founders of the party, who became the indisputable leader in 1937, hailed from Bikfaya, in the northern Matn, and was a descendant of a family of local notables.[1]

The party supported popular causes, such as urging the government to decrease unemployment, and to prevent big companies from raising prices, as well as campaigning against corruption in the administration. It was basically an antiestablishment political organization, from early 1939 onwards. By mid-1942 it claimed a membership of 35,000.[2]

The Phalangist Party played an important role in the movement for the independence of Lebanon. It mobilized the Maronite masses, as the Najjada Party mobilized the urban Sunnis against the French authorities, when President al-Khuri, Prime Minister Riyad al-Sulh, and other prominent Lebanese politicians were arrested on November 11, 1943. Pierre Jumayil was arrested as an instigator of demonstrations, and was released when the movement for independence succeeded, on November 22, 1943.

During the period from 1943 to 1958, the Phalangist Party was almost exclusively regional, appealing to the Maronites of the northern Matn and of the eastern section of Beirut. At the time, it was in strong competition for members with the Syrian Social Nationalist Party (SSNP) of Antun Sa'ada, which was also popular in the mountain region of the northern Matn.[3]

Although the Phalangist Party had deputies elected to the parliaments of 1951, 1953, and 1957, the party appealed most to the youth, and was not yet a full-fledged member of the political establishment. It cooperated with President Bishara al-Khuri's regime, and was used by him in the famous Jumaiza incident of June 9, 1949, to punish the militant SSNP.[4] After the leader of the SSNP, Antun Sa'ada, was executed in July 1949, official support for the Phalangists increased and this trend culminated in the elections of 1951, when they won their first seats in Parliament. When opposition to Bishara al-Khuri's presidency gained momentum in 1952, the Phalangist Party was the last to abandon the president, and to rally to the opposition, as he noted in his memoirs.[5]

When Sham'un (who was known for his strong ties with the Arab world, and with the Hashimites in particular) came to power in 1952, he did not, at first, get the support of the Phalangists. They were not particularly happy, for instance, with the freedom he had given the SSNP, especially after it had been banned in Syria, in early 1955, to organize and hold rallies in Beirut and the provinces. However, during the last two years of Sham'un's presidency, the Phalangist Party supported him; Joseph Shadir joined the cabinet last (March–September 1958) and supported Sham'un's anti-Nasir, pro-Western foreign policy. They were not, on the other hand, too enthusiastic about Sham'un's attempt to amend the Constitution, and run for the presidency for a second term. The issue that linked them to his political ambitions was their common fear of Nasir's Arab nationalism, and their desire to safeguard Lebanon as an independent political entity and prevent it from being incorporated into a larger political and regional unit. This fear was increased by the formation of the United Arab Republic in February 1958, which merged Egypt and Syria under 'Abd al-Nasir. The Civil War which ensued in Lebanon, in May–October 1958, gave the Phalangists the opportunity to use their militias, which they had been training. They took on the role of defending the Lebanese system from Nasir's alleged intervention on the side of his Lebanese supporters, and this made them more popular with the Maronites, whose apprehensions with respect to Arab nationalism had augmented over the past few years.

The Phalangists launched what they called a "counterrevolution" (al-Thawra al-Mudadda), when Shihab assumed the presidency on September 23, 1958.[6] One wonders if Shihab himself did not encourage them to do so in order to qualify them to represent the Lebanese nationalists in the place of Sham'un. Significantly, in the first cabinet after the Phalangists' counterrevolution, Pierre Jumayil was appointed as one of the four cabinet ministers representing those who were against the 1958 "Revolution" led by Karami, Salam, Junblat, and others.

During the period from 1958 to 1967, the Phalangist Party cooperated with the Shihabist regime, and thus became an integral part of the political establishment. Shihab bolstered up the Phalangists as a counterpoise to Sham'un, who was politically isolated, and whose power was curbed throughout most of the Shihabist era. The political reputation of the Phalangists and their role in the Civil War of 1958 made them ideal representatives of the Maronite community and of the ideological school of Lebanese nationalists. In the elections of 1960, the leader of the Phalangists, Pierre Jumayil, was elected for the first time to Parliament, in the first constituency of Beirut, representing the predominantly Christian section of Beirut. Pierre Jumayil brought with him a total of six party members as deputies in Parliament: two from Beirut, three from Mount Lebanon, and one from the South. The Phalangist Party had become almost overnight one of the largest political parties represented in the 99 member Parliament of 1960.[7]

The Phalangists acquired the reputation of consistent loyalty to the regime, and to the Lebanese political system, because of their alliance to Shihab and their almost uninterrupted representation in all cabinets during Shihab's presidency between 1958 and 1964. By having representation in the cabinet, the Phalangists were able to offer services *(khadamat)* to their party members and sympathizers and thus competed effectively with the traditional Christian leadership.

Shihab's objectives were, among other things, to develop the backward regions of Lebanon, to create a system of social justice, and to strengthen the role of the bureaucracy and the executive at the expense of the traditional leaders and the legislature.[8] The Phalangists benefited from these programs, which were aimed, in part, at undermining the power of the traditional leaders among the Christian communities, as ipso facto that enhanced their own role as a well-organized modern party.

During the years 1966–67, the Phalangists began to be disillusioned with Shihabism. Shihabist members of Parliament started, in early 1964, to organize themselves as a parliamentary bloc *(al-Nahj al-Shihabi)*, to rely on the support of the Deuxième Bureau (the military intelligence), and the army in general, to get elected, and to get political benefits for themselves. The Phalangists' disillusionment, however, according to a prominent member of the party, was primarily due to the fact that by 1967 Shihabism had "changed the traditional foreign policy of Lebanon which had been characterized by neutralism on the regional and international levels."[9] Moreover, the Phalangists claimed that the Shihabist establishment was flirting with leftists, including the Lebanese Communist Party.[10] Thus the Phalangists were disenchanted with the Shihabists, from the mid-1960s on, both because of their foreign policies, and their reliance on the army and the Deuxième Bureau. They eventually turned against Shihabism. But it was the turbulent events of the Arab countries east of Lebanon which affected most significantly their attitude towards Shihabism. The Phalangists' reaction to the regional upheavals between 1966 and 1968 was not unlike their previous reaction in 1956–1958. All their old fears were revived, and as a result they adopted the narrow conception of Lebanese nationalism, expounded by Emile Iddi during the French Mandate, and the early years of independence, and by Camille Sham'un since late in 1956. This culminated in the formation of *al-Hilf al-Thulathi* (the Tripartite Alliance) between the Phalangists, Raymond Iddi's National Block, and Sham'un's National Liberal Party, and they ran together in the elections of 1968.[11]

The Phalangists benefited tremendously from the Shihabist regime. Their alliance with Shihabism was symbolized by Maurice Jumayil, a relative of Pierre Jumayil and an important member of the Phalangist Party, whose work on development and planning was very much in the line of the Shihabist era from 1958 to 1968. By the late 1960s, the Phalangist Party had become a formidable political force, with influence spreading to the southern and northern regions of Lebanon. Ironically, the Shihabism upon which the Phalangists had relied for so long, had become, by the late 1960s, their target of attack. The very raison d'être of the Tripartite Alliance of the 1960s was its anti-Shihabist plank. When Sulayman Franjiya was elected and the Shihabist candidate Ilyas Sarkis was defeated in the presidential elections of August 1970, the Lebanese Army was purged of its Shihabist officers, and this marked the demise of Shihabism as a political force in Lebanon.

The Phalangist Party relied more and more on its militias from the late 1960s onward, as the armed presence of the Palestinians became firmly established in Lebanon, and was guaranteed by the Cairo Agreement of 1969. The ejection of the Palestinian guerrillas from Jordan between September 1970 and December 1971 increased the importance of Lebanon for the Palestinian guerrillas. Their growing number aroused the suspicions and fears of the Phalangists, who viewed them as a state within a state. The Phalangists demanded control of the Palestinian armed presence in Lebanon, a demand which received the support of other political parties and groups, such as Sham'un's National Liberal Party, the Maronite League, and smaller groups such as the Guardians of the Cedars. During Franjiya's presidency, the fighting which took place in May 1973 between the Lebanese Army and the Palestinian guerrillas, in the wake of the assassination of three prominent Palestinian leaders by an Israeli raid in the heart of Beirut, in April 1973, was another important landmark which made the Phalangists and other groups prepare for the showdown with the Palestinian guerrillas in Lebanon. Thus, during the period between 1967 and 1975, the Phalangist Party became overconcerned with the armed presence of the Palestinians and Lebanese. During this period, they shared their fears and their goals with other parties and groups, and especially with Sham'un's National Liberal Party. They began seriously cooperating with them.

The Phalangists became the defenders of the political establishment, par excellence, although they participated with other political parties of both the Right and the Left, to discuss, in the early 1970s, the development of a modern political party system based on party affiliation, rather than on sectarian and *mahsubiya* loyalty. Thus the Phalangist Party, at the time, was dual in character: on the one hand it was a well-organized party with militias and a sophisticated electoral machine, and on the other, its appeal was basically sectarian.

Despite the fact that the Phalangist Party was a modern organization, it was more sectarian than the traditional Christian leadership. The Phalangist Party never had a Phalangist deputy, who belonged to any of the Muslim sects, representing it in Parliament, while the old Constitutional Bloc of Bishara al-Khuri had many Muslim deputies. Sham'un himself had Muslim members representing his party or allied with it, such as the Shi'ite Mahmud 'Ammar and the Druze Bashir al-A'war. Both, however, were elected in predominantly Christian constituencies. The most important Muslim in Sham'un's Party was the Shi'ite Qadhim al-Khalil, vice-president of the National Liberal Party, and an ex-deputy for the Tyre constituency. Raymond Iddi's National Bloc also had Muslim members, such as the Shi'ite Ahmad Isbir, who was a deputy representing the Jubail constituency on Iddi's list. Thus, although the Phalangist Party had become more "national" in character during the years 1967–1975, it had remained more sectarian than the traditional Christian leadership with which it had been in competition, but which it had now largely replaced.

THE NATIONAL LIBERAL PARTY

Camille Sham'un, the founder and president of the National Liberal Party, had a long history of political activism before the establishment of his own party in 1959. Camille Sham'un was born in 1900, in Dair al-Qamar, a town of the Shuf area, a descendant of a family of scribes to the feudal lords, and of government officials. He studied law and became a prominent member of Bishara al-Khuri's Constitutional Bloc in the 1930s.[12] His British connections during the Second World War were valuable to Bishara al-Khuri, and vital to the independence of Lebanon in 1943. He was known for his pro-Arab stands, and his "Arabism," as well as his pro-British leanings, which endeared him to many Arab rulers, and in particular to the Hashimite rulers of Iraq and Jordan. Until 1951, Sham'un was regarded as a leading member of al-Khuri's Constitutional Bloc.

The National Socialist Front which emerged, in 1952, in opposition to Bishara al-Khuri, held the same views as the president did on the role of Lebanon in the Arab world. The National Socialist Front, led by Junblat, Sham'un, Tuwaini, and others, was concerned with domestic reform in the administration and the government, as well as with the removal of al-Khuri's corrupt entourage, and especially of his powerful brother, nicknamed Sultan Salim.[13] It was not concerned with foreign policy.

After the resignation of President Bishara al-Khuri, in September 1952, there were two major candidates for the presidency: Camille Sham'un and Hamid Franjiya. Both were members of the Constitutional Bloc, but the traditional

Muslim leaders preferred the former because of his strong, pro-Arab credentials.[14]

Sham'un, unlike al-Khuri, did not have a stable working partnership (between 1952 and 1956) with a strong Muslim leader as prime minister. On the contrary, he kept changing prime ministers, and thus weakened the position of the prime minister in the Lebanese political system. His partnership with Sami al-Sulh, on the other hand, during the period 1956–1958, although more stable, was very unequal in terms of political power, as Sami al-Sulh was a weak prime minister who had no political support among the Sunni community.

During the period 1956–1958 Sham'un followed a foreign policy that was consistent with his former pro-Arab stands and his pro-British leanings. However, this was done when new developments were taking place in the Arab world. He was definitely in favor of the pro-Western Kingdoms of Iraq and Jordan, and turned against the tide of the anti-Western Arab nationalism in many parts of the Arab world, which Nasirism had led to emerge. Nasir's defiance of the West with his nationalization of the Suez Canal, and his remaining in power in spite of the Suez War in 1956, made him a hero overnight in the eyes of the Arab masses, and in particular with the urban Muslim masses in Lebanon. Sham'un was aware of these new trends in the Arab world but remained a staunch ally of his pro-Western friends like Nuri al-Sa'id of Iraq. He also thought that if he rode the pro-Western tide and accepted the Eisenhower Doctrine, he would be able to amend the constitution, and get reelected to the presidency. He rigged the elections of 1957, and a large number of traditional leaders, such as Ahmad al-As'ad, Kamal Junblat, and others, lost their seats in parliament. The union of Egypt and the Syrians, as the new United Arab Republic, in February 1958, in conjunction with the rigging of the elections, encouraged the traditional Muslim leaders to declare a "revolution" (al-Thawra) against Sham'un's regime, and the Civil War of 1958 began.

Sham'un relied domestically on the Lebanese nationalists, and exploited the fears and suspicions primarily of the Maronite community by accusing pro-Nasirites of undermining the independence of Lebanon, and of aiming at making it a satellite or even a "province" of the United Arab Republic.[15] The Phalangist Party and the Syrian Social Nationalist Party (both of which feared the Nasirite wave of Arabism), as well as Raymond Iddi's National Bloc and other pro-Western politicians like Charles Malik, supported Sham'un's stands. However, some prominent Christian leaders were against him, such as Rene Mu'awwad and Hamid Franjiya in Zgharta, the Constitutional Bloc leaders in Mount Lebanon, and the leaders of the Third Force, Henri Far'un, Charles Hilu, and others. Moreover, the Maronite Patriarch, Mar Bulus al-Ma'ushi, was openly against Sham'un, especially with regard to his ambitions for a second term as president of Lebanon.

Sham'un's term ended on September 22, 1958. By then, he had already built a popular political base for himself among the Maronite masses, based in part on his charisma and his strong ties with certain important leaders, mostly

Christian, but with some Muslim leaders as well, especially Shi'ite, in the various regions of Lebanon, whom he tried to play against rival traditional leaders, during his presidency. To this category belonged Sam'an al-Duwayhi in Zgharta, Jean Harb in Batrun, 'Adil 'Usairan in Zahrani, and Qadhim al-Khalil in Tyre. With this political base, a combination of charisma among the Maronite Christians and traditional electoral alliances, Sham'un's National Liberal Party, formed in 1959, was able to win four seats in Parliament in 1960, and six seats in 1964.[16] Nevertheless, during Shihab's regime, Sham'un and his allies in Parliament remained outside the pale of the political establishment.

Sham'un's power increased when he allied himself with the other two parties of the Tripartite Alliance, the Phalangist Party and the National Bloc, and especially after the parliamentary elections of 1968, which marked the beginning of the decline of Shihabism in Lebanon. Even President Charles Hilu, who had been elected in 1964 to continue the work of President Shihab, became disillusioned with Shihabism towards the end of his term. By the late 1960s, the National Liberal Party had also acquired a clear ideology, centered first on the safeguarding of the free enterprise system, against incursions from the radical Left *(al-Yasar al-Mutatarrif)*, whether in Lebanon or in the Arab countries to the east. Their second platform was the struggle against the Shihabist military establishment *(al-Militariya)*, which was accused of allying itself with the radical Left.[17] The National Liberal Party tended to represent the interests of the Christian big bourgeoisie. Sham'un himself was either president or member of the board of at least five joint-stock companies: the Iron and Steel National Company, the Universal Company, Almaza Company, the National Woolen Products, and Protein Company.[18]

Sham'un's return to the political scene as a major figure coincided with the declining popularity of Shihabism. This was due to the heavy-handed way the military establishment had dealt with some of the traditional Christian and Muslim leaders, and had interfered in politics, in parliamentary elections and in the selection of cabinet ministers. The parliamentary elections of 1968 witnessed the growing power of the Tripartite Alliance and of Sham'un in Parliament.[19] From then on, Sham'un could no longer be ignored. The presidential elections of 1970, which led to the election of Sulayman Franjiya, the leader of the Centrist Bloc (whose views fell between those of the Tripartite Alliance and the Shihabist parliamentary bloc), was, in a way, a victory for Sham'un. During Franjiya's presidency, when the army was de-Shihabized (that is, when Shihabist officers were removed from key positions), Sham'un managed to place some of his supporters in the highest echelons of the army such as, for example, General Iskandar Ghanim, who became the commander of the Lebanese Army. Under Franjiya, even Prime Minister Sa'ib Salam had to be reconciled with Sham'un before he could form his cabinet. Sham'un's ability to influence events and people, and in particular the president himself, was significant when the clashes of May 1973 took place between the Lebanese Army and the Palestinians. The relationship of Sham'un to Franjiya is of paramount importance in understanding the developments that led to the Civil War during Franjiya's presidency.

SULAYMAN FRANJIYA

Sulayman Franjiya's role in the Conservative Lebanese Front would not have been so important if it were not for his position as president of the republic between 1970 and 1976. He replaced his brother, Hamid Franjiya, as head of the Franjiya clan in Zgharta, when the latter had a stroke that paralyzed him in the late 1950s. Hamid Franjiya had been a lawyer by profession and had had many years of experience in national politics. He had been a member of the Constitutional Bloc and an unsuccessful candidate for the presidency in 1952. Sulayman Franjiya, on the other hand, was known for his parochial views and possessed neither training in nor knowledge of national or international affairs. It was therefore a surprise to many Lebanese to see him elected to the presidency, defeating the Shihabist candidate, Ilyas Sarkis.

The defeat of Sarkis was, in part, due to the decline in the popularity of Shihabism in Lebanon. The reasons for this decline were many. First, some of the traditional leaders resented the reforms initiated by Shihab, such as, for example, the strengthening of the executive. Second, they also resented the continued interference of the army in politics, under both Shihab and President Charles Hilu, which led, under Hilu, especially after 1964, to a duality of power (al-Izdiwajiya)–the president on the one hand, and the Deuxième Bureau (the military intelligence) on the other. The leading Lebanese daily, *Al-Nahar*, repeatedly emphasized the theme of "duality," and popularized it through the caricatures of Pierre Sadiq. Third, both the conservative parties of the Tripartite Alliance and the leftist parties which were under surveillance, were critical of the antidemocratic tendencies of the Shihabist establishment. Consequently, Franjiya's election was hailed by many as the triumph of political freedom and democratic rights. In fact, his election was a shift to the Right.

Franjiya widened his political base while in power and, in the parliamentary elections of 1972 the Franjiya Bloc, led by his son Toni Franjiya, had seven members. His influence expanded in al-Kura, Bsharri, and his son-in-law was elected in 'Akkar.[20] Nevertheless, Franjiya's political base was still regional in character.

Sulayman Franjiya came from a region where there was a tradition of clan allegiance, and where feuds were frequently violent and bloody (as in the incident at the Mizyara Church in 1957). Moreover, the leadership was not motivated by a clear ideology. The Franjiya clan, headed by Hamid, and then by Sulayman, was against Sham'un during the 1958 Civil War, and both brothers had to flee to Syria during that time, although they were not pro-Arab nationalists. Personal relations and clan feuds largely determined their political attitudes.

For instance, Sham'un's support, during his presidency, of their rival clan, the Duwayhis in the Zgharta region, led them to oppose him strongly in the 1958 Civil War.

However, during the 1975-76 Civil War, the five clans of the Zgharta region—the Franjiyas, Mu'awwads, Duwayhis, Karams, and Bulos—closed ranks, and fought under the banner of the Conservative Lebanese Front. Their local militias were called the Marada Brigade *(Liwa' al-Marada)*, and the Zgharta Liberation Army *(Jaish al-Tahrir al-Zghartawi)*. And consequently the bone of contention between Sham'un and the Franjiyas disappeared.

OTHER ORGANIZATIONS OF THE CLF

There were a number of other organizations and groups that were an integral part of the Conservative Lebanese Front. Among the most important was Al-Tanzim (the Organization), established by the president of the Medical Association, Dr. Fu'ad Shamali, who was also a member of the executive board of the Maronite League *(al-Rabita al-Maruniya)*. Al-Tanzim was a small but well-organized militia. It was suspected that it was financed by the Maronite League.[21] When a unified military command of the Lebanese Front was formed in August 1976, the representative of the Tanzim, George 'Idwan, held the second highest position.

Another important group was the Guardians of the Cedars *(Hurras al-Arz)*, founded in the early 1970s, with a strong anti-Palestinian plank. Their leader during the Civil War, and until August 1976, was the famous poet and writer Sa'id 'Aql, although the militia was under the leadership of Etienne Saqr. They adhered to a strongly chauvinistic conception of Lebanese nationalism and were vehemently against the armed presence of the Palestinians in Lebanon.[22] They were also, however, against the traditional leaders and couched their somewhat fascistic ideology in anticapitalistic terms, reminiscent to some extent of petit-bourgeois organizations in Europe in the earlier decades of this century.

Several other regional organizations were also members of the Conservative Lebanese Front. The most important was the Zahli group *(al-Tajammu' al-Zahli)*, led by the Maronite deputy of Zahla, Ilyas al-Harawi, which had its own local militias. Another local militia was that of the Lebanese Youth Movement *(Harakat al-Shabiba al-Lubnaniya)*, in the Dikwana suburb of Beirut, headed by the charismatic leader Marun al-Khuri. There were other local militias, such as the one led by Henri Sufair in Rayfun (Kisrawan region), and the local militias of the Bsharri region of northern Lebanon, led by traditional Maronite leaders.

Another important component of the Conservative Lebanese Front (CLF) was the Maronite clergy represented by the head of the Maronite Order of Monks, Father Sharbal Qassis. The public political role of the Maronite clergy in the Civil War of 1975-76 was unprecedented, especially when compared to the role they played in the 1952 and 1958 crises. The open political support given by the bulk of the Maronite clergy to the CLF was reminiscent of their role in the events of the period between 1840 and 1860. The influence of the local Maronite priests on the villages and small towns was tremendous, and therefore their political activities were crucial in rallying support for the CLF throughout the Civil War.

THE NATIONAL BLOC

Although the CLF had the support of the majority of the Maronites and the Maronite leaders, the National Bloc, headed by Raymond Iddi, was a notable exception. After Emile Iddi's death in 1949, his son, Raymond Iddi, took over the leadership of the National Bloc and continued its unabated opposition to Bishara al-Khuri's regime. In the parliamentary elections of 1951, the National Bloc had only two deputies. Later, however, when Sham'un was president, it played a more important role. It had four deputies in Parliament in 1957, and participated in Sami al-Sulh's cabinet of March–September 1958. Its leader, Raymond Iddi, was definitely a Lebanese nationalist, not unlike the Phalangists. Therefore, it was not surprising that the National Bloc attracted, in the late 1940s and early 1950s, individuals who in their youth had been members of the Phalangist Party.

Raymond Iddi's aspirations to the presidency began in the 1950s, when he ran against Fu'ad Shihab, knowing that he had no chance of winning, but just, as he claimed at the time, to keep the democratic principle of opposition alive. There was a short honeymoon with Shihabism when Raymond Iddi served on the four member cabinet in the first year of Shihab's presidency. However, in the early 1960s, he moved to the opposition and against the Shihabist regime, and the deputies representing the National Bloc in Parliament decreased from seven in 1960 to two in the Parliament of 1964. This opposition culminated when the National Bloc joined the Tripartite Alliance. This move was motivated by purely domestic reasons, unlike the Phalangists and Sham'unists.[23]

The duality of power under the Shihabist regimes (including Hilu's), and the interference of the army in the political system, prompted the National Bloc to join with the two other parties. It was clear, however, that Raymond Iddi was continuing to take a nonaligned stand on the cold war issues and on communism. The other two parties of the Tripartite Alliance did not. The National Bloc even attempted, by the late 1960s, to project the image of a social democratic party, in marked contrast to the National Liberal Party of Sham'un, for instance.[24] Raymond Iddi explained that his alliance with the Phalangists and Sham'unists was solely to save the country from the growing influence of the military under the Shihabists' rule. It was not, he claimed, an alliance against the reforms initiated by Shihab.[25]

By the late 1960s, the National Bloc, under Raymond Iddi, had become more moderate in its views, very much like its old rival, the Constitutional Bloc of Bishara al-Khuri. This was in contrast to the more militant Lebanese nationalist parties, the Phalangist Party and Sham'un's NLP. This tendency became clearer in the 1970s, especially during the Civil War of 1975-76. Nevertheless, Raymond Iddi remained a consistent critic of the Cairo Agreement of November 1969, between the Lebanese government and the PLO. He argued that the Cairo Agreement would either lead to Israeli occupation of southern Lebanon, or to so much fighting and destruction that most of its inhabitants would be forced to flee to the cities. Otherwise, Iddi was very much against the organized militias of some of the militant parties, and openly described the Phalangists as fascists in character.

During most of Franjiya's presidency, Iddi was in the opposition both in Parliament and in the cabinet except for the first two years. His chances of becoming president rose in the mid-1970s, in part due to his independent personality, which appealed to many, and in part to his frequent visits to southern Lebanon, which increased his popularity. However, Iddi was not an organizer—his party remained a cadre party and not a mass party using Duverger's term, with only regional strength in Mount Lebanon, and in particular in Jubail.

In early 1975 he formed an alliance with Sunni leaders Sa'ib Salam and Rashid Karami, a classical move for presidential aspirants. During the Civil War he remained in western Beirut, and became a founding member of the National Union Front (see Chapter Three below). He continued to oppose the Conservative Lebanese Front, and was especially critical of the role played by President Franjiya and the Phalangist Party in the Civil War. Iddi, former ex-Shihabists, and/or ex-members of the Constitutional Bloc, such as Jean 'Aziz, Manuel Yunis, and Shaikh Michel al-Khuri, represented the moderate Maronite leadership, which would have been an alternative to the Conservative Lebanese Front, but lacked mass support among the Maronites themselves.

THE CLF DURING THE CIVIL WAR

The first phase of the Civil War, which began on April 13, 1975 with the ambushing of a bus passing through the Phalangist stronghold of 'Ain al-Rummana, put the Phalangist Party and its allies on the defensive. The Phalangist Party refused, at first, to give up those who had been responsible for the ambushing of the bus, and this triggered the first round of fighting, in which the Phalangist Party bore the brunt of the fighting against the PRM and their Lebanese allies in the suburbs of Beirut—'Ain al-Rummana, al-Shiyyah, Furn al-Shubbak, and Dikwana. However, the attempt by Junblat and his supporters to isolate the Phalangist Party politically, resulted in the closing of ranks of all the conservative parties and groups, namely, the Phalangists, the Maronite League, Sham'un's

NLP, and the Maronite Order of Monks. The Phalangists, realizing that Prime Minister Rashid al-Sulh was under pressure from Junblat and the PRM, asked their own representatives in the cabinet to resign, hoping the whole cabinet would fall. Thus, by putting the blame on the weakness of the prime minister and by then demanding his resignation, the Phalangist Party was attempting to divert attention from itself.[26]

This worked only in part. The resignation of al-Sulh was accompanied by a statement read in Parliament blaming the Phalangists for ambushing the bus in April 1975. It also accused them of provoking the PRM because they were against the armed presence of the Palestinians in Lebanon.[27] The Phalangist Party's reaction to this was that Prime Minister al-Sulh had prematurely decided that it was guilty, which was not for him to decide but for the judiciary to decide.[28] The Phalangist Party maintained that all the incidents would not have occurred had the prime minister, who was also minister of the interior, been able to exercise his authority, and to establish law and order.[29]

President Franjiya had the full support of the conservative parties, namely, the Phalangists and Sham'un's NLP, when he announced the formation of a military cabinet on May 23, 1975. This decision reflected the general view of the conservative parties that only a strong cabinet could reestablish "stability and security" in Lebanon.[30]

After the failure of the military cabinet, the Phalangist Party and Sham'un countered Junblat's insistence upon a cabinet without Phalangist representation by demanding a cabinet of parliamentarians representing both Sham'un's NLP and the Phalangist Party. The latter also accused Junblat of obstructing the formation of a new cabinet by putting forth such conditions. Pierre Jumayil, the leader of the Phalangist Party, insisted until late June that a "national union cabinet" had to be formed to include the Phalangist Party, the NLP, and Junblat himself.[31] However, under political pressure from many sides (the Syrians, Junblat, and even Sham'un), the Phalangists reluctantly accepted the formation of a new cabinet on July 1, 1975, in which they were not represented.[32]

After a lull of about two months, clashes took place in Zahla, Tripoli, and Zgharta in late August and early September 1975. Conservative political leaders and groups demanded the army's intervention to stop the fighting. Pierre Jumayil accused those whom he described as elements of the "international Left" (al-Yasar al-Duwali), of undermining the Lebanese state by opposing the involvement of the army to stop the fighting. However, some limited intervention of the army to stop the combatants in the Tripoli-Zgharta regions did take place, after General Hanna Sa'id became commander of the army on September 9, 1975, replacing General Iskandar Ghanim.

As the fighting intensified, especially in the commercial center of Beirut and its suburbs ('Ain al-Rummana, Shiyyah, Nab'a and Sin al-Fil), efforts were made to assert the authority of the government and reestablish law and order. The formation of the National Dialogue Committee (Lajnat al-Hiwar al-Watani) was an attempt to resort to political discussion of the issues which divided the major political groups and parties in the Civil War. On the eve of the formation of the National Dialogue Committee, Pierre Jumayil gave a press interview in which he raised some of the fundamental issues in the crisis. First, he maintained that the National Pact formula of 1943 was well suited to Lebanon, and denied that Phalangists and other conservative parties were in favor of the partition of Lebanon. He added that the solution of the crisis in Lebanon was to "put a limit to the incursions of the international Left" in Lebanese affairs,[33] a theme he brought up time and again throughout the Civil War. He also raised some major questions, which he believed had to be answered before any political solution to the crisis could be found, namely, whether Lebanon was to have a socialist or a capitalist system, and whether Lebanon was to be a Christian or a Muslim national homeland.[34] He thus put forward the issues which the conservative parties and organizations were most concerned with, and which they most wanted to be resolved.

During this second phase of the Civil War it was clear that the views of Franjiya, Sham'un, and the Phalangist Party had become so close with respect to the role of the army in the fighting, and the Palestinian armed presence in Lebanon, that a "natural" alliance began to be formed between them. It was also noted that Sham'un was having a growing influence on decision making in the Ba'abda Presidential Palace, where he lived from early July 1975 on.[35] From mid-September 1975 it was obvious that Franjiya had sided completely with the Phalangists and Sham'un. There was also some evidence to show that the Phalangist Party and Sham'un, in alliance with Franjiya, were trying during that period to escalate the conflict so that a state of emergency would be called and the army could then be used to intervene in the fighting. This was based on their assumption that, first the army could keep law and order in the country and second, because of the existence among the Palestinian Resistance Movement of the rejectionist elements and groups, the PRM would be unable to keep all its forces under control, even if it wished to, and that consequently the army was needed for that purpose.

The third phase of the Civil War began with the meetings of the National Dialogue Committee and its various subcommittees, to find a political solution to the conflict. Both Sham'un and Pierre Jumayil were members of the NDC. Jumayil, whose party was the leading member of the Conservative Lebanese Front, emphasized two preconditions to the finding of a political solution. First, reforms or changes were to be preceded by the establishment of law and order in the country. Second, he emphasized the importance of Lebanon's territorial sovereignty and the need for the Lebanese government to reassert its authority over the whole of Lebanon.[36]

The fighting on the 'Ain al-Rummana-al-Shiyyah front, which had almost stopped, began again during that period on the Nab'a-Sin al-Fil front, and the Dikwana-Tal al-Za'tar front. Junblat accused the Phalangists of shifting the fighting to involve Palestinian camps in order to show the Arab foreign ministers who were meeting in Cairo that the Lebanese conflict was between the Lebanese and the Palestinians.[37] This, according to Junblat, was to gain the support of the Arab countries and "Arabize" the conflict.

Franjiya complained about the inability of Karami's cabinet to stop the fighting, and implied that, had the military cabinet of May 1975 remained in power, law and order would have prevailed and the government would not have had to face the problem of whether or not to use the army.[38]

The Phalangist Party and some of the other conservative groups, such as the Maronite League and the Lebanese Maronite Order of Monks, put the blame for the crisis on the Palestinians. Jumayil spoke at the meeting of the NDC on November 3, 1975 about the five percent group of Palestinians who dominated their compatriots, and insisted that the NDC discuss the problem of the Palestinians in their meetings. He added that the Lebanese government could still control them, if there was mutual trust between the Lebanese Christians and Muslims.[39] Jumayil continued, on a conciliatory note, that although fifty percent of the Christian community in Lebanon were entertaining the idea of partition, the Phalangist Party itself was against it.[40]

Junblat accused the Phalangist Party, the other conservative groups, and Sham'un of preparing themselves for another round of fighting, and of bringing in foreign mercenaries to train their militias.[41] The arrival of a ship loaded with weapons and ammunition to Aqua Marine in Juniya in early November 1975 gave some validity to Junblat's accusations. When Prime Minister Karami asked Commander of the Army Hanna Sa'id to confiscate the arms and take over the ship, the army was unable to take any action against the militias of the Phalangist Party and of Toni Franjiya. This confirmed the suspicions of both Karami and Junblat that the army was not impartial in the conflict but that it sided with the conservative groups, and did not obey the orders given to it by Karami, as the minister of defense (as well as the prime minister).[42]

The Phalangists' reaction to those accusations was expressed in a manifesto issued on November 6, 1975, in which they stated that the flow of arms and weapons to any party or political group, other than the Lebanese government, had to be stopped. They added that the reason some Lebanese had weapons was that certain groups, over which the government had no effective authority, were heavily armed themselves. The Phalangist Party pointed out that the NM and the PRM had been getting a large number of rocket launchers, artillery, and other weapons. It then urged Prime Minister Karami to assert the authority of the government over the whole of Lebanon, and not just over those regions in which the Christians were the majority.[43] The manifesto also emphasized that the campaign against the role of the army in the Aqua Marine incident was the continuation of the plan to paralyze the army and prevent it from, in the Phalangists' words, protecting the Lebanese people and their property.[44]

In spite of this crisis and the strained relations between Karami and both the Phalangist Party and Sham'un, the cabinet survived. The High Coordination Committee (HCC), composed of members from all parties, which had been established in October 1975 to keep law and order in Lebanon, also survived the Aqua Marine crisis.

It was noted at the time, that Sham'un and the Phalangist Party were cooperating very closely and were expressing similar views during the HCC meetings. Raymond Iddi regarded himself and his National Bloc Party as neutral, and maintained his alliance with Karami and Salam.[45] Iddi said that the government in the aftermath of the Aqua Marine incident, was suffering from a duality in the exercise of political authority. On the one hand, there was the division between Karami as minister of defense and Sham'un as minister of the interior, and on the other, there was the split between Prime Minister Karami and President Sulayman Franjiya.[46]

The discussions of the National Dialogue Committee led to certain recommendations. In the meeting held on November 4, 1975, which representatives of Sham'un and the Phalangist Party did not attend, the annulment of Article 95 of the Constitution, and Article 96 of the employees statute (Legislative Decree 112, dated June 6, 1959), was recommended in order to abolish sectarianism in the civil service and in the formation of cabinets.[47] The political bureau of the Phalangist Party attacked the NDC, saying that they had no legal authority or representation to recommend the abolition of sectarianism in public affairs and the civil service. It added that as long as there was a cabinet, and the Chamber of Deputies was in session, these institutions alone were entitled constitutionally to make decisions on such matters.[48]

Strong criticism was also leveled against the NDC by the Maronite League and the Lebanese Maronite Order of Monks. These groups said that the NDC was unrepresentative and that political dialogue was not possible in an atmosphere of "terror, pressure, and the existing occupation of a large section of [Lebanese] territory."[49] Some of the constitutional amendments suggested by the NDC, according to Sharbal Qassis, the head of the Lebanese Maronite Order of Monks, showed "a flagrant attempt to destroy the National Pact."[50]

President Franjiya and the Phalangist Party tried successfully to move the discussion of reform and constitutional amendment from the NDC to the cabinet. There Franjiya could preside, Sham'un would be there, as a member of the cabinet; however, Junblat's NM would have no representative.[51] In this respect, Franjiya, Sham'un, and their allies were able to undermine the role of the NDC. Karami demanded a new interpretation of the Constitution, rather than a repeat or an amendment of certain articles, and emphasized the role of the cabinet in deciding these matters. Karami's attitude was in harmony with Pierre Jumayil's statement that "no change in the Constitution was needed but simply an interpretation and clarification of certain points."[52]

It was obvious that, by mid-November 1975, a new front of conservative, predominantly Maronite, parties and groups was emerging, although not yet formally organized. There were the Phalangists, Sham'un's NLP, President Franjiya, Shamali's Tanzim, the Guardians of the Cedars, the Maronite League, the Lebanese Order of Maronite Monks, and other Maronite orders of monks. Simultaneously, Maronite priests and some intellectuals formed the "Kaslik Congress" meeting in Kaslik, where the Maronite University of the Holy Spirit is located. They began issuing statements and preparing studies in support of the conservative conception of Lebanese nationalism. The role of the Maronite Patriarch Khuraish was politically neutral and therefore above the divisions in his community and in Lebanon. However, the fact that Maronite monks openly and fully supported one side (which was unprecedented in its degree of activism and involvement) without the patriarch clearly and unequivocally disassociating himself from them, or exercizing his religious authority to curb their activities, was of great significance.

The statements issued by the Kaslik Congress expressed a strongly conservative view on most of the issues involved in the conflict. The memorandum submitted to members of the Chamber of Deputies, by the permanent Congress of the Lebanese Maronite Order of Monks and the Maronite League, dated November 6, 1975, shows the way some of the conservative Maronites interpreted Lebanese nationalism, and what constituted in their eyes the very basis of the Lebanese entity.

The Lebanese formula of the National Pact, according to this memorandum, consisted of four major principles. The first principle, expressed in the statement referring to Lebanon's neutrality, was interpreted by the writers of the memorandum to mean that non-Muslim sects would never give priority to those interests that were against those of the Arab and Islamic world, while the "Muslim sects would never give priority to Arab and Islamic interests over the interests of the Lebanese state."[53]

The second principle, taken from Riyad al-Sulh's cabinet program of 1943, was that Lebanon was "a free, independent, and sovereign country."[54] This originally referred to the principle that Lebanon would not be tied to or used by imperialist forces. The memorandum interpreted this to mean that any form of "imperialism," from the West or from the East (the Arab hinterland), would be unconstitutional.

The third principle of the 1943 National Pact, according to the writers of the memorandum, was that, although Lebanon was to have an Arab character, it could select from Western civilization that which would be beneficial to itself.[55] This principle, according to the memorandum, was meant to reassure the Christians that "Lebanon was not organically linked to the Arab countries,"[56] and would continue to have a distinctive character, and retain its particular identity.

The fourth principle of the National Pact, according to the memorandum, was that the president of the Republic would be a Maronite Christian, and that his executive powers would not be in any way either curbed or restricted. Both these elements were necessary, for a Maronite president without his powers would not constitute an effective guarantee for the security of the Christians of Lebanon.

The memorandum came to the conclusion that the National Pact of 1943 was not to be interpreted in terms of the relationship between a minority and a majority. Rather, an interpretation ought to be an attempt to reconcile two different conceptions of the nature and role of Lebanon, as a political entity held by the two major parties in the conflict.[57]

In the light of these four principles, the writers of the memorandum examined the problem of the armed presence of the Palestinian Resistance Movement in Lebanon. They argued that the demand expressed by the NM and the traditional Muslim leaders, to cooperate with the PRM, and provide it with support and protection, introduced a new element that upset the balance of the National Pact. First, they asked why Lebanon had to support and cooperate with the PRM when, according to Article 1 of the Constitution, "the Lebanese state is a neutral state in all the meanings of the word neutral."[58] Second, they argued that the Palestinian armed presence impinged upon the internal and external sovereignty of the Lebanese state. Giving the Palestinians a free hand in pursuing its objectives unconditionally and without reservations, was, according to the writers of the memorandum, a ploy used by the NM and the traditional Muslim leaders, to tilt the balance in their favor. That would lead, they argued, to Lebanon "sacrificing" itself for the Palestinian cause, and suffering from the existence of a "dual authority,"[59] on its own territory.

The writers of the memorandum regarded the ability of the PRM to recruit members from among the Lebanese, as evidence that the loyalty of the Muslims of Lebanon went beyond the borders of Lebanon. They argued that since the establishment of the Arab kingdom in Damascus in 1920, the rise of Nasirism, the Ba'th Party, and, finally, the Palestinian resistance of the late 1960s, the loyalty of the Muslims had always been to an entity larger than Lebanon.

To revive the old formula of the National Pact, the writers believed that it was necessary to make all Lebanese declare their loyalty to Lebanon as a permanent entity, politically independent from both the East and the West.[60] They also thought it was necessary to reexamine the rights of freedom of the press and freedom of assembly and organization in the light of Lebanon's interests, so that these rights would not be abused and lead eventually to undermining the state. They believed ownership of property by non-Lebanese ought to be examined as well, and the number of aliens resident in Lebanon ought to be controlled. Moreover, representation according to ratios, of the various sects in the cabinet and the Chamber of Deputies, ought to be kept, as the Constitution had stipulated, and the sect of the president of the Republic and his constitutional powers ought to remain unchanged. Finally, the writers of the memorandum believed, the institutions of the government and the state were to be strengthened and the rule of law was to be enforced.[61]

The latter part of November 1975 was characterized by the decline in the importance of the NDC and its subcommittees, as dialogue and discussions of political reform and national reconciliation shifted to the cabinet. The meeting of the NDC on November 24, 1975, failed—Sham'un boycotted the meeting, while Raymond Iddi and Sa'ib Salam who did attend, left in protest of the absence of Minister of Interior Sham'un. It was reported that Sham'un boycotted the meeting because the majority of the members of the NDC wanted the kind of political reform to which he, as well as Franjiya and their allies, were opposed. Pierre Jumayil came to the NDC meeting and was more conciliatory in his attitude. Nevertheless, he emphasized the urgency of security matters, which, he believed, had to take precedence over any fundamental changes made in the political system of Lebanon—a reiteration of his former position.[62] It is interesting to note that 'Asim Qansu, head of the pro-Syrian Organization of the Ba'th Party, maintained that the Phalangist Party was a victim of the other conservative parties and groups, such as the National Liberal Party, and the Guardians of the Cedars, as well as of President Franjiya himself.[63]

The statement of November 29, 1975, issued by President Franjiya, was a result of his agreement with Prime Minister Karami on the basic issues, such as reform, expanding the cabinet, and regulating relations between the Lebanese authorities and the PRM.[64] It was significant that President Franjiya, who had never before made any public address or statement, decided to be more conciliatory. This move was probably aimed at demonstrating the superfluousness of the NDC, as he, together with the cabinet, seemed to have ironed out most of the problems that were at the roots of the conflict. The presence of the French envoy, Maurice Couve de Murville, who had arrived a few days earlier, may have been an additional factor in leading Franjiya to change his public attitude.

However, the decisions stated on November 29, 1975 were not implemented. In fact, by early December 1975 the fighting escalated in Beirut, especially in the commercial area and the hotel district. The NDC had become inactive, and the High Coordination Committee was unable to convene because some of the representatives of the NM boycotted it, although representatives of the National Liberal Party, the Phalangists, the PRM, and Qansu's Organization of the Ba'th attended.[65] Both the attempts, first to convene a national conference for the reconciliation of the parties to the conflict, and second, to expand the cabinet, failed also, and Karami threatened to resign.

On the other hand, the political and military coordination between Sham'un, the Phalangist Party, and Franjiya increased. The Phalangists were leading their allies in the commercial areas and hotel district fighting, while Franjiya's Zghartan Liberation Army was the major force fighting the NM and the Palestinians in Tripoli and the surrounding areas.[66]

After Pierre Jumayil's visit to Damascus on December 6, 1975, the Phalangist Party became more conciliatory in its public statements. In one statement, issued on December 16, it emphasized the importance of revitalizing the government institutions, and it expressed optimism that all parties, whether represented in the High Coordination Committee or not, were willing to stop the fighting. The statement included a reference to the need for "fundamental and comprehensive reform in political, economic, and social matters," and the possibility "of meeting the proponents of genuine reform on common grounds, and in an atmosphere of rational, open, and honest dialogue."[67] It also called for the "implementation of the agreements signed between the Lebanese state and the PLO, the only legitimate representative of the Palestinian people," specifying the Cairo Agreement and the Protocol of Milkart,[68] which is a detailed appendix of the Cairo Agreement added in May 1975. Nevertheless, the Phalangists still regarded the issues of security and sovereignty as the basic preconditions to enable the parties concerned to realize their goals for reform.[69]

The change which took place in the attitude of the Phalangist Party was brought about by the overtures the Syrians made to them. In late November, the pro-Syrian leader of the organization of the Ba'th Party, Qansu, described the Phalangists as the victims of their allies, Franjiya and Sham'un, implying that the latter were escalating the conflict, while the Phalangists were not (see p. 82). Jumayil's visit to Damascus on December 6, 1975, was an indication of Syria's willingness to cooperate with the Phalangist Party. However, the indiscriminate killing of almost two hundred Muslims by the Phalangists on December 6, 1975, in retaliation for the slaying of four Phalangists in al-Fanar, impeded the process of rapprochement between the Phalangist Party and the Syrians (see p. 82).

The differences between Franjiya and Karami continued in spite of their apparent reconciliation and cooperation. On the one hand, Franjiya attacked the PRM, saying that it did not abide by the Cairo Agreement, while on the other hand, he was criticized by Karami, Salam, and the NM, and was accused of collusion with the head of the military intelligence (the Deuxième Bureau), to escalate the fighting. Salam demanded the dismantling of all militias, as well as the resignation of Franjiya.[70]

On December 22, 1975, the Lebanese Research Committee of the Kaslik group issued another memorandum on general proposals for a reform program. It covered many areas—political, judicial, administrative, socioeconomic, and educational—and it was couched in less polarized terms than its first memorandum of November 6, 1975. It accepted the view that there was an internal dimension to the conflict in Lebanon, but believed that it was due to misgovernment on all levels, rather than to the nature of the political system itself. It also changed, somewhat, its attitude toward the Lebanese Constitution, and agreed that it could be changed in accordance with the people's needs. More specifically, the memorandum maintained that the president and the prime minister could be equal partners in the Lebanese political system, although the president was to retain his right to choose the prime minister. They believed that, up to this time, the president's dominant role in choosing the prime minister had been due primarily to the political fragmentation of the Chamber of Deputies, and the absence of a homogeneous majority in Parliament.[71] Furthermore, the memorandum rejected the proposal for the abolition of political sectarianism on the grounds that it would not eliminate sectarianism, but rather would enable the majority religious groups to dominate the system, to the detriment of the minority groups.[72]

On December 24, 1975, Pierre Jumayil gave a press conference to explain the Phalangists' point of view with respect to the conflict. Jumayil claimed that "international communism" *(al-Shuyu'iya al-Dawliya)* had exploited the contradictions existing in the Lebanese society, and had convinced the Palestinians that "whoever was not a Marxist was necessarily an enemy of the Palestinian Revolution."[73] Jumayil claimed that international communism had adopted the demands of the Muslims and made the assurances that had been given to the Christians in the 1940s appear to be unwarranted privileges, and a monopoly over political power. And consequently, according to Jumayil, it might have been possible to establish a good and well-organized modus vivendi between the PRM and the Lebanese, had it not been for the intervention of international communism, which had paralyzed the governing institutions of the Lebanese state, especially the army, and was aiming at taking over power in Lebanon.[74] He added that change in Lebanon by revolution was very difficult, if not impossible. The victory of one side would automatically mean the subjugation of the other, and that finally there could be no other alternative but to go back to the old principle of "no victor and no vanquished," a slogan that had been adopted after the 1958 Civil War.[75]

A Maronite summit was held on December 31, 1975, in the Presidential Palace, that included Sham'un, Jumayil, Qassis, and Franjiya. It was reported that the aim of the Maronite meeting was not to study the demands of the Muslims and Junblat's National Movement, but to "establish a united front both militarily and politically," that would include the Phalangist Party, Sham'un's NLP, the Maronite Order of Monks, the Maronite League, as well as the parties, organizations, and individuals allied to them.[76] This represented the first attempt to formalize the alliance between all the groups and parties that had found themselves on the same side with respect to the Civil War and the issues involved.

The views of the leaders who met in the Maronite summit meeting did not change much. Qassis, for example, regarded the proposed solutions and demands of the NM as "lean and absurd."[77] Jumayil, on the other hand, maintained that the demands neither endorsed nor reflected the spirit of the National Pact, and that consequently there could be no realistic hope of accepting them, especially as the fighting was still going on. Sham'un insisted on safeguarding the National Pact, and refused any changes in the terms of the pact.[78] This was somewhat of a reversal of previous stands, with respect to the Phalangist Party, especially after the statements that had been made when Jumayil returned from Syria. These stands were probably a response to the formation of the new Conservative Front after the Maronite summit.

The Lebanese-Palestinian conflict began again on January 7, 1976, when a food blockade was enforced on the Tal al-Za'tar Palestinian camp by the Phalangists.[79] Amin Jumayil, Pierre Jumayil's son, maintained that the blockade was to prevent the Palestinians from isolating certain Christian quarters, such as Ashrafiya, 'Ain al-Rummana, and Furn al-Shubbak, from the rest of the Christian stronghold to the east and north of Beirut.[80] In turn, the Palestinians and their leftist allies attempted to break the blockade on Tal al-Za'tar and Jisr al-Basha. This led to fierce battles in the eastern suburbs of Beirut, that later spread to the commercial areas and the hotel district. The intensity of the fighting prompted the Phalangist Party and Sham'un to again demand the army's intervention to stop the conflict.[81] However, both Sham'un and Jumayil refused Karami's suggestions to put an end to this critical situation. Those suggestions included guaranteeing the delivery of food supplies to the Tal al-Za'tar camp under the supervision of the army, the reviving of the High Coordination Committee, and the formation of a new National Dialogue Committee composed of both politicians and nonpoliticians.[82]

The renewal of the fighting, which took on a Palestinian-Lebanese character, was regarded by the Palestinians and their allies as an attempt by the Phalangist Party and the other conservative parties to force the issue of the Palestinian armed presence in Lebanon during the UN Security Council discussion of the Palestinian issue in early January 1976. Furthermore, when the Dubay Palestinian camp, and later the slums of the Karantina and the Maslakh areas, were overrun by the Phalangists, the Palestinians and leftists interpreted this to be motivated by the desire to clear all Muslim and Palestinian enclaves within the predominantly Christian areas of Beirut, so as to prepare for partition, and the establishment of a Maronite-dominated state in the Christian heartland of Lebanon.[83]

The Maronite summit, which was held on January 13, 1976 in the Presidential Palace in Ba'abda issued a statement describing the conflict in Lebanon as a "conflict between the Lebanese, especially the Christians, and those Palestinians (both Muslim and Christian) who did not abide by the agreements with the Lebanese state, but formed an alliance with the leftists." Those in turn were described as having taken the Lebanese Muslims as a cover.[84] However, the Maronite summit emphasized the historical contribution of the Maronites to the Arab renaissance, and their awareness of their role and responsibility towards the Arab world.[85] This was definitely a change in their former attitude: that the

Maronite community in particular, and the Christians in general, represented a different culture *(hadara)* from the Muslims of Lebanon. This statement was probably directed at the Arab countries and at Syria, in particular, in the hope that either an Arab commission of inquiry would be formed, or that the Arab countries would act as arbitrators in the conflict and find a solution to the Palestinian question.[86]

The Maronite conservative leaders decided, on January 31, 1976, to formally organize themselves into a front that they called *Jabhat al-Hurriya wal-Insan fi Lubnan*. In literal translation this is The Front of Freedom and Man in Lebanon (FFML). This intellectually pretentious name was probably proposed by the poet and writer Sa'id 'Aql (head of the Guardians of the Cedars), and by Professor Charles Malik, the Lebanese philosopher. Both were founding members of the FFML, as were Jumayil, Sham'un, Sharbal Qassis, Shakir Abu Sulayman, and Fu'ad Shamali, the head of the Tanzim. The establishment of the FFML was accompanied by a public declaration stating that the "basic conditions for any solution was a permanent cease-fire and the regaining of complete sovereignty, both militarily and politically, by the Lebanese authorities over all the Lebanese territories."[87] This statement was regarded as a hardening of the position of the conservative parties. Nevertheless, the FFML and Franjiya accepted the Syrian initiative to mediate, and worked with the Tripartite High Military Committee (composed of Lebanese, Syrians, and Palestinians), to normalize everyday life in Lebanon by the removal of barricades and armed militias from the streets in the major cities, and even in some rural areas.

While the Syrians were succeeding in finding a compromise solution acceptable to the parties concerned and the articles of the Constitutional Document were being formulated, Jumayil spoke of the minority status of the Christians in the Muslim Arab world. He maintained that to the Christians, an independent Lebanon meant a guarantee of personal freedom and freedom of religious belief.[88] Jumayil thus formulated the fears and anxieties of the Christian minorities in Lebanon. According to him, Riyad al-Sulh, the Sunni prime minister, and one of the formulators of the National Pact of 1943, had genuinely understood the fears of those minorities. He was aware that the more the Christians were given assurances of personal and religious freedom, the greater their allegiance would be to Arabism. Jumayil pointed out that when the Palestinians became revolutionized and concentrated their efforts in Lebanon after 1970, they entered the Lebanese political life, and in so doing they upset the political and sectarian balance in the country. This, he explained, revived the fears of the Christians that had been dispelled by the National Pact.[89]

The attitude of the Phalangist Party toward the Constitutional Document was favorable. An extraordinary session of the Political Bureau and the Central Council of the Phalangist Party was held on February 21-23, 1976. They issued a statement reiterating the party's strong attachment to the Lebanese formula, and the National Pact. They also accepted however, the Arab character of

Lebanon *(intima'ahu al-'Arabi)*, as well as the Constitutional Document, which included political reforms in the Lebanese system. On the other hand, the Phalangists questioned the possibility of implementing the Constitutional Document when the executive, the army, and the security forces were unable to function properly. The Phalangist Party added that the relations between the Lebanese authorities and the Palestinian Resistance Movement ought to be regulated, and that the Palestinians' interference in the internal affairs of Lebanon ought to be stopped. "The sovereignty of the state was not necessarily in opposition to the safeguarding of the Palestinian Resistance Movement,"[90] they added.

Sham'un, on the other hand, was not particularly enthusiastic about the Constitutional Document. He was able, however, in the cabinet discussion which preceded its declaration, to represent the views of the conservative parties, by insisting on reaffirming his support for the customary practice of dividing the leading political offices on a sectarian basis, and for retaining the presidency of the Republic for the Maronites.[91]

Jumayil was against the revival of the National Dialogue Committee, but he was ready to meet with Nasirites, Palestinians, and some members of the leftist organizations. He and the Phalangist Party supported the Syrian efforts to stop the fighting. The party actively participated in the Tripartite High Military Committee, which was, according to Jumayil, the strongest deterrent force acceptable to all sides, because it was composed of three armies—the Lebanese Army, the Syrian Army, and the Palestinian Liberation Army.[92] The Syrians also proposed the formation of a new cabinet or the expansion of the existing cabinet. Jumayil preferred to retain the six-member cabinet, which he believed would, in conjunction with the High Military Committee, establish law and order in the country. However, he maintained, if they were unable to do so, then the government "should resort to the Arab League, the UN, or the devil" to find a solution to the conflict.[93]

Sham'un was also in favor of retaining the existing cabinet, in which he occupied the important post of minister of the interior, and consequently objected to the Syrians' proposed change in the cabinet. He maintained that the implementation of the Cairo Agreement, as well as national reconciliation, ought to precede the formation of a new cabinet. However, he did praise the Syrian effort to enforce a cease-fire.[94] Another reason that both he and Jumayil were against such proposed changes was that they wished to prevent the inclusion of members of the leftist parties in any new or expanded cabinet.

The official attitude of the FFML, on the other hand, was that if any expanded cabinet was to be formed, then some of the leading members of the Front, such as Sa'id 'Aql, Charles Malik, and Fu'ad Shamali, had to be included in the new cabinet.[95] Nevertheless, the FFML was in favor of a maximum of 12 members so that, apart from the 6 members already in the cabinet, they would have 3 members of their own representing the Front, and the other side would also have 3 members, including Junblat. In this way, they believed, other progressive and leftist groups would not be represented.

President Franjiya fully supported the Syrian proposals, and was described by Sham'un, in his diaries, as being obsessed by the idea of forming a new cabinet.[96] Junblat, on the other hand, wanted a cabinet of more than 20 members, so that his allies would be represented.[97] Fu'ad Shamali, the head of the Tanzim, and Sa'id 'Aql, the leader of the Guardians of the Cedars, were also in favor of changes in the cabinet. They wanted a "young cabinet with extraordinary powers," because they believed that there was a need for new blood in the political leadership of Lebanon. And therefore, in this respect only, Shamali and 'Aql were in agreement with Junblat and his NM.[98]

In January–February 1976, the defection from the Lebanese army of some officers, headed by First Lieutenant Ahmad al-Khatib, who had considerable support among the soldiers, weakened the army. Consequently, the demand for the use of the army to intervene in the fighting, by the Phalangists and Sham'un and others, was no longer voiced. They laid greater emphasis, as a result, on the role of the High Military Committee, headed by the Lebanese Army Commander, Hanna Sa'id, from March 2, 1976. The fact that the army began to suffer from internal division led the FFML to back the Syrian role in Lebanon more strongly, as well as that of the High Military Committee, which was Syrian-sponsored when originally formed on January 22, 1976.[99]

The most outspoken critic of Franjiya, the FFML, and the Syrians was the Maronite leader, Raymond Iddi, who continued to be allied with Prime Minister Rashid Karami and Sa'ib Salam. Iddi described the Syrian involvement in Lebanese affairs as a "Syrian mandate" over Lebanon, which did not endear him to the pro-Syrian organizations in Lebanon. Iddi also openly attacked Sham'un and Franjiya, stating that they were the cause of Lebanon's disaster. He also feared that the country was moving toward partition.[100] Iddi had always criticized the presence of militias. He linked the crisis to the private militias, such as those of Franjiya, of Jumayil, and of Sham'un. However, when faced with the growing strength of some of these militias in Jubayl, his own stronghold, he advocated in early March 1976 that his own National Bloc partisans begin to train and to arm themselves, in order to prevent the domination of the Jubail region by the Phalangists and Sham'unists, as they had already dominated Ashrafiya and other regions.[101]

The attitude of the leaders of FFML toward the split in the army was either one of disbelief or an inability to face the new reality. Jumayil, who did admit to the existence of a serious split in the Lebanese army, construed it as the logical result of the continued attack on the army by partisans of Junblat's National Movement.

Brigadier 'Aziz Ahdab's declaration of a temporary military rule to force the resignation of the president and of Karami's cabinet, was met with opposition from the conservative parties. Jumayil was against the move, although he had good personal relations with Ahdab himself. Sham'un described Ahdab's move as reminiscent of coups d'etat in other parts of the Arab world. He also seemed to doubt Ahdab's military capabilities, although he and Jumayil praised the Brigadier's strong nationalist views.[102]

A petition in support of Ahdab's demand for the resignation of President Franjiya was signed by 66 of the 99 members of Parliament. President Franjiya, however, refused to accept the signed petition. He held the view that he represented legitimacy, and would not be accused of blunders he had not committed. After all, he argued, it was the negative attitude of Prime Minister Karami that had, in refusing to declare a state of emergency and use the army before it became divided, aggravated the crisis.[103]

Franjiya had the complete support of Sham'un and Jumayil. They said that demand for the resignation of the president was yet "another round in a series of actions aimed at undermining the legitimate institutions and constitutional foundations of the country."[104] The resignation of President Franjiya, according to the Phalangists, was no guarantee for the future, nor did it constitute a solution to the crisis, as "his resignation would only create a new vacuum in the constitutional structure of Lebanon."[105]

Franjiya entertained the idea, during the first few days of Ahdab's movement, of forcing Karami to resign and forming a military cabinet instead. In other words, he wished to shift the blame to Karami for failing at his task.[106] Sham'un said that the cabinet ought to resign because it was there that political responsibility constitutionally lay.[107] Sham'un feared that if President Franjiya resigned, the NM would make greater demands, which in turn would eventually lead to the "complete destruction of the political and social system" of Lebanon.[108]

It was significant that the Maronite Patriarch Khuraish gave limited support to President Franjiya. He maintained that the situation in Lebanon was not "the sole responsibility of the president of the Republic, but more that of the series of cabinets which were effectively and legally in charge of the security, stability, and the running of the country's affairs."[109] The Phalangist leader Jumayil expressed similar views by accusing the prime minister and ministers of former cabinets of intentionally or unintentionally shirking their responsibilities, and thus heightening the tensions that led to the crisis.[110]

Raymond Iddi, the Maronite leader, maintained that the president's resignation would not create a vacuum, if it did not become effective until a new president was elected by Parliament. He argued that since two-thirds of the representatives of the nation (66 out of 99 deputies), had, in their petition, demanded the resignation of the president, they expressed the will of the majority of the Lebanese, to which the president ought to submit.

Others, such as the deputies of Zahla and the northern Biqa', suggested that the precedent established by the resignation of President Bishara al-Khuri in 1952 could be followed. The cabinet would have to resign first; then a new interim cabinet would be formed, headed by a Maronite. Only then would the president have to tender his resignation, and Parliament would convene, without delay, to elect a new president.[111]

The effect of the emergence of al-Hatib's Lebanon's Arab Army (LAA) and Ahdab's movement on the Phalangist Party, Sham'un, Franjiya, and their allies was basically twofold. First, it hardened their attitude toward the issue of the resignation of the president. Sham'un strongly defended President Franjiya (which was reminiscent of the way he had defended his own presidency, at the time of the Civil War of 1958), declaring that "the Head of State is above suspicion," and that it was the cabinet that "was responsible vis-a-vis the public and the legislative authorities."[112]

The attitude of the Guardians of the Cedars on this issue was somewhat different. They were against all traditional leaders, and in fact supported Ahdab's movement (although not Khatib's LAA), partly because the head of the Guardians of the Cedars, Sa'id 'Aql, was a personal friend of Ahdab. Nevertheless, the Guardians of the Cedars blamed Karami for the army's disintegration because he occupied the post of prime minister, as well as that of the minister of defense.

The second effect of Ahdab's movement and the emergence of the LAA on the conservative parties was to increase their dependence on Syria. This was especially true of President Franjiya and the Phalangists, but less so of Sham'un or the Maronite League, or the Guardians of the Cedars.[113] The Phalangist delegation of George Sa'ada and Karim Baqraduni visited Damascus on March 18, 1976, and laid the basis for cooperation between the Phalangist Party and the Syrian regime.

The coordination between Ahdab's movement and the Lebanon's Arab Army in northern and southern Lebanon led to a greater involvement of some Lebanese Army officers with the militias of the Phalangists, Sham'un, and Franjiya. The army barracks of Fayadiya and Sirba rallied to the Conservative Lebanese Front. Other Christian army officers who at first had supported Ahdab now joined forces with local conservative militias in Mount Lebanon and in Zgharta, Bsharri, and al-Batrun in northern Lebanon.[114]

On March 25, 1976, President Franjiya was forced to leave his presidential residence, after it was bombed by artillery. This removed the last appearance of President Franjiya's nonpartisan involvement in the Civil War. From then on, he became a full member of the alliance forged between the Phalangist Party, Sham'un, the Maronite League, the Maronite Order of Monks, Shamali's Tansim, and Maronite militias. On the same day, President Franjiya presided over a meeting of some Maronite deputies and declared that he would remain in office until the end of his term.[115] According to Raymond Iddi, Franjiya told the gathering of Maronite deputies that there was "a conspiracy against Lebanon by a number of Arab and foreign countries which did not aim at the person of Sulayman Franjiya but at Lebanon as a whole."[116] Iddi, who was a strong critic of Franjiya, defied him to name the countries that were conspiring against

Lebanon. Iddi made fun of Franjiya's insistence on staying in office, on the grounds that he was not sure that a new president would be able to stop the Civil War. Iddi pointed out that Franjiya no longer represented the whole of Lebanon, especially since he had moved to Kisrawan, the Christian stronghold, and had taken the town of Zuq Mikha'il and then al-Kufur, as his headquarters.[117]

Pierre Jumayil issued a manifesto addressed to all Lebanese on March 25, 1976, calling them to join him in saving Lebanon from those who would destroy it, not only as a political state, but also as a socioeconomic system.[118] As the divisions between Junblat's NM and the traditional Muslim leaders, particularly Karami, became clear, Pierre Jumayil issued a second manifesto on March 27, 1976 to the Muslims of Lebanon, reminding them that they constituted the other integral part of the Lebanese formula of the National Pact. He blamed the Muslims for being so receptive to leftist views, which, he claimed, were, in the last analysis, against both Christianity and Islam.[119]

Jumayil continued attacking the leftists and accusing them of disrupting the existing political and economic system of Lebanon. He reiterated his faith in individual initiative *(al-mubadara al-fardiya)*, which, he maintained, had played a major role in the development and progress of the country. The existing political and economic system, he argued, was the only one suitable for Lebanon. It was based on services of a commercial, social, and cultural nature, and offered opportunities for investment of foreign and Arab capital. If these features were to be changed, the system would not be able to survive, as this was the foundation on which it was built.[120]

By late March 1976, the conservative parties expressed their apprehension about the course of the fighting, especially in Zahla, the northern Matn, and the hotel district in Beirut. On March 27, 1976, a meeting was held in Bkirki, which included the Maronite patriarch, Franjiya, Sham'un, Jumayil, and Qassis. Some expressed the opinion that perhaps the resignation of the president of the Republic would create an atmosphere more conducive to political reconciliation. Sham'un feared that if the conservative forces were overrun in certain strategic areas, such as al-Kahhala in the 'Alay district and Bulunya in the northern Matn, the gateway to Kisrawan, this would lead to the total collapse of their forces in east Beirut, as well as in Mount Lebanon as a whole. Thus, the military side of the conflict led the conservative leaders to concentrate their attention on military operations, to meet the challenge from the forces of the NM and their Palestinian allies.[121] On the whole, the conservative parties were able to hold their position, in spite of the offensive launched against them by the NM and the PRM. Al-Kahhala remained in the hands of the conservative forces. The Phalangist Party was able to hold its own in the commercial areas of Beirut in spite of losing the hotel district. However, on April 2, 1976, the conservative forces lost 'Aintura in the northern Matn, after some fierce battles with the NM and the Palestinian Resistance Movement forces. But, on April 14, the Phalangist forces were able to overrun the stronghold of the Syrian Social Nationalist Party of Duhur al-Shwayr.[122]

The conservative parties did not, at that stage, consider themselves as losing ground militarily. However, faced with the formidable joint forces of the PRM, the Lebanon's Arab Army, and the NM, they became more willing to compromise. On March 22, 1976, the cabinet decided to send legislation to Parliament amending Article 73 of the Constitution, and which would allow Parliament to select a new president within six months (instead of two) preceding the end of the term of the incumbent president. In fact, Parliament met on April 10, passing the legislation required for the amendment by a unanimous vote. Franjiya was unhappy with the fact that the legislation had passed without any debate.[123] At a stormy meeting on April 22, 1976, Jumayil, Sham'un, and Qassis urged Franjiya to countersign the legislation passed by Parliament amending Article 73 without further delay. Jumayil told Franjiya that a president who could not exercise his authority was merely a "shadow" president. Therefore, it was wise to elect a new president as soon as possible who would appoint a new cabinet, which in turn would be able, gradually, to reestablish law and order in the country. Sham'un wanted President Franjiya to countersign the legislation so that it would become law, and a new president would be elected, without necessarily having President Franjiya resign before the end of his term, but rather leaving that issue open and dependent on the course of events.[124]

Since Franjiya had been forced to move from the Ba'abda Presidential Palace to al-Kufur, his power to influence events had waned. He ceased to be regarded by the NM and the traditional Muslim leaders as a real president of the Republic. Furthermore, Franjiya, in comparison to his two major allies, Jumayil and Sham'un, was a junior partner, as his militia and followers were less numerous and less powerful than were those of the Phalangist Party and Sham'un.

There were two basic reasons for the interest of Jumayil and Sham'un in the immediate election of a new president. First, it was better for them to have presidential elections then, than at a later date, when their own military position might be worse, and consequently they might be in a weaker position to influence the situation. At a meeting with Sham'un and Franjiya, on April 6, 1976, Jumayil expressed that fear, and said that new military confrontations might not produce favorable results for the conservative forces. It would be better, he added, "to solve our problem in an honorable manner," rather than being forced, later, to accept the dictates of the NM or the PRM.[125] Second, they believed that the principle of legitimacy would be safeguarded by having a new president elected before Franjiya resigned or was forced to resign.

Moreover, Sham'un was interested in running for the presidency. According to Sham'un, both Franjiya and Jumayil had encouraged him at first to run for the presidency, but later Franjiya lost interest in the matter, while Jumayil had taken a rather negative attitude toward his candidacy.[126]

The Phalangist Party found no difficulty in endorsing the candidacy of Ilyas Sarkis for the presidency. Sarkis, the old Shihabist, was on excellent terms with the Phalangist Party, when the party was a pillar of the Shihabist regime in its heyday. Sarkis was also supported by Syria and by Prime Minister Karami. Only Sham'un was not particularly enthusiastic about Sarkis, because he reminded Sham'un of the years he was left out in the cold, throughout the era of Shihabism. Nevertheless, Sham'un and his parliamentary bloc voted for Ilyas Sarkis on May 8, 1976.[127] The reasons for Sham'un's eventual acceptance of Sarkis were twofold: first, he preferred Sarkis to the other candidate, Raymond Iddi, who was openly critical of the Conservative Lebanese Front.[128] Second, Sham'un probably realized that with the disintegration of the army, which had originally been a Shihabist stronghold, Sarkis would be a Shihabist president without a power base, therefore not threatening Sham'un's political power.

The fifth phase of the Civil War, which preceded the Syrian military intervention, witnessed the arrival of two important foreign envoys. One was L. Dean Brown, the president of the Middle East Institute in Washington, D.C., and former ambassador to Jordan, who arrived in Lebanon on March 31, 1976, and stayed most of April and until early May, after the elections of the new president took place. The other was the French envoy, Georges Gorse, who arrived on April 7, and left on April 16. Both envoys were in favor of the Syrian role, and regarded the election of a new president as a step in the right direction.[129] The Phalangist Party and Franjiya, who had already developed good relations with Syria, were relying on Syria to find a solution to the conflict. Jumayil accepted the Syrian troops, who, in conjunction with troops from Arab and other friendly nations, were to establish law and order.[130]

From late March 1976, Sham'un sought some kind of international mediation or intervention. He contacted the U.S. chargé d'affaires in Beirut on March 25, 1976, to ask if the UN Security Council could intervene.[131] The reply he received from the chargé d'affaires did not satisfy him—he found it too general and somewhat negative in character. The reply included three major points. First, the Lebanese were responsible for the conflict, as well as for the involvement of a foreign power in Lebanese affairs, and, consequently, only they could find a way out. Second, the Syrian proposals were apparently the most suitable ones for the situation. And third, the United States did not believe that resorting to the UN Security Council would lead to any positive result.[132] Sham'un's reaction to these statements was that they added nothing new to the situation, and that they ignored the basic cause of the conflict, namely, the Palestinian question.[133] Sham'un wanted intervention by the United States, France, or the UN Security Council, a reenactment of the U.S. Marines landing in Lebanon in the summer of 1958. He felt that Lebanon had been abandoned by Europe (particularly France) and by the United States. Sham'un belonged to the generation of politicians whose outlook had been molded by the Cold War of the 1950s—

the decade of the Baghdad Pact and the Eisenhower Doctrine. Sham'un summed up, in his diaries, his attitude toward L. Dean Brown's mission to Lebanon, in the following manner: "In spite of his [Brown's] long stay in Lebanon, and the contacts he had made with the various politicians, and his consultations with Washington, he had no positive proposal to offer. His visit ended in failure . . . ."[134] Concerning the French envoy, Georges Gorse, Sham'un was even less complimentary. He described his mission as not serious, and not aimed at finding a solution to the crisis. According to Sham'un, sending the envoy was just a show to indicate that the French diplomacy was actually concerned about Lebanon. This was demonstrated in the fact that Gorse had been sent on the heels of the American envoy.[135]

However, on May 22, 1976, President Valery Giscard d'Estaing, during his visit to the United States, offered to send French troops to Lebanon to keep law and order if he were asked to by President-elect Sarkis. Jumayil welcomed the French offer, suggesting that either Syria or France send troops to fill the vacuum caused by the disintegration of the Lebanese Army and internal security forces.[136] Sham'un also welcomed the offer, writing in his diaries that he was more than ever convinced that only an international "presence" could put an end to the Civil War. Later, however, he dismissed the idea as unrealizable, especially after the French foreign minister declared that the French proposal was conditional. French troops would be sent only if they were accepted by all parties in the conflict, as well as by the Arab countries.[137]

It was clear, by the end of the fifth phase of the Civil War—that is, by the end of May 1976, that, in spite of the election of a new president, Franjiya refused to step down. He argued that he did not consider himself responsible for the Civil War; therefore, he saw no reason to resign. His resignation would appear to be an admission of his responsibility for the continuing conflict. Sham'un, on the other hand, maintained that if law and order were reestablished in the country, and the Cairo Agreement implemented, President Franjiya would resign.[138] It would seem that the conservative parties, including the Phalangist Party, were hoping to use the issue of the resignation of President Franjiya for political bargaining with the NM and its allies.

Meanwhile, President Sarkis was trying to convene round-table talks at which the major parties and organizations could reconcile their differences, and find some common ground on which to bring about a solution to the crisis. However, his attempts to convene those talks failed when a series of very significant events took place.

SIXTH PHASE

Fighting broke out on May 23-24 in Jubail between the partisans of Raymond Iddi's National Bloc and those of the Phalangist Party. A stormy meeting took place in Bkirki, the seat of the Maronite patriarch, on May 25, 1976, between Iddi and Pierre Jumayil. On the same day, an unsuccessful attempt was made on Iddi's life, when he was on his way back to Beirut. Two days later on May 27, 1976, Kamal Junblat's sister, Linda Junblat, was assassinated in her house in eastern Beirut, the stronghold of the conservative parties.[139] Fighting erupted between the northern branch of the Lebanon's Arab Army, led by Ahmad al-Mi'mari, and the militias and soldiers belonging to the predominantly Maronite village of 'Andaqt and al-Qibbiyat. The sixth phase of the Civil War began with the Syrian military intervention of June 1, 1976, immediately following these incidents.

The attitude of the conservative Lebanese Front toward the Syrian intervention was basically one of acceptance. Franjiya and Jumayil were enthusiastic. They felt that the objective of the Syrian intervention was to curb the NM and end the Civil War by establishing law and order. In a statement issued on June 5, 1976, the conservative parties praised the role of Syria in its attempt to end the war in Lebanon.[140] Sham'un, however, described the reaction of a section of the Christian population to the Syrian intervention as reserved. This was his attitude, as well as that of some of the supporters of the conservative parties.

During the first few days immediately following the Syrian intervention, there appeared to be a rapprochement between the NM and the conservative parties, as they perceived the common threat of Syrian intervention. Bashir Jumayil and Kamal Junblat met on June 2, 1976. The next day, Fu'ad Lahhud, a member of Sham'un's parliamentary bloc, tried to bridge the gulf that separated Sham'un and Junblat. But all these attempts failed to produce any result when the conservative parties received assurances from the Syrians that they would safeguard the independence and territorial integrity of Lebanon.

The PLO's success in convening an emergency meeting of the foreign ministers of the Arab League on June 8, 1976, made the conservative parties rally more enthusiastically to the support of Syria's intervention. President Franjiya, in an open letter to the secretary-general of the Arab League, maintained that he regarded the Syrian military intervention as part and parcel of the implementation of the Constitutional Document of February 1976, in which Syria guaranteed that the Palestinians would abide by their previous agreements with the Lebanese authorities. He argued that the Syrian military presence was temporary and would end when peace and security were reestablished in Lebanon.[141] Franjiya accused the Palestinian militias of fighting in Mount Lebanon far from their camps, and of interfering in the internal affairs of Lebanon. Why, he asked, was the Syrian military intervention in Lebanon considered a foreign intervention, while the Palestinian military involvement was not? [142]

The leaders of the conservative front also complained of the quick response that 'Arafat's appeals had produced from the Arab countries, while Lebanon had not received any when it had wanted to put its case before the Arab League. They asked "why it was permissible for the Palestinians to resort to the Arab

League without fearing the 'Arabizing' or 'internationalizing' of the conflict
... while this was not allowed for the Lebanese? "[143] Franjiya's complaints and
those of the other members of the conservative front against the Palestinians
were a theme that recurred in the appeals they made to the Christian masses so
that they would rally to their support.

The decisions taken by the Arab League on June 9, 1976, were opposed by
Franjiya, mainly because he had been bypassed in the process. In their statement
calling for national reconciliation, ignoring the incumbent president, the Arab
Foreign Ministry stated that this was to be done under the auspices of President-
elect Sarkis. The Arab League resolution to establish an Arab Security Force in
Lebanon to take the positions of the Syrian troops had given the power of pull-
ing out those forces from Lebanon, if necessary, to the President-elect Sarkis,
and not to Franjiya. It is, consequently, not surprising that President Franjiya
would reject the Arab League's decisions as unacceptable. He claimed this was
because Lebanon was not bound by any Arab League resolution, which meant,
technically, that according to Article 7 of the League's Charter, resolutions
passed by the Arab League were binding on a particular member only if it volun-
tarily accepted them.

Jumayil called for the Arab League to act as arbitrator and not be partial
to either side. He complained that Lebanon had had more than its share in
shouldering the responsibility for the Palestinians. He wondered whether any
Arab country would have accepted such a large contingent of Palestinians or
agreed to the infringement of its sovereignty, and the existence of the Palestinians' organized military forces.[144] The leaders of the conservative front also
regarded the decisions of the Arab League of June 9-10, 1976, as null and void.
They were not binding on Lebanon nor could they be implemented. Their statement of June 11 denounced the role played by some Arab countries who supported the NM and the PRM and at the same time tried to appear as neutral in
the conflict. It is interesting to note that the Maronite Patriach Khuraish publicly
supported the position of the conservative front, especially with respect to
Franjiya's open letter to Arab kings and presidents, and to the secretary-general
of the Arab League.[145]

However, the conservative front did eventually accept the decisions of the
Arab League. This was after Secretary-General Mahmud Riyad of the Arab
League personally explained the decisions to President Franjiya, Sham'un, and
Jumayil. According to the understanding of the conservative front, the Arab
security force were first to put into effect the Cairo Agreement; second, they
were to cooperate with the Syrian forces and not to replace them; third, the
endorsement of the Syrian government would be required prior to any deployment of Arab security forces; and fourth, the Lebanese authorities would be
able to accept or reject the forces of any particular Arab country, as well as
decide on the size of these forces.[146] The explanations of Mahmud Riyad, the
respect and consideration given to Franjiya as president of the Republic, and the

assurances given about the continuation of the Syrian initiative were sufficient to make the conservative front accept the decisions of the Arab League.

President Franjiya tried to reassert his waning powers by dismissing Minister of Foreign Affairs Phillipe Taqla, who was abroad, and replacing him by Sham'un. He also appointed the latter deputy prime minister. It was a decision that was strongly criticized by the traditional Muslim leaders and by Raymond Iddi, as well as by the NM. This was a last attempt by Franjiya to show that he was still the president, and that he could make decisions. The new appointments enabled the conservative front to send their own representatives to the Arab League as well as to the United Nations.[147]

The first result of the Arab League's decision, as well as the mediating effort of the Libyan Prime Minister Jallud, was the withdrawal of Syrian troops from the southern suburbs of Beirut—that is, from Khalda and al-Awza'i—on June 22, 1976. Sham'un reacted swiftly, and on the very same day, by launching a military offensive on Palestinian camps, and in particular on Tal al-Za'tar and Jisr al-Basha.

The fundamental reason for this offensive was given by Sham'un in his diaries. He interpreted the Syrian withdrawal as the first step in Syria's reconciliation with Arab countries, as well as with the PRM and the NM, and wanted to prevent this at all costs. He also felt that the Arab League had not found a solution to the Palestinian presence in Lebanon, and wanted to bring up the issue again, dramatically. Sham'un's timing of the offensive could not have been more opportune. It was on the eve of a meeting, to be held in Riyadh, of the prime ministers of Saudi Arabia, Egypt, and Syria, and the foreign minister of Kuwait. By attacking Tal al-Za'tar, he reaffirmed that the conflict was, as the conservative parties had always maintained, a Palestinian-Lebanese conflict. Therefore, if the conflict had to be solved, the problem of the Palestinians had to be dealt with.

Another major reason for this attack may have been Sham'un's desire to win back the leadership of the conservative parties, which he felt he had been losing to the Phalangists. He decided to steal the thunder from his major rival in the conservative front, and launched this offensive to boost his popularity among the front's supporters. He wrote in his diaries for June 22, 1976: "The battle to occupy Tal al-Za'tar, the most important battle of the fourteen months war, has begun."[148]

The competition between Sham'un's militia and the Phalangist Party militia characterized the sixth phase of the Civil War. Sham'un took the initiative in attacking Tal al-Za'tar and Jisr al-Basha in cooperation with some of the units of the regular Lebanese Army, under the command of Major Fu'ad Malik, and some other militias, such as those of the Guardians of the Cedars, al-Tanzim, and Marun Khuri's Lebanese Youth Movement. The Phalangists waited four days before joining the battle on June 27, 1976, against Tal al-Za'tar and Jisr al-Basha. Sham'un's militias, called the Tigers of the National Liberal Party

(Numur al-Ahrar), denied the Phalangist Party's claim that it had led the battle to occupy the strategic hill of Talat al-Mir, near Tal al-Za'tar. They also maintained that the Phalangist Party had been forced to join them "under pressure from Lebanese public opinion."[149]

The differences between Sham'un's NLP and the Phalangist Party were not always expressed in a peaceful manner. Violent clashes took place between the two parties in Juniya on July 27, 1976. It was decided to form a unified military command on August 30, 1976, to prevent incidents between the major parties of the conservative front.

The objective of launching an offensive against the Palestinian camps, according to the Phalangist Party, was not the rejection of the Palestinian military presence in Lebanon, but rather an attempt to confine this presence to certain areas, in accordance with the Cairo Agreement and the Milkart Protocol. Tal al-Za'tar represented, to the conservative front, a defiant enclave in their own stronghold of the eastern part of Beirut and its suburbs, and had been a source of friction since 1969.[150] Moreover, Tal al-Za'tar was located in a very important industrial area in which an estimated 40 percent of Lebanese industries were situated. Whenever any incident occurred, the operation of these industrial establishments was affected, and this led to industrial unrest because many of this camp were employed in these factories.[151]

The forces of Sham'un, and those of the other parties of the conservative front, were able to occupy the Jisr al-Basha camp on July 1, 1976. On the other hand, the attempt by the NM and their Palestinian allies, in early July, to drive out the conservative forces from al-Kura and Batrun, failed. In fact, local militias, under the command of Army Colonel Victor al-Khuri were able, in a few days, to defeat the NM and the PRM forces in those areas of northern Lebanon. The conservative forces were also able to occupy the suburb of Nab'a on August 4, which was the stronghold of the Syrian Social Nationalist Party and the Lebanese Communist Party. On August 12, Tal al-Za'tar fell into the hands of the conservative forces. This victory, which Sham'un claimed, constituted a landmark in the Civil War. It is interesting to note that Sham'un's diaries, which he had begun while besieged in his Sa'diyat Palace in mid-January 1976, stopped after the fall of Tal al-Za'tar. It was as though he had his personal revenge for the occupation of Damur and the destruction of his palace. He did not resume his diaries until October 16, 1976, on the very day of the Riyadh Summit, which was to be crucial in eventually putting an end to the Civil War.[152]

Throughout the sixth phase of the Civil War, the Phalangist Party took a more conciliatory stand than did Sham'un. Several meetings were held, for instance, between the Phalangist leaders and some Palestinian leaders during the months of June and July, to cooperate in the running of day-to-day activities (such as fixing electric wires and telephone cables and sharing flour for bread), as well as to carry on a political dialogue. Sa'ib Salam, the traditional Muslim leader, crossed to eastern Beirut on August 7 to hold talks with Pierre Jumayil. However, after the fall of Tal al-Za'tar, the meetings between the Phalangists and the leading members of the PRM virtually stopped.

The conservative front's first priority was the continuation of the Syrian military and political role in Lebanon. Even Sham'un, who had been reluctant to cooperate with the Syrians, began to do so from July onward. He also refused to attend the Arab foreign ministers meeting held in Cairo on July 12, 1976. The decisions made at that meeting were merely a reiteration of the Arab League's decisions of June 9–10—namely, enforcement of the cease-fire, strengthening of the Arab Security Forces, as well as an expression of support for the normalization of relations between the PLO and Syria. No mention was made of the question of Syrian military intervention in Lebanon, which satisfied the conservative front.[153] On the other hand, Syria, in the Arab League meeting, supported the conservative parties' demands concerning the enforcement of the Cairo Agreement, and the noninterference of the PLO in the internal affairs of Lebanon.

Sham'un, who had accepted the Syrian military intervention, refused to join the talks in Shtura in early August 1976 between Syrians, Palestinians, and Lebanese from all parties concerned, under the auspices of the Arab League. He also criticized the Salam-Jumayil meeting of August 7, 1976. After the fall of Tal al-Za'tar, Sham'un and other conservative leaders, with the exception of the Phalangist leader, called for the liberation of the whole of Lebanon. Etienne Saqr, the military leader of the Guardians of the Cedars, called for the expulsion of all Palestinians from Lebanon.[154]

The disagreement between President Sarkis, who had taken office on September 23, 1976, and the Palestinians and the NM, was about the latter refusing to withdraw from their position in Mount Lebanon, except as part of a comprehensive political solution to the conflict. Consequently, the Syrians launched a second military offensive against the NM and the PRM positions in Mount Lebanon on September 28, 1976. The conservative parties welcomed this military intervention, which confirmed their views that only force would make the PRM and the NM "flexible." The second Syrian military intervention, therefore, strengthened the position of the conservative front, and in a way deepened the gulf between them and the NM and the PRM.

An emergency six leaders Arab summit took place in Riyad, with the leaders of Egypt, Syria, Saudi Arabia, Kuwait, Lebanon, and the PLO. The formation of the Arab Deterrent Force (ADF) composed of 30,000 men was one of the resolutions of the Riyad summit, which was of great concern to Sham'un. In the first place, he thought the force was too large for a mere deterrent force. Second, Sham'un wanted troops from only Syria, Jordan, and Saudi Arabia. In fact, more than two thirds of the ADF was Syrian. Third, he believed that the deployment of these troops ought to be confined to regions which were under "aggression," and not to areas in which there was no conflict. In other words, he did not want the ADF to deploy its forces in the regions under the control of the conservative parties. Finally, although Sham'un was in favor of the predominantly Syrian ADF, he was wary of the way Syria was trying to build a Lebanese Army (called the Vanguard of the Lebanese Arab Army) as an auxiliary of the Syrian troops.[155] These issues were to remain sources of tension between Syria and the conservative front, even after the 1975-1976 Civil War came to an end.

NOTES

1. Joseph Ashqar, *Pierre Jumayil fi Khidmat Lubnan* (Beirut: Dar al-Tiba'a wal-Nashr al-Lubnaniyya, 1950), p. 30. Bulaybil claimed that the Jumayil family acquired the feudal title of "shaykh" in 1711. See Edmond Bulaybil, *Taqwin Bikfaya al-Kubra wa Tarikh Usariha* (Bifaya: Matba'at al-'Ara'is, 1935), pp. 64-65.

2. Iskandar al-Riyashi, *Qabl wa Ba'd 1918 ila 1941* (n.p., n.d.), pp. 64-65; Ashqar, op cit., pp. 34-35; see also John P. Entelis, *Pluralism and Party Transformation in Lebanon: Al-Kata'ib, 1936-1970* (Leiden: E. J. Brill, 1974), pp. 48-50.

3. See, for example, Jubran Jurayj, *Ma'a Antun Sa'ada* (n.p., n.d.), pp. 97-98.

4. Labib Yamak Zuwiyya, *The Syrian Social Nationalist Party: An Ideological Analysis* (Cambridge, Mass.: Harvard University Press, 1966), p. 87.

5. Bishara al-Khuri, *Haqa'iq Lubnaniyya*, vol. 3 (Harisa: Matba'at Basil Ikhwan, 1961).

6. Entelis, op. cit., pp. 178-81; Michael C. Hudson, *The Precarious Republic: Political Modernization in Lebanon* (New York: Random House, 1968), pp. 143-44.

7. Camille K. Chehab, "Les Elections Legislatives de 1960," mimeographed (Beirut, 1960), pp. 17-78.

8. See Hudson, *The Precarious Republic*, op. cit., chap. 8, especially pp. 308-25; Kamal S. Salibi, "Lebanon under Fuad Chehab 1958-1964," *Middle Eastern Studies* 2 (April 1966): 218-26.

9. Rashad Salama, "Hizb al-Kata'ib al-Lubnaniyya," in *Al-Qiwa al-Siyasiya fi Lubnan* (Beirut: Dar al-Tali'a, 1970), p. 12.

10. Ibid., p. 28.

11. Jalal Zuwiyya, *The Parliamentary Election of Lebanon, 1968* (Leiden: E. J. Brill, 1972), p. 77.

12. Riyashi, *Qabl wa Ba'd*, op. cit., pp. 116-17.

13. Camille Chamoun, *Crise au Moyen Orient* (Paris: Gallimard, 1963), pp. 241-44; Sulayman Taqiy al-Din, *Al-Tatawwur al-Tarikhi lil-Mushkila al-Lubnaniyya: 1920-1970* (Beirut: Dar Ibn Khaldun, 1977), pp. 80-81.

14. Hudson, *The Precarious Republic*, op. cit., pp. 274-75.

15. Chamoun, *Crise au Moyen Orient*, op. cit., pp. 395-98.

16. Chehab, "Les Elections Legislatives de 1960," op. cit.; idem, *Les Élections Legislatives de 1964* (Beirut, 1964), pp. 38-80.

17. Joseph Mughabghab, "Hizb al-Wataniyyin al-Ahrar," in *Al-Qiwa al-Siyasiya fi Lubnan* (Beirut: Dar al-Talia'a, 1970), p. 12.

18. See *Annuaire des Sociétés Libanaises par Actions* (Beirut: MECICO, 1969).

19. See Zuwiyya, *The Parliamentary Elections*, op. cit., p. 92. Sham'un's bloc in Parliament consisted of nine deputies.

20. Jean Ma'luf and Joseph Abi Farhat, *Al-Mawsu'a al-Intikhabiyya al-Musawwara fi Lubnan 1861-1972* (Beirut: Dar al-Tali'a al-Lubnaniyya, 1972).

21. See *al-Hawadith* 1013 (April 9, 1976), pp. 41-42.

22. Ibid. 1046 (November 26, 1976), pp. 44-45.

23. Ramzi Abi Faraj, "Hizb al-Kutla al-Wataniyya al-Lubnaniyya," in *Al-Qiwa al-Siyasiya fi Lubnan*, op. cit., pp. 44–45.

24. Ibid., pp. 36–39, 42–43.

25. *Al-Anwar*, August 1, 1975, p. 4.

26. Fu'ad Matar, *Suqut al-Imbraturiya al-Lubnaniyya*, vol. 1; *Al-Sharara* (Beirut: Dar al-Qadaya, 1976), pp. 13–14.

27. *Al-Nahar*, May 16, 1975, p. 2.

28. Ibid., p. 14.

29. Ibid.

30. Ibid., May 24, 1975, p. 10.

31. Matar, op. cit., pp. 43, 59.

32. *Al-Nahar*, June 29, 1975, p. 10.

33. Ibid., September 25, 1975, p. 3.

34. Ibid.

35. Kamal S. Salibi, *Crossroads to Civil War: Lebanon 1958–1976* (London: Ithaca Press, 1976), p. 111.

36. *Al-Nahar*, September 30, 1975, pp. 2, 8; ibid., October 19, 1975, p. 2.

37. Ibid., October 16, 1975, p. 2.

38. Ibid.

39. *Al-Anwar*, November 4, 1975, p. 2.

40. Ibid.

41. Ibid., November 6, 1975, p. 2.

42. Ibid., November 7, 1975, pp. 1, 8.

43. Ibid.

44. Ibid.

45. Ibid., November 8, 1975, p. 8; ibid., November 9, 1975, p. 1.

46. Ibid., November 10, 1975, p. 1.

47. Matar, op. cit., pp. 207–08.

48. Antoine Khuwairi, *Hawadith Lubnan 1975*, vol. 1 (Junya: Al-Bulusiya Press, 1976), pp. 415–16.

49. *Al-Anwar*, November 16, 1975, p. 8.

50. Ibid., p. 1.

51. Ibid.

52. Ibid., November 17, 1975, p. 2.

53. Ibid., November 7, 1975, p. 3.

54. Ibid.

55. Ibid.

56. Ibid.

57. Khuwairi, *Hawadith Lubnan 1975*, op. cit., p. 375.

58. *Al-Anwar*, November 7, 1975, p. 3.

59. Ibid.

60. Ibid.

61. Khuwairi, *Hawadith Lubnan 1975*, op. cit., p. 376.

62. *Al-Anwar*, November 25, 1975, p. 3.

63. Ibid.

64. Matar, op. cit., pp. 223–25.

65. *Al-Anwar*, December 15, 1975, p. 2.

66. Ibid., pp. 1, 6.

67. Ibid., December 17, 1975, pp. 2, 5.

68. Ibid., p. 5.

69. Ibid.

70. *Al-Anwar*, December 18, 1975, pp. 2, 4.

71. Ibid., December 23, 1975, p. 3.

72. Ibid.

73. Ibid., December 25, 1975, p. 3.

74. Ibid., p. 6.

75. Ibid.

76. Ibid., January 1, 1976, pp. 2, 8.

77. Fu'ad Matar, *Suqut al-Imbraturiya al-Lubnaniyya*, vol. 2: *Al-Makhad* (Beirut: Dar al-Qadaya, 1976), p. 39.

78. *Al-Anwar*, January 1, 1976, pp. 2, 8.

79. Camile Sham'un, *Azmat fi Lubnan* (Beirut: Al-Fikr al-Hurr Press, 1977), p. 20.

80. *Al-Nahar*, January 7, 1976, p. 1.

81. *Al-Anwar*, January 11, 1976, p. 2.

82. Ibid., pp. 2, 7.

83. Ibid., January 16, 1976, p. 3.

84. *Al-Nahar*, January 14, 1976, p. 6.

85. Ibid.

86. *Al-Anwar*, January 16, 1976, p. 2.

87. Antoine Khuwairi, *Al-Harb fi Lubnan 1976*, vol. 1 (Junya: Al-Bulusiya Press, 1977), p. 110.

88. *Al-Anwar*, February 4, 1976, p. 2.

89. Ibid.

90. Khuwairi, *Al-Harb fi Lubnan*, op. cit., p. 212.

91. Sham'un, *Azmat fi Lubnan*, op. cit., pp. 48–49.

92. *Al-Anwar*, February 29, 1976, p. 2.

93. Ibid.

94. Sham'un, *Azmat fi Lubnan*, op. cit., p. 56.

95. *Al-Anwar*, March 1, 1976, p. 2.

96. Sham'un, *Azmat fi Lubnan*, op. cit., p. 54.

97. *Al-Anwar*, March 2, 1976, p. 1.

98. Ibid., March 4, 1976, p. 8.

99. Ibid., March 3, 1976, pp. 2, 8.

100. Ibid., March 5, 1976, p. 3.

101. Ibid., March 4, 1976, p. 2.

102. Sham'un, *Azmat fi Lubnan*, op. cit., p. 60.

103. Ibid., p. 62.

104. *Al-Nahar*, March 15, 1976, p. 3.

105. Ibid.

106. Ibid., p. 1.

107. *Al-Anwar*, March 15, 1976, p. 2.

108. Sham'un, *Azmat fi Lubnan*, op. cit., p. 62.

109. *Al-Anwar*, March 16, 1976, p. 6.

110. *Al-Nahar*, March 17, 1976, p. 2.

111. Ibid.

112. *Al-Anwar*, March 18, 1976, p. 6.

113. Ibid., March 19, 1976, p. 2.

114. Ibid., March 27, 1976, p. 1.

115. Khuwairi, *Al-Harb fi Lubnan*, op. cit., pp. 429–30.

116. *Al-Anwar*, March 27, 1976, p. 2.

117. Ibid., pp. 2, 6.

118. Khuwairi, *Al-Harb fi Lubnan*, op. cit., pp. 433–34.

119. *Al-Anwar*, March 29, 1976, p. 2.

120. Ibid., March 31, 1976, p. 2.

121. Sham'un, *Azmat fi Lubnan*, op. cit., pp. 71–74, 77.

122. *Al-Nahar*, April 15, 1976, p. 4.

123. Sham'un, *Azmat fi Lubnan*, op. cit., p. 85; *Al-Nahar*, April 11, 1976, pp. 3–4.

124. Sham'un, *Azmat fi Lubnan*, op. cit., p. 82.

125. Ibid.

126. Ibid., pp. 82, 91.

127. *Al-Nahar*, May 9, 1976, p. 3.

128. Ibid., May 5, 1976, p. 3. Sarkis and Iddi were the two major candidates, but there were others who were regarded as presidential candidates, such as Michel al-Khuri, Jean 'Aziz, and Pierre Hilu.

129. Ibid., April 17, 1976, p. 3; Antoine Khuwairi, *Al-Harb fi Lubnan 1976*, vol. 2 (Junya: Al-Bulusiya Press, 1977), pp. 94–95.

130. *Al-Nahar*, May 12, 1976, p. 2.

131. Sham'un, *Azmat fi Lubnan*, op. cit., p. 72.

132. Ibid., p. 75.

133. Ibid., p. 76.

134. Ibid., p. 95.

135. Ibid., p. 84.

136. *Al-Nahar*, May 24, 1976, p. 2.

137. Ibid., May 29, 1976, p. 4; Sham'un, *Azmat fi Lubnan*, op. cit., pp. 101–03.

138. *Al-Nahar*, May 23, 1976, p. 1.

139. Ibid., May 26, 1976, pp. 1, 4; ibid., May 28, 1976, pp. 1, 4.

140. Khuwairi, op. cit., vol. 2, pp. 321–23.

141. *Al-Nahar*, June 9, 1976, pp. 1, 4.

142. Ibid., p. 4.

143. Ibid.

144. Ibid., June 10, 1976, p. 2.

145. Ibid., June 11, 1976, p. 2.

146. Sham'un, *Azmat fi Lubnan*, op. cit., p. 110; *Al-Nahar*, June 17, 1976, p. 2.

147. Ibid., p. 1.

148. Sham'un, *Azmat fi Lubnan*, op. cit., pp. 113, 110–11.

149. *Al-Nahar*, June 28, 1976, p. 4.

150. Joseph al-Hashim, *Sawt Lubnan fi Harb al-Sanatayn* (Beirut: Marshvrat Idha'at Sawt Lubnan, 1977), pp. 261–62.

151. Sham'un, *Azmat fi Lubnan*, op. cit., p. 116.

152. Ibid., pp. 19, 131–33.

153. *Al Nahar*, July 14, 1976, p. 4; ibid., July 15, 1976, pp. 1, 4.

154. Antoine Khuwairi, *Al-Harb fi Lubnan 1976*, vol. 3 (Junya: Al-Bulusiya Press, 1977), pp. 157–59, 528–29; *Al-Hawadith* 1046, November 26, 1976, pp. 44–45.

155. Sham'un, *Azmat fi Lubnan*, op. cit., pp. 136–37, 140–41.

3

THE NATIONAL MOVEMENT AND TRADITIONAL MUSLIM LEADERS

The leadership of traditional Muslims has its roots in both a feudal, largely mountain socioeconomic structure, and a notability of the urban areas.[1] The latter are more prominent because the bulk of the Sunni population live in the major cities, that is, Beirut, Tripoli, and Saida, and the prime minister has been, by custom, a Sunni, in accordance with the National Pact of 1943. Traditional Muslim leadership of feudal origin has been either Shi'ite—al-As'ad's in the South and Hamada's in the northern Biqa'—or Druze—Junblat's in the Shuf and Arslan's in the Gharb. The only notable exception is the Sunni Mar'abi feudal family of 'Akkar.

The political system that emerged in Lebanon since its independence and the National Pact of 1943 helped maintain traditional leadership, including the traditional Muslim leaders, while that selfsame group of notables were superseded elsewhere in the Arab hinterland, particularly in Syria, since the late 1950s and early 1960s. In other words, the political sectarianism and the division of political posts among the various sects, which was adopted on the eve of Lebanon's independence, bolstered up the traditional leadership of those who built this new political system. This leadership was based on a sectarian and *mahsubiya* system (that is, one based on the rendering of services to constituents in return for their political allegiance), that became one of the pillars of modern Lebanese political life. Although some of the traditional leading Muslim families lost some of their political power in the process, such as the Da'uqs, and the Bayhums in Beirut, other families of notables continued to be prominent, such as the Karamis of Tripoli and the Salams of Beirut.

Traditional leadership tended also to be inherited, passed on from father to son. Rashid Karami followed his father, 'Abd al-Hamid Karami. Kamil al-As'ad took over the leadership of the al-As'ad family after his father, Ahmad al-As'ad, died. Majid Hamada became the head of the family after his father's death in

January 1976. Similarly, after Kamal Junblat was assassinated in March 1977, the leadership was pass automatically to his son, Walid Junblat. The system thus perpetuates the leadership of certain families in certain regions.

The Lebanese political system was dominated by traditional leadership until the Civil War in 1975. Of the 12 most prominent and influential political figures in Parliament, prior to the Civil War, 7 belonged to traditional Muslim leading families: 3 were Sunnis—Rashid Karami, Sa'ib Salam, and Sulaiman al-'Ali—2 were Shi'ite—Kamal al-As'ad and Sabri Hamada—and 2 were Druze—Kamal Junblat and Majid Arslan. Five of the 7 belonged to the *muqata'jis* (feudal lords) of the mountains and 2 were notables of urban centers.[2]

Traditional Muslim leaders were affected by radical political movements in Lebanon as well as in the Arab hinterland. In the late 1950s, most of them rode the wave of Arab nationalism introduced by Nasir, to mobilize the Muslim masses, and joined in the so-called "Revolution" *(al-Thawra)* of 1958 against President Camille Sham'un. Of the above-mentioned seven traditional Muslim leaders, only Arslan and al-'Ali supported Sham'un, while the other five led the armed uprising against him.

Nasirite Arab nationalism contained convenient slogans designed to mobilize the masses and offer them a vehicle to express their grievances in a system in which they had little say. The adoption of "scientific socialism" as the ideology of Nasir's Egypt created some apprehensions among the notable families of the cities who, nevertheless, continued to pay lip service to Nasirism in order to gain local support.

The challenge to traditional leadership began during the 1958 Civil War. Ma'ruf Sa'd of Saida was able to win the parliamentary elections of 1960, not because he belonged to a family of notables, but because of his militant role in the Civil War. Under Shihab and the Shihabist regime that followed, that is, between 1958 and 1968 (the last two years of President Hilu's rule, 1968–70, were characterized by a complete break between Hilu and Shihab and the Shihabist apparatus of the Deuxième Bureau), some traditional leaders cooperated with the Shihabi regime, while others stood at loggerheads with the government. Consequently, rival leaders were promoted, such as al-Bazzi against the al-As'ad family, 'Uthman al-Danna and 'Abdallah al-Yafi against Salam. Hamada, Karami, Junblat, and Arslan, who cooperated with the Shihabists, became leaders of the Shihabist Nahjist Bloc in Parliament.

However, the fundamental challenge came from organized political parties of various colors that weakened the authority of the traditional Muslim leadership, as had happened earlier to some of the Christian traditional leadership. Muslim urban communities were affected by organized political parties with an ideology that appealed to the educated and literate members of these communities. As the Lebanese Communist Party and the Syrian Social Nationalist Party had appealed first to the Christian communities, especially those in mixed sectarian districts, such as the northern Matn and Kura, so did the Arab Nationalist

Movement and the Ba'th Party begin to appeal to the Sunni petite bourgeoisie in the major urban centers.

MAJOR NATIONAL MOVEMENT ORGANIZATIONS

The first attempt to form a leftist front, a precursor of the National Movement led by Kamal Junblat during the Civil War, was the formation of the Front of Progressive Parties, Organizations and Personalities (FPPOP) in the summer of 1965. The Front originated in the congress on the crisis of the marketing of apples and agricultural production, which was held on September 26, 1965, in the village of Btikhnay. Three political parties founded the FPPOP—the Progressive Socialist Party of Junblat, the Lebanese Communist Party, and the Arab Nationalist Movement. Some progressive Shihabists, such as Jamil Lahhud and Nuhad Sa'id, joined too. This leftist front pursued a policy of support for the reformist Shihabist majority in Parliament. This improved the image of the Left, as it gained political respectability. But the alliance also incurred strong criticism from the rightists, such as the Phalangist Party, who accused the Shihabist movement of favoring the political Left.[3] The June war of 1967 and the changes that took place in its aftermath led to the eventual disintegration of the FPPOP. There were three major reasons for this. First, due to his attitude, Kamal Junblat, a traditional leader supporting leftist groups, was gradually isolated from the political scene. The Lebanese authorities put tremendous pressure on him and others to stop holding rallies, as they feared he might unleash uncontrollable forces. The second reason was the differences that emerged among the members of the Front over the strategies to be used concerning the Palestinian question. And third was the fact that the Arab Nationalist Movement had undergone fundamental transformations in its outlook, ideology, and organization.[4]

The Arab defeat in June 1967 had a tremendous impact on the political and ideological development of the Arab world. The Arab Nationalist Movement gave birth to a number of organizations; then it ceased to exist in its original pan-Arab form. In late 1967, the Popular Front for the Liberation of Palestine (PFLP) was formed by George Habash, formerly the leader of the Arab Nationalist Movement (ANM). In Lebanon, two organizations were formed out of the former ANM. First, the Organization of Lebanese Socialists (OLS) was established in early 1969, led by Muhsin Ibrahim and Muhammad Kishli, who, through their organ *al-Hurriya* (Freedom), tried to form the nucleus of a revolutionary Marxist-Leninist political party. The tract, which was written by Muhsin Ibrahim to justify the formation of the organization, is one of the most enlightening in the history of the party.[5] Second, at the same time, a splinter group of the PFLP formed a new organization, the Democratic Popular Front for the Liberation of Palestine (DPFLP), headed by Nayif Hawatmeh, which developed close ties with the Organization of Lebanese Socialists. The leader of the PFLP, George

Habash, formed out of his Lebanese followers, among the members of the former ANM, a party called al-Hizb al-'Amal al-Ishtiraki al-'Arabi (the Arab Socialist Action Party) which also adoped a Marxist-Leninist ideology, and became critical of the original petit bourgeois orientation of the ANM.

A group of ex-Ba'thists, headed by the Lebanese intellectual Fawwaz Tarabulsi, formed a political organization known by its organ, *Lubnan al-Ishtiraki* (Socialist Lebanon), which was first issued in 1967. During the next few years, it analyzed both the Lebanese and Arab political scene from a Marxist point of view. In its criticism, it spared neither the Lebanese Communist Party nor Junblat's Progressive Socialist Party.

This was typical of the infighting and squabbling among the various leftist organizations in the period of revolutionary outbursts that immediately followed the defeat of June 1967. Arab intellectuals and militants advocated armed struggle in Cuban, Vietnamese, or Chinese style, as a more effective substitute to regular warfare where Israel continued to have the upper hand. Guerrilla activities increased across the Jordan River Valley, and so did the power of Palestinians in East Jordan and in the Palestinian camps in Lebanon. The Dhufar revolutionaries were gaining ground in their fight against the sultan of 'Uman. This period of revolutionary outbursts, from 1967 to 1970, coincided with the successes of the Vietnamese revolutionaries, and student movements in Europe and in the United States.

However, this revolutionary period was short-lived. By the end of 1970, it was clear that the Arab world was entering a new phase, characterized by a decline in revolutionary fervor and the growing dominance of conservative forces. The acceptance of the cease-fire in August 1970 by President Nasir, and the end of the war of attrition on the Suez Canal, in addition to the clashes between the Lebanese army and the Palestinian guerrillas, which had already begun in 1969, and had led to the signing of the Cairo Agreement, between the chief of the Lebanese Army, Emile Bustani, and the PLO leader Yasir 'Arafat, ushered in a new period. A first step in allying the various leftist and progressive parties and organizations, as well as some of the traditional Muslim leaders in Lebanon, was achieved by rallying around the issue of the Palestinian guerrillas, and their continued presence in Lebanon. This alliance was strongly reinforced by King Husain's successful attack on the Palestinian guerrillas in Jordan, which began in September 1970 and was completed by the end of 1971.

Thus, the rise of the Palestinian Resistance Movement had deep repercussions on the Lebanese political system. It led to the reemergence of old, and the formation of new, leftist organizations of all shades. Later, when Jordan was no longer a field of operation for the Palestinian guerrillas, many sought haven in Lebanon, where they had greater freedom. "Hurriyat al-'Amal al-Fida'i" (freedom of action for guerrillas) became the slogan of the rallying forces for the Lebanese Left in alliance with some of the traditional Muslim leaders.

With the growing strength of the Left, there were indications as early as the parliamentary elections of 1972, that the power of the traditional Muslim leaders in the urban centers had been weakened. Najah Wakim, the candidate of the Nasirite organization, the Union of the Forces of Working People, was elected in the third constituency of Beirut, in defiance of the strong *mahsubiya* of Sa'ib Salam and 'Abd-Allah al-Yafi. In the same election, the Ba'thist leader, Dr. 'Abd al-Majid al-Rafi'i, was elected in Tripoli and the ex-Ba'thist leftist, Dr. Ali al-Khalil, won a seat in Tyre, getting the largest number of votes from the city of Tyre itself.

By 1972, the leftists and the progressive forces united in a front called *Jabhat al-Ahzab wal Qiwa al-Wataniya wal-Taqaddumiya* (the Front of National and Progressive Parties and Forces, FNPPF), headed by the traditional Druze leader and president of the Progressive Socialist Party, Kamal Junblat. He was also chosen to be secretary-general of the Arab Front in support of the Palestinian Revolution, which convened its first congress in November 1972.

The FNPPF, or, as it was better known during the Civil War, the National Movement *(al-Harakat al-Wataniya)*, was comprised of six major parties or organizations, and at least another six minor parties and organizations. First, there was Kamal Junblat's party, the Progressive Socialist Party (PSP), formed by Junblat on May 1, 1949.[6] The PSP was secular and reformist in character. Although its mainstay of power was the Druze traditional allegiance to the feudal Junblat family, the party managed to gain the support of many Christians as well, including such prominent figures as Fu'ad Rizq, Farid Jubran, and George Hanna.[7] Its reformist and anticorruption plank in 1951 made it play a decisive role in the formation of the National Socialist Front, which was instrumental in forcing the president of the Republic, Bishara al-Khuri, to resign. It was also instrumental in the selection of Camille Sham'un, a member of the National Socialist Front, to become the new president on September 23, 1952. The PSP's nonaligned stand in foreign affairs led it to cooperate with the Arab Ba'th Socialist Party of Syria. Later, they urged Arab countries to refrain from joining in any pacts with Western powers, such as the Baghdad Pact. Junblat's PSP, along with other political parties, and with the support of many traditional Muslim leaders, took arms in 1958 to fight the pro-Western President Camille Sham'un. Concomitantly, it became increasingly more Arab nationalist in its outlook. Its Arabism gradually developed with the rising tide of Nasirism and Arab nationalism in the Arab world. By the early 1970s, the PSP had come to believe in a federal unity among Arab states, in which Lebanon remained an independent political entity, and retained its special characteristics and role in the Arab world.[8]

The PSP revolved around the charismatic leadership of Kamal Junblat. Its ideology was inseparable from that of its founder and leader. During the Shihabist era, 1958–68, the PSP supported President Fu'ad Shihab, and later cooperated with the Shihabists under President Charles Hilu. Its meeting ground with Shihabism was the reformism of the latter, its relatively unaligned stand with respect to foreign policy, and a special relationship with Nasir's Egypt. Although Junblat continued to support Fu'ad Shihab personally, and would have backed him if he had wished to run again for president in the elections of 1970, he was critical of the Shihabist apparatus, and especially of the military intelligence (the Deuxième Bureau) and its interference in internal politics. As a strong believer in parliamentary democracy, Junblat was concerned with the army's growing role in Lebanese politics. Therefore he voted for President Sulayman Franjiya in the presidential elections of August 1970, who was running against the Shihabist candidate, Ilyas Sarkis. Junblat, a strong supporter of the Palestinian Resistance Movement (which had clashed with the Lebanese army in 1969, leading to the Cairo Agreement in October 1969), felt that Sulayman Franjiya would be a weaker president and consequently would be more amenable to influence, unlike Sarkis, who would have the strong backing of the military establishment.

In August 1970, Minister of the Interior Junblat was able to "legalize" the Lebanese Communist Party, the Arab Ba'th Socialist Party, and the Syrian Social Nationalist Party, preparing to take over himself the leadership of all leftist and progressive parties and organizations in Lebanon. Their eventual alliance became known, during the Civil War, as the National Movement.

The second major organization which became an integral part of the National Movement was the Independent Nasirites Movement (INM, *Harakat al-Nasiriyin al-Mustaqallin*), and its military arm, *al-Murabitun*. The movement got its support from the lower middle class in the urban centers, and especially from the Sunni community. It was their leader, Ibrahim Qulailat, who began organizing a militia in his Beirut quarter (Mahallat Abu Shakir), and allied himself, from the late 1960s, with Junblat. On September 3, 1973, the army raided the headquarters of the INM. This action of the Lebanese authorities was strongly criticized by Junblat and other leaders.[9] From the time of that incident, Ibrahim Qulailat and his INM received considerable support, and eventually played a major role in the Civil War. Its militias, the Murabitun, fought on many fronts in Beirut and its suburbs, and were also responsible for the maintenance of law and order in most of the areas of western Beirut.[10] The INM was the counterpart of the Phalangist Party for the Sunni community of Beirut, and was in some ways comparable to 'Adnan Hakim's Najjada Party during the period from the late 1930s to the early 1950s.

The third major party of the National Movement was the Lebanese Communist Party (LCP). Its roots can be traced to the Lebanese People Party formed on October 24, 1924, by a group of Lebanese intellectuals and workers in Bikfaya, in the northern Matn. It was led by a Maronite, Fu'ad Shamali, who presided over labor unions of tobacco workers and tradesmen. Among its first recruits were workers and members of the petite bourgeoisie in Zahla, a major commercial and industrial town.[11] The LCP, after a checkered history in the

1930s, began a new stage in its development with its First Congress, held in December 1943–January 1944, under the leadership of Farajallah Hilu.[12] By 1947, the LCP's membership had increased tenfold, reaching 200,000,[13] including workers, peasants (both small and medium landowners), and especially members of the petite bourgeoisie in the sectarianly mixed provincial areas. The LCP had its ups and downs, due primarily to its attitude toward Arab nationalism and the Palestine question. Its ultraleftist and unsympathetic attitude toward Arab nationalism resulted in a strong decline in its popularity during the periods from 1948 to 1951 and from 1959 to 1963. The LCP's Second Congress, held in July 1968, marked a fundamental change in the attitude of the party toward Arab nationalism.[14] It criticized its former attitude as dogmatic, admitting that, until the mid 1960s it had been unable to understand the nationalist dimension of the Palestine problem, and had tended to belittle the forces of nationalism in the Arab world.[15] The LCP also joined other Arab Communist parties in supporting the Palestinian Resistance Movement, and even tried to form, in 1970, the Partisans' Forces (Quwwat al-Ansar), a Communist militia whose aim it was to fight with the PRM against Israel.[16]

During the Civil War, the LCP had at least one thousand armed fighters— they lost about 200. It was active on most fronts, as its membership lived in all the regions of Lebanon. However, its major forces were in the suburbs of Beirut, al-Shiyyah, Burj Hammud, and in the Kura district in northern Lebanon. Its support tended to come from the Greek Orthodox communities, which traditionally had kept strong links with Russia, dating as far back as the nineteenth century. The LCP's secularism tended also to attract members in districts that were sectarianly mixed, such as al-Kura, Jubail, northern Matn, some parts of the Biqa', the Mina district in Tripoli, and Marjicyun in southern Lebanon.

The fourth major party in the National Movement was the Organization of Communist Action or OCA *(Munazzamat al-'Amal al-Shuyu'i)*, which was formed in May 1970 from two groups. One was the Organization of Lebanese Socialists, itself an offshoot of the Arab Nationalist Movement, and the other was the Socialist Lebanon Organization, a group of ex-Ba'thist intellectuals who organized in the mid-1960s, adopting revolutionary Marxism-Leninism as their ideology, under the leadership of Fawwaz Tarabulsi.[17] The new OCA was headed by Muhsin Ibrahim, a schoolteacher and former prominent member of the Arab Nationalist Movement. The OCA continued to issue the weekly *al-Hurriya* (formerly the ANM's paper), in partnership with the DPFLP. Despite the many divisions the OCA suffered during the early 1970s, it managed to get support from workers and students in the Beirut suburbs, in the South, and in al-Biqa'. Compared to other parties of the National Movement, the OCA's membership was small, but its militia participated in the fighting on most fronts. It lost about 75 of its members in combat during the Civil War.[18] The importance of the OCA was reflected when Muhsin Ibrahim, the OCA's secretary-general, was chosen in the election of the secretary-general of the Central Political Council of the National Movement.

In recent years, the OCA and the LCP made inroads into the Shi'ite migrant community in what is known as the poverty belt *(hizam al-faqr)* that surrounds Beirut on the southern and eastern sides. These parties also got recruits from intellectuals and students of both eastern and western Beirut, appealing to Maronites, Catholics, as well as to Sunnis. Their popularity in the al-Biqa' Valley and southern Lebanon greatly increased during the early 1970s.

The fifth major party is the Syrian Social Nationalist Party, SSNP *(al-Hizb al-Suri al-Qawmi al-Ijtim'i)*. It was established in 1932 by Antun Sa'ada. In the mid-1950s and late 1950s, the SSNP took an anti-Arab nationalist stand, cooperated with the Hashimite regimes of Iraq and Jordan, and fought on the side of Sham'un in 1958. On December 31, 1961, the SSNP in Lebanon attempted an unsuccessful coup, led by a Maronite army officer from 'Akkar, Fu'ad 'Awad, against the Shihabist regime. This resulted in the arrest and imprisonment of most of the leaders of the SSNP. It was not until the late 1960s that most of them were pardoned and released from prison. Since the emergence of the Palestinian Resistance Movement in the post-1967 period, the SSNP has given its full support to the Palestinians. They found a meeting ground with the leftist and progressive political parties and movements, as well. Moreover, Kamal Junblat's role in "legalizing" the party in 1970, which was done partly for electoral purposes in his Shuf district, cemented the alliance between the SSNP and the PSP of Junblat, and prepared the ground for the SSNP to become a full-fledged member of the National Movement. Although the SSNP continued to adhere to its Syrian nationalist ideology, that is, believing in the unity of the countries of the Fertile Crescent, it began to change. The party line repeatedly quoted its founder, Antun Sa'adi, who said, "We do not [verbally] call for Arab unity but we work for it."[19]

The SSNP was strongly nationalist and secular and had a reformist program. Its secularism could be best seen in the membership of Greek Orthodox, Shi'ites, Druze, Maronites, and Sunnis, in the party. Its strength was in the Kura, the Biqa', the northern Matn, and the South. It also received support from Lebanese emigrants in Africa and South America. Two of its former presidents were Lebanese emigrants in West Africa: Asad Ashkar, and Mas'ad Hajal. During the Civil War, the SSNP militias fought on many fronts, in the hotel district in Beirut, in Sin al-Fil suburb, in northern Matn, in al-Kura, and in Mount Lebanon as well. The divisions which took place in the party in March 1975 paralyzed its military effectiveness in many areas, especially in Jal-al-Dib and the northern Matn areas, but the majority of the members rallied behind the leadership of In'am Ra'd, who had made the SSNP, during the Civil War, an essential and integral part of the National Movement.

Another major political force in the National Movement was the Ba'thist parties. One was the Organization of the Ba'th Party, OBP (Munazzamat Hizb al-Ba'th), led by 'Asim Qansu, a Shi'ite from Biqa'. Its popularity varied with the attitude of Syria toward the National Movement. In the early phases of the Lebanese Civil War, the OBP was inseparable from the National Movement. However, as early as November 1975, it began to take an independent stand and formed what was to be called *al-Jabhat al-Qawmiya*, the Nationalist Front. This included Kamal Shatila's Union of the Forces of Working People, Musa al-Sadr's *Harakat al-Mahrumin*, the Movement of the Disinherited, a faction of the SSNP headed by Ilyas Qunaizih, and some traditional leaders, such as Kamil al-As'ad.

The other Ba'th party was the Arab Socialist Ba'th Party, whose strongholds were Beirut, Tripoli, and other urban centers, as well as in the Biqa'. One of the major figures of the party was Dr. 'Abd al-Majid al-Rafi'i of Tripoli, who was elected to Parliament in 1972, using, in part, his traditional links to the Jisr family, and his services as the physician of the community, for electoral purposes. The party got many recruits from the Sunnis and Shi'ites of Tyre, Ba'albak, and Nabatiya, as well as the Greek Orthodox of the Biqa'. The program of the party was Arab nationalist, secular, and reformist, appealing to the intelligentsia and the petite bourgeoisie. From the late 1960s on, the ASBP was interested in forming a new progressive front, uniting Nasirites, Communists, and members of the former Arab National Movement, the PSP, as well as other progressive groups.[20]

MINOR NATIONAL MOVEMENT ORGANIZATIONS

There were also some minor parties or organizations that constituted an integral part of the NM. The most important of these were four Nasirite organizations (three in Beirut and one in Saida) and the Lebanese counterpart of the PFLP, the Arab Socialist Action Party (ASAP). In the early 1970s, the Arab Socialist Union *(al-Ittihad al-'Arabi al-Ishtiraki)* in Lebanon was formed. It was led by members of the intelligentsia. Its rank and file were recruited from the poorer quarters of Beirut. The Arab Socialist Union in Lebanon (ASUL) gained force during the early months of the Civil War, but split into two groups in late 1975. One group was headed by Khalid Shihab and another by Kamal Yunis. The first became known as the ASU-Nasirite Organization, with forces concentrated in Beirut: Ras Beirut, the commercial center, and the suburb of al-Shiyah. The second group became known as the ASU-the Nasirite Organization's Executive Committee. Its main forces operated in 'Ain al-Muraisa, Ras Beirut, and the Basta quarters. Later, it merged with local militias in the traditional Sunni quarters of western Beirut, where they gained greater popular support. The third Nasirite organization in Beirut was the Union of the Forces of Working People-the Corrective Movement (UFWP-CM), a splinter group which was formed in October 1974 out of the Union of the forces of the Working People, a Nasirite organization that was formed in January 1965. The latter, headed by Shatila, supported Syria from December 1975 on, and later was no longer a constituent member of the NM. The UFWP-CM, on the other hand, remained a member of the NM and participated in the fighting on several fronts—in the hotel district, al-Shiyyah, Ra's al-Nabi' and in Mount Lebanon in 'Alay and Bdadun.

The Populist Nasirite Organization (PNO), led by Mustafa Sa'd, son of the late Nasirite leader and ex-deputy, Ma'ruf Sa'd, was a very important regional organization in Saida, forming, with some other parties, the backbone of the Regional Political Council of the NM in southern Lebanon. The PNO played a crucial role in the fighting before Damur fell into the hands of the PRM and the NM. After that, Saida continued to be a key city for the supply of arms, ammunition, and food to the NM. The port of Beirut was closed for a long period of time. Therefore, the port of Saida was used as a main trade outlet for the territories, under the control of the NM, throughout the later stages of the Civil War. The PNO was involved in the fighting in Jizzin and participated in the fighting in Mount Lebanon.

The Arab Socialist Action Party (ASAP), which was formed in July by George Habash,[21] held its first congress in August 1972. By the beginning of the Civil War it had already established itself in the urban centers, especially in Tripoli, Saida, Tyre, and Beirut. During the Civil War, it fought on many fronts in al-Shiyyah, Ra's al-Nabi', Sfayr, Tripoli, and in Mount Lebanon. Its representative in the Central Political Council of the NM was given the important post of deputy chief of military operations.

This brief survey of the major, and minor, organizations in the NM would be incomplete without mentioning Imam Musa al-Sadr's *Harakat al-Mahrumin* (the Movement of the Disinherited), which, in the early stages of the Civil War, fought side by side with the NM. Imam Musa al-Sadr had emerged as the spiritual leader of the Shi'ites because of the weakening of their traditional leaders, such as Kamil al-As'ad and Sabri Hamada. The presence of the Palestinian guerrillas in the South and the frequent Israeli raids against their areas forced many southerners to seek refuge in the cities, especially in the suburbs of Beirut. These rural migrants, dissatisfied with their traditional leaders, became easy targets for leftist and radical movements. Musa al-Sadr's movement also exploited the situation using his charismatic personality and his recently acquired title of president of the Higher Shi'ite Islamic Council, established in 1969. By the mid-1970s, he had already mobilized some sections of the Shi'ite population under the banner of his Movement of the Disinherited, symbolizing the gap that separated the poor Shi'ite masses from their traditional leaders. The Higher Shi'ite Islamic Council represented the Shi'ite religious leadership in the political establishment, a leadership that lagged behind the Sunni and the Druze by more than one decade. It competed effectively with the traditional political leaders, further undermining their power, which had already been eroded by the leftist and progressive parties of the NM. Al-Sadr's Movement of the Disinherited and its militia, Amal, fought side by side with the NM until the latter became at

loggerheads with Syria. Al-Sadr's pro-Syrian stand made him part company with
the NM in the spring of 1976.

THE NATIONAL MOVEMENT
DURING THE FIRST PHASE

The incidents that took place in Saida on February 25, 1975, which led to
the fatal wounding of the Nasirite leader, Ma'ruf Sa'd, gave the first impetus to
the parties and organizations that eventually formed the National Movement to
come together and mobilize the masses in their support. On the same day,
April 13, 1975, of the 'Ain al-Rummana incident in which a busload of Palestinians and Lebanese coming back from a Palestinian rally was ambushed and
most of the passengers were killed, these parties established a unified command.
It included, apart from Junblat's Progressive Socialist Party, leaders of the
Lebanese Communist Party, the pro-Iraqi Ba'th Party, the Syrian Social Nationalist Party, and Ibrahim Qulailat's Independent Nasirites' Movement.

The National Movement participated in the fighting that followed the 'Ain
al-Rummana incident, but the main brunt of the fighting was taken by the PRM.
The NM pursued a policy of isolating the Phalangist Party, putting the blame on
it for that incident. Junblat's representatives in the cabinet, 'Abbas Khalaf and
Khalid Junblat, submitted their resignations in protest. However, when it became
clear that Rashid al-Sulh, the prime minister, was openly holding the Phalangists
responsible for 'Ain al-Rummana, the NM changed its attitude and backed
al-Sulh's cabinet, hoping that after the Phalangist and the National Liberal ministers and their allies resigned, as they did on May 7, the cabinet would be
reshuffled in favor of the National Movement.

The National Movement went even further in trying to isolate the Phalangist Party. The Arab Front in support of the Palestinian Revolution, which
included progressive parties and organizations all over the Arab world, and whose
secretary was Kamal Junblat, held a conference on April 26, 1975, condemned
the Phalangist Party, and advocated its isolation in the Arab world.

There was some evidence that the Phalangist Party was unwilling to
cooperate fully with al-Sulh's cabinet in investigating the 'Ain al-Rummana
incident. However, Junblat's attempt to make political capital of the incident by
calling for the isolation of the Phalangist Party was doomed to failure. The Phalangist Party had been, since 1958, an integral part of the political establishment.
Moreover, Junblat's strong representation in Rashid al-Sulh's cabinet should have
backed the prime minister's demands for a judicial inquiry in the 'Ain al-Rummana incident, rather than resort to a confrontation with the president of the
Republic himself. Junblat and the National Movement, however, could not
resist the temptation to exploit the antigovernment popular feelings that followed
the Saida and 'Ain al-Rummana incidents. This led, ironically, to the weakening

of their strong position in government since the formation of al-Sulh's cabinet on October 31, 1974.

After the resignation of the Phalangist, National Liberal, and other ministers from al-Sulh's cabinet, Junblat rallied to the support of Rashid al-Sulh, trying to convince President Franjiya to keep him in power. Prime Minister al-Sulh, having lost more than half of the cabinet ministers, decided, in turn, to resign, after giving a full account of the reasons for his resignation to the Chamber of Deputies. By putting the blame on the Phalangists for 'Ain al-Rummana, al-Sulh played into the hands of those who wanted to escalate the crisis.

The National Movement believed that the ministerial crisis was really a crisis of the political system itself, and demanded changes and reforms. The traditional Muslim leaders, who were not unhappy about the resignation of Rashid al-Sulh, who they regarded as Junblat's man (he owed his seat in Parliament to Junblat's supporters in the second constituency of Beirut), were demanding an equal participation in the political decision making of the president of the Republic. Rashid Karami, the prominent Sunni leader of Tripoli, maintained that the position of prime minister had lost its importance.

By mid-May 1975, the National Movement had participated in the fighting, which had involved primarily the Phalangists and their allies, on the one hand, and the PRM on ther other. The Ghubairi and Shiyyah suburbs of Beirut also were involved in the fighting; that is the predominantly Shi'ite population who were mostly emigrants from other regions of Lebanon. These areas were not strongholds of the traditional Muslim leaders of Beirut, but were hotbeds of radical parties that belonged to the National Movement, as well as for some of the supporters of the quasi-traditional head of the Shi'ite sect in Lebanon, Imam Musa al-Sadr. These suburbs were part of the poverty belt surrounding Beirut and which include some of the Palestinian refugee camps. In these areas, the support for the PRM did not mean only defending the rights of the Palestinians, but also meant support for a revolutionary ideology that had been passed through the radical organization of the PRM. This ideology had found receptive ears among the impoverished masses in al-Shiyyah and the Tal al-Za'tar and Jisr al-Basha camps (the latter two also included some non-Palestinians), and in the Nab'a, Karantina, and Maslakh slum areas. It was not accidental that the supporters of the PRM, and, in particular, of the PFLP, the PDFLP, and their Lebanese counterparts, such as the Arab Socialist Action Party (ASAP), the Organization of Communist Action (OCA), and the Lebanese Communist Party (LCP), found recruits there. In this, as in many other cases, political issues acquired a social dimension as well. It was sufficient to contrast the people of these slum areas with the basically petit bourgeois and middle class suburbs of 'Ain al-Rummana, Furn al-Shubbak, Sin al-Fil, and Dikwana, which attracted, since the 1950s, predominantly Christian, albeit Maronite, migrants from Mount Lebanon. These areas, as we have seen above, constituted the strongholds of the Phalangists and National Liberals.

After the resignation of Rashid al-Sulh, Junblat demanded that the next cabinet change its composition of traditional leaders, especially with respect to the Christian representatives. He supported Rashid Karami for the post of prime minister. President Franjiya surprised the political establishment, and the public, by announcing on May 23 that a military cabinet, handpicked by Franjiya, had been appointed. It was to be headed by the retired Brigadier Nur al-Din al-Rifa'i, and included six other military officers. The chief of the army, General Iskandar Ghanim, was minister of defense. The only civilian, Lucien Dahdah, Franjiya's son-in-law, was appointed minister of foreign affairs. It was noted that the fighting intensified on the eve of the appointment of the military cabinet. It seems that President Franjiya came under pressure from the Phalangists and from Camille Sham'un to appoint any Sunni, other than Rashid Karami (who had the backing of a large number of deputies), who would accept the use of the army in putting an end to the fighting. A cabinet of military officers, including the chief of the army, who was minister of defense, was best suited for that purpose, they believed. However, such a move by President Franjiya was politically disastrous, because all the suspicions of the NM, the PRM, and the traditional Muslim leaders were aroused. The National Movement, with its various political parties and organizations, could hardly welcome a military cabinet that wanted to curb its political activities, thereby threatening the atmosphere of freedom which they had enjoyed since the Shihabist Deuxième Bureau era had ended, when Franjiya came into power in September 1970. The NM and the PRM remembered the events of May 1973, when the Lebanese army bombed Palestinian camps. It was the same chief of the army, General Iskandar Ghanim, now to be minister of defense, whose responsibility for the Lebanese army's inaction when Israel raided Beirut on April 10, 1973 had been the bone of contention between President Franjiya and Sa'ib Salam, the ex-prime minister.

Junblat attacked the formation of the military cabinet on several grounds. First, the prime minister designate should have consulted the various blocs and parties in the Chamber of Deputies, as was the custom, before forming his cabinet. Second, this military cabinet was unprecedented in the history of Lebanon, and would encourage military officers to take power. Third, the NM was against any form of military rule and was proud that Lebanon had never had any, as had many of the countries of the Arab world. Lebanon, it claimed, was the only country that had a democratic parliamentary system. Fourth, this action taken by the president was a blow to the Muslim community, which had expected full participation in political decision making. Finally, Junblat maintained that a military cabinet would be regarded as a threat to the Palestinian armed presence in Lebanon, and would be construed as a preparatory stage for the eventual liquidation of the PRM in Lebanon.[22]

The outcome of the announcement of the formation of the military cabinet was the closing of ranks between the NM and the traditional Muslim leaders. Sa'ib Salam and Kamal Junblat, who had been at loggerheads, made peace. The

NM, through Junblat and others, participated in the huge rally of Muslim spiritual leaders and politicians that took place in Dar al-Fatwa, the headquarters of Mufti Hasan Khalid, the religious head of the Sunni Muslim community.[23]

The military cabinet lasted only three days, after which it resigned, on May 26, 1975, due to tremendous opposition. By then it was clear that Rashid Karami was the candidate of the traditional leaders of the Muslim communities, as well as the National Movement and the Syrians. Thus, Karami was imposed on President Franjiya (who seemed to have been convinced of the efficiency of his military cabinet), by the other three groups. The Syrian minister of foreign affairs played a crucial role in paving the way for Karami's candidacy. Junblat, who visited President Franjiya, insisted of emphasizing that, in spite of this crisis, their personal relations were good. Junblat, in a prophetic note said that the "cabinet crisis had been on the verge of bursting into a kind of national rebellion against the government authorities."[24]

After Rashid Karami was asked to form a cabinet on May 28, 1975, the NM wanted to make sure that no representatives of the Phalangist Party would be included, and that no military officer would be appointed to the two most crucial ministries—the interior and defense, controlling the internal security forces and the Lebanese army, respectively. It also called for the formulation of a new national pact that would deal with the issue of the Arab identity of Lebanon, and Lebanese-Palestinian relations. This pact would also have to attempt to render the legislative and executive institutions more representative, and set a plan for the development of backward areas and economically depressed sections of the population.[25]

Junblat tried to force the traditional Muslim leaders to back him by claiming, in a statement issued on June 1, 1975, after they all met at the residence of the Sunni Mufti Hasan Khalid, that Imam Musa al-Sadr and other Muslim leaders endorsed the decisions of the NM to isolate politically the Phalangist Party, and to oppose its participation in any future cabinet. Al-Sadr, Sa'ib Salam, and some of the Muslim leaders denied those claims. These were the first external signs of the differences in the attitudes and objectives of the NM and those of the traditional Muslim leaders.

Junblat was very critical of the army leadership as well. He voiced the widespread opinion that the army command was dominated by pro-Phalangist and pro-National Liberal elements. His strong attacks on the Phalangist Party and on the Lebanese army made the formation of the new cabinet by Karami an even more difficult task. It was only after the intervention of traditional Muslim leaders and the spiritual head of the Druze community, Shaikh 'Aql Muhammad Abu Shaqra, that Junblat toned down his attacks. He began a secret dialogue with Sham'un via the vice-president of the National Liberal Party, Qadhim al-Khalil. Junblat, to help Karami in his task, declared that his party, the PSP, would not participate in the new cabinet, hoping that the Phalangist Party would not participate either. This maneuver weakened Junblat's position, especially with respect to his former strength in Rashid al-Sulh's cabinet of October 1974-May 1975.

The cabinet was formed by taking into consideration the NM's insistence on the political isolation of the Phalangists, but leaving the final decision in the hands of Karami and other traditional Muslim leaders. However, Junblat was overruled by Khaddam, the Syrian foreign minister, whose mediation was very decisive in the formation of Karami's six-member cabinet. Junblat feared that the important portfolios of the defense and interior would be held by Amir Majid Arslan, the head of the rival feudal family of the Druze community, or by the former president, Camille Sham'un, the rightist leader. Therefore, the names of the members of the cabinet were announced first, and only later were the portfolios assigned. When the announcement of the formation of the cabinet was made on July 1, 1975, Prime Minister Karami also became the minister of defense, although Sham'un was assigned the ministry of the interior. The other members of the cabinet either leaned toward the right, like Arslan, and, to a lesser extent, the former Speaker of the House 'Adil 'Usairan, or were centrists like the other two members of the cabinet, Phillipe Taqla, minister of foreign affairs, and Ghassan Tuwaini, the well-known journalist and owner of the publishing house of Dar al-Nahar. In the new cabinet, the NM was not represented, while its rival, the conservative front, was well represented. Another of the recurring ironies of the Civil War was that, although it was the NM that bore the brunt of the actual fighting against the conservative forces, it did not have a strong voice in the political establishment, in contrast to the traditional Muslim leaders. Soon after the formation of this cabinet, Junblat criticized Karami for not consulting him about the choice of its members, although he reluctantly gave his support to the cabinet.[26]

THE NATIONAL MOVEMENT'S PROGRAM FOR REFORM

During the months of July and August 1975, the NM busied itself with drawing up a reform program to make the Lebanese political system more representative and less sectarian. The program was eventually announced by Junblat on August 18, 1975.

Junblat, in an interview given to the *Falastin al-Thawra* magazine, the organ of the PLO, on January 1, 1976, maintained that the Lebanese Civil War originated in the attempt by President Franjiya, the Phalangist Party, Sham'un, and General Ghanim, the chief of the army at the time, to crack down on the Palestinian Resistance Movement in Lebanon, using both the right-wing militias and the Lebanese army. Junblat also claimed that the NM was able to transform a Lebanese-Palestinian conflict into a conflict among the Lebanese over the nature of the political system, and that this was achieved, according to him, by putting forward, in August 1975, a program for political reform, *al-Burnamij al-Marhali lil-Islah al-Siyasi*.

In fact, the NM, led by Junblat, took advantage of the armed Palestinian presence in Lebanon, and the strong feelings in its support that existed among various sections of the population, to make demands from the government for fundamental changes in the Lebanese political system. In this way, also, the NM stole the thunder from traditional Muslim leaders by advocating political reform, and thus managed "to prevent the traditional leaders from putting forward their own proposals."

The NM's insistence on a program for political reform lay in the nature of the crisis of the Lebanese political system, which was a crisis of political participation. The political establishment, in the eyes of the NM, did not any longer represent the majority of the Lebanese people. There is some evidence to back this claim, although it applies more to the Sunni, Shi'ite, and Greek Orthodox communities, than to the Druze and Maronite communities. The critics of the political system leveled their criticism on the basis that a self-perpetuating dominant ruling class had been unwilling or incapable of introducing reform in the system. Some of the critics, including the NM, depicted the rule of the dominant class as one of "political feudalism," *al-Iqta' al-Siyasi*. This was not meant to refer to the feudal origin of this class (although the political power of some of its members went back as far as the feudal era in Lebanese history, that is prior to the mid-nineteenth century), but rather to its ability to perpetuate itself and prevent the infusion of new blood at the top of the system. Although there was a high turnover rate among the parliamentary elite, of the 12 most important and powerful members of the Chamber of Deputies of 1972, 11 had either exercised political power directly, or had inherited it from members of their family who had been in power since the French Mandate. The only exception was the rise of Pierre Jumayil, the leader of the Phalangist Party, as a prominent Maronite leader, especially after 1958.[27] Moreover, the turnover in terms of families represented in the Chamber of Deputies as a whole, that is, the number of seats per family, had not basically changed since 1922.

The NM's statement on the rigidity of the Lebanese political system was especially true of the representatives of the Muslim communities. Perhaps the best illustration of the fact that most of the traditional Muslim leaders had ceased to represent their communities was the ability of the NM to upstage them, during the Civil War, in terms of popularity, military force, and in the ability to put forward a coherent program for political reform.

The NM program for reform was divided into seven major parts. The first was entitled "Toward the Abolition of Political Sectarianism."[28] The NM believed that the ultimate goal of reform should be complete secularism of the Lebanese political system, with the elimination of all forms of sectarianism from the various levels of Lebanese political life. However, the first stage would have to be the abolition of political sectarianism in the Chamber of Deputies, in the local and municipal councils, in the civil service, and the army.

The second major part of the NM's program of reform was entitled the "Democratic Reform of Popular Representation," which involved fundamental changes in the electoral laws of Lebanon. The NM proposed to make the whole of Lebanon one constituency, to adopt the principle of proportional representation, to abolish the system of the division of seats on a sectarian basis, to increase the number of seats to a one deputy for every 10,000 eligible voters basis, and, finally, to lower the voting age to 18. Other changes along those lines were put forward to render elections less amenable to influence. The NM also proposed a greater decentralization of the administrative units of Lebanon and a greater increase in the allocation of power to elected local and municipal councils.

The third major part of the NM's program dealt with the separation and balance of power between the legislative, the executive, and the judicial branches of government. All legislation was to be the prerogative of the Chamber of Deputies. A new elected Upper House was to be established, representing the various professional, economic, social, and cultural organizations. The NM also proposed that the power of the president of the Republic to dissolve the Chamber of Deputies be restricted by prior conditions, such as when the chamber rejected the budget in toto, or when the cabinet received a vote of no-confidence twice in the same year. It also proposed the introduction of a national referendum or plebiscite on fundamental issues.

On the executive level, the president would be elected by a joint session of the Chamber of Deputies and the Upper House. The Chamber of Deputies would also select the prime minister, while the president would have no other choice but to officially endorse the selection. The prime minister would then choose his cabinet, after consulting with the various parliamentary blocs. The appointment of the cabinet would then be approved by both the prime minister and the president of the Republic. Although the president would have the power to dismiss the cabinet, this would have to be followed by general parliamentary elections. On the judicial level, the independence of the powers of the judiciary would be safeguarded. A supreme court would be established to examine the constitutionality of laws. A special court would be formed to prosecute presidents and ministers. Finally, a voluntary civil personal status law would be promulgated, to provide an alternative to those who would choose not to follow their own sect's laws, such as marriage, divorce, and inheritance.

The fourth and fifth parts of the NM's program dealt with the reform of the civil administration and the reorganization of the army respectively. In the case of the latter, the program emphasized the abolition of sectarian discrimination of army recruits, and of the practice of sectarian divisions in the internal organization of the army. It asserted the importance of noninterference of the army in internal politics, and the necessity for civil political authorities to control the army.

The sixth part of the NM's reform program dealt with the protection of the individual's basic rights and liberties, such as the right to organize parties and trade unions without any restrictions, complete freedom of the press and publication, and the elimination of any kind of discrimination against women. Moreover, the NM wanted to include the Declaration of Human Rights in Lebanon's legislation, and change all other laws that were not in conformity with those rights.

The seventh part of the program advocated the formation of a constituent assembly of 250 members, elected by popular vote, on a nonsectarian basis, representing the various political currents in the country, to conduct a dialogue on the proposed reforms, and enact the constitutional laws needed for its realization.[29]

After a lull of almost two months, the fighting erupted again in Zahla on August 28, 1975. Junblat and the NM accused the Phalangist Party of starting the fighting. They also accused Karami's cabinet of not being firm enough to put a stop to the clashes.[30] On September 2, 1975, Junblat demanded the resignation of Karami's cabinet, especially as the new round of fighting began in northern Lebanon, between militias from Zgharta, which belonged to President Franjiya, and the militias in Tripoli, Karami's constituency. The significance of the fighting was that it erupted immediately after the signing of the Second Sinai Interim Agreement between Egypt and Israel, which was condemned by both Syria and the PLO.

As the fighting between Zgharta and Tripoli escalated, Karami and his cabinet began to think about using the army to stop the fighting. The NM issued a statement warning Karami against using the army, saying that it would eventually support one side (the conservative militias) against the other.[31] However, on September 10, 1975, Karami's cabinet decided to relieve General Iskandar Ghanim of his post as chief of the army, replacing him with Hanna Sa'id. This was to prepare the ground for a limited mobilization of the Lebanese army, to be used to separate the combatants in the North, especially those in Tripoli and Zgharta. The NM continued to oppose the use of the army. It called for a one-day strike to protest such a move, and to express its support for the NM militias in Tripoli and in the North.[32] However, Junblat came under pressure from Karami and other traditional leaders, as well as from the Sunni spiritual leader, Hasan Khalid, to cancel the strike. When Junblat realized that labor unions, merchants, and industrialists were also against the strike, he called it off. The difference in outlook between the NM and the traditional Muslim leaders surfaced again, and 'Arafat, the PLO leader, had to reconcile Karami and Junblat. When they met, Junblat insisted that his reform program be adopted by the cabinet, but Karami wanted only to introduce some changes, especially with respect to electoral laws.[33]

When the fighting escalated in Beirut and involved the kidnapping of noncombatants as well, the NM put the blame again on the Phalangist Party. It argued that it was being encouraged to continue the fighting by the use of the army in the North. It claimed that the fighting in Beirut, which had begun on September 17, was aimed at forcing Karami to permit the army to intervene in Beirut. The NM, coordinating its effort with Karami, decided that the only solution to the crisis was political and not military, and so called for an immediate cease-fire.[34] The NM said it was ready to abide by the cease-fire if the other side would. Thus, the NM, on the eve of September 18, 1975, wanted reconciliation based on political reform and opposition to military intervention in the conflict.

Instead, on September 18, 1975, the fighting intensified. The Phalangist Party bombarded the downtown commercial center of Beirut—which led to the burning and destruction of some of the old *suqs*—as well as other sections of the commercial areas.[35] As we have noted above, it was clearly an attempt by both the Phalangist Party and Sham'un's party to escalate the conflict and force the army to intervene. Sham'un threatened to resign if the army was not brought in, after all else had failed.

Syrian mediators, Minister of Foreign Affairs Khaddam, and Syrian Chief of Staff General Hikmat al-Shihabi stopped the conflict from leading to a ministerial crisis, over and above its military and security dimensions. The outcome of the Syrian efforts was the formation of the National Dialogue Committee (NDC) on September 24, 1975, which had a membership of twenty, equally divided between the Christian and Muslim sects.[36]

THE NATIONAL DIALOGUE COMMITTEE

The formation of the National Dialogue Committee (NDC) ushered in a new phase of the Civil War. The NM had at least three representatives on the NDC: Kamal Junblat, 'Abbas Khalaf, and the leader of the pro-Syrian Organization of the Ba'th Party, 'Asim Qansu.

Raymond Rabbat, the distinguished university professor and intellectual, was not unsympathetic to the NM. The lack of representation of the NM in Karami's cabinet was compensated for in the NDC. The only opposition to the NDC came from the pro-Iraqi Ba'th Party, probably because the leader of its rival pro-Syrian Ba'th Party, Qansu, was one of the members of the NDC. The statement issued by the NM, expressing its acceptance to participate in the NDC, included some reservations concerning the efficacy of such a body, and some criticism about the sectarian basis on which it had been formed.[37] Nevertheless, the very formation of the NDC, as well as the selection of its members, was a partial victory for the NM.

On October 13, 1975, the NDC formed 3 subcommittees. One was for political reform, one for economic reform, and one for social reform. Excluding the 5 members of the NDC who were also members of the cabinet, and the president of the Chamber of Deputies, Kamil al-As'ad, who refused to attend the meetings—he believed that it was he and not the prime minister who ought to preside over the NDC—the remaining 14 members of the NDC were divided into the 3 subcommittees. The economic reform and social reform subcommittees, which had 4 and 3 members respectively, were not particularly important. They had among their members only 2 prominent politicians, René Mu'awwad and 'Asim Qansu. On the other hand, the political reform subcommittee had 6 members, all of whom, except for Edmond Rabbat, were prominent politicians.[38] The political reform subcommittee included 2 traditional Sunni leaders, 'Abdallah al-Yafi, who presided over the subcommittee, and Sa'ib Salam, the leader of the NM, Kamal Junblat, the leader of the Phalangist Party, Pierre Jumayil, and the leader of the National Bloc, Raymond Iddi. It was clear from the debates of the political reform subcommittee that the conservative parties and, in particular, the Phalangist Party, were in a poor position. Pierre Jumayil was the only representative of the conservative parties in the political reform subcommittee.

The basic argument in the subcommittee concerned the issue of sovereignty. Junblat maintained that there were two kinds of sovereignty. One is sovereignty over territories and the other is popular sovereignty—that is, the participation of the people in political institutions. The first, as we have seen above, was the main concern of the conservative parties. They saw the armed presence of the Palestinians in Lebanon as an infringement of Lebanon's territorial sovereignty. The NM countered this by holding that there was no absolute sovereignty; all agreements (such as the Cairo Agreement between the Lebanese authorities and the PRM) were limitations on this kind of sovereignty. It was the second type of sovereignty which, according to Junblat, was the most important. "Seventy per cent of the Lebanese [people] do not regard themselves as represented in the [political] system," he claimed.[39] Then he added that the political system would either have to become nonsectarian, in which case a minority and a majority in parliament would emerge, free of any sectarian ties, or else the existing sectarian system would have to be equitably applied, by basing it on the actual sectarian realities of Lebanon.[40] Here Junblat was playing the game typical of his background and position in Lebanese politics. He kept one foot in the leftist, secular movement and another foot in the sectarian political establishment. The first appealed to the secular and nonsectarian members and sympathizers of the NM, while the second appealed to the Muslim communities (which then constituted the numerical majority in Lebanon). Junblat was a product and a symbol of this paradoxical symbiosis.

Both the NM and the traditional Muslim leaders were in favor of the NDC, especially after the political reform subcommittee became active. On the other hand, the conservative parties and organizations were definitely against it as a forum instituted for political debate in order to find an acceptable solution to the crisis. When Sham'un attacked the NDC and insisted that the Chamber of Deputies discuss all matters pertaining to political, economic, and social reform, Prime Minister Karami pointed out that the NDC had been formed with the purpose of finding a political solution to the crisis.[41]

The attitude of the NM toward the events of late October 1975 was that the conservative parties had stood in the way of a cease-fire, in spite of the formation of a joint committee, under the supervision of 'Arafat, the PLO leader, and Sham'un, the minister of the interior, to put the cease-fire into effect by mid-October. The NM accused the conservatives of timing their attacks with certain political events. When, for instance, the Arab Front, in support of the Palestinian Resistance, held its meetings in Damascus, on October 22 and October 23, 1975, fighting and kidnapping resumed in Beirut, initiated by the Phalangists and the Sham'unists. Prime Minister Karami accused Sham'un of being party to the fighting and of having his own militia not abiding by the cease-fire.

The objective of the NM during this third phase was simply to push for political reform through the NDC. It was interested in having a lasting cease-fire so that the atmosphere for a political dialogue would be congenial, and so that these objectives might be realized. The NM insisted that all factions of the conservative side should be represented in the High Military Coordination Committee (HMCC), so that they would abide by its decisions. The expanded HMCC was convened in early November, and all the political parties and organizations (both Lebanese and Palestinian) were represented.

The NM emphasized the social dimension of the conflict in Lebanon as well as the political, because Junblat realized that the NDC had been, in its discussions, favorable to the reform program put forward by the NM. He therefore insisted that those changes in the political system, and the amendments to the Constitution, be dealt with through the NDC, not in Parliament, which had become, according to Junblat, a weak institution, unrepresentative of the people.[42]

However, it became apparent that the conservative parties and President Franjiya were unhappy with the NDC. Rumors began to circulate that the NDC subcommittees were to be abolished, and that the cabinet would continue the discussions on political reform. The immediate reaction of the NM was to reiterate its adherence to the reform program of August 1975. It also stated that it regarded the NDC and its subcommittees as a suitable medium for the discussion of the reform of the political system. It insisted on its continued existence, if such reforms were to be made. However, the president of the political reform subcommittee realized that the weakness of the NDC lay in the fact that it had no legislative power, but simply the power to recommend proposals for political reform.[43]

It was becoming clear that the conservative parties were trying to undermine the NDC. The meeting of the NDC, which was held on November 24,

1975, was boycotted by Sham'un and Jumayil, who reiterated his view that order and security should precede political reform. Junblat, after the meeting was adjourned, attacked both President Franjiya and Sham'un. He maintained that it was unprecedented for a president of a republic and a minister of the interior to have under their command, other than the army and the internal security forces, respectively, their own private militias. Junblat added that those in power ought to be the guardians of the state and of the rule of law, and not partisans themselves involved in the conflict.[44] Sa'ib Salam, the ex-prime minister, openly accused Franjiya and Sham'un of deliberately undermining the NDC and consequently in having an interest in escalating the fighting.[45]

An important landmark of the third phase of the Civil War was the reconciliation of Franjiya and Karami at the end of November 1975. Both had been at loggerheads over the issues of sovereignty and reform. Franjiya had emphasized the primacy of territorial sovereignty *(al-Siyada)*, implying that the armed presence of the PRM extended geographically beyond what the Cairo Agreement had stipulated. Karami, on the other hand, had emphasized reform, though milder in form than that advocated by the NM. He believed that it should precede the issue of the Palestinians, and territorial sovereignty. Karami, in his statement of November 29, made known the reconciliation included both elements: reform and territorial sovereignty. This reconciliation and attempt to reach an agreement may have been prompted by the presence of the French envoy, Maurice Couve de Murville, who had arrived ten days earlier to study the Lebanese situation, and also perhaps to find some solution acceptable to both sides.

The statement of November 29, 1975, was a precursor of the Constitutional Document of February 14, 1976. It was less clear and less specific than the Constitutional Document itself, although it expressed the view that Lebanon was an integral part of the Arab world, although its special characteristics distinguished it from its Arab hinterland. The logical sequel to the statement of November 29 was Karami's decision to expand the cabinet. The NM insisted that political reform precede the formation of a new cabinet. This again is an illustration of the type of relationship that existed between Karami, who usually had the support of other traditional Muslim leaders, and Junblat's NM. Karami was willing to expand the cabinet and convene a national conference of the most prominent political leaders to find a solution to the crisis. Junblat, on the other hand, was not interested in what he called "tribal reconciliation" *(sulh 'asha'iri)*, but rather in political reform, which was shelved for some future date. Political reform, according to Junblat, ought to have been the basis of reconciliation.[46]

When the disagreement between Karami and Junblat came into the open in early December 1975 and after the somewhat successful visit of Pierre Jumayil to Syria on December 6, 1975, the NM had begun to show internal dissension. Representatives of the pro-Syrian Organization of the Ba'th Party (OBP), Kamil Shatila's Nasirite Union of Forces of the Working People (UWPF), and Imam

Musa al-Sadr's Movement of the Disinherited met and took a different stand from that of the NM. They supported Karami in his effort to form a new cabinet, and attacked the attempt by those they described as extreme leftists to blackmail Karami in order to achieve their objectives. Those groups, which were also pro-Syrian groups, were in favor of convening a congress representing all the parties concerned to find a solution to the crisis.[47]

Syria's attempt to draw the Phalangist Party closer to a position of reconciliation was clearly demonstrated when it invited Pierre Jumayil and an official party delegation to Damascus in December 1975. The Phalangist Party was still regarded as an outcast party, since the Arab Front in Support of the Palestine Revolution (AFSPR), had decided, in April 1975, to isolate it politically.[48] It was, therefore, quite an affront to the NM, and to Junblat in particular, when Syria, which had endorsed the decision of the Arab Front, invited an official party delegation, headed by Pierre Jumayil.

The Syrian attempt to split the conservative parties, by playing the Phalangist Party against the other conservative groups and parties, was not very successful. On the day of Jumayil's visit to Damascus, four bodies of Phalangist members were discovered in the al-Fanar area. This led to a series of executions by the Phalangists in the commercial areas of Beirut, where people were abducted and shot merely on the basis of their religion. The day was dubbed the Black Saturday by the press. The NM reacted by launching an offensive against the Phalangists in the hotel district of Beirut. The pro-Syrian parties issued a manifesto condemning the "brutal massacre committed by some Phalangist members against innocent people," and demanded the surrender of those responsible for the bloody events.[49]

In late November 1975, it became apparent that the pro-Syrian elements in the NM began to take distinct separate stands from the NM, although they still cooperated with it. That the differences did not become sharper was due to four reasons. They were, first, the Black Saturday events and the intensified fighting that resumed immediately after; second, the Phalangist attack and forced eviction of the residents of the Ghawarina quarter in Antilyas, which was regarded as a stronghold of the Lebanese Communist Party and the Organization of Communist Action;[50] third, on December 16, Sham'un's National Liberals and the Phalangists attacked and attempted to evict the residents of Sibnay village in the Ba'abda area where Junblat's Progressive Socialist Party had a local branch;[51] and fourth, President Franjiya's criticism, on different occasions, of the Left and the Palestinians, and his complaints that the latter did not abide by their agreements with the Lebanese authorities. This prompted Karami to counter Franjiya's allegations by pointing out that the PRM had an interest in, and was keeping law and order, and was participating in the High Military Coordination Committee since its inception. Karami emphasized that the conflict in Lebanon was basically a conflict among Lebanese, and that therefore the solution lay in the hands of the Lebanese parties to the conflict.[52] All these factors made the NM and the pro-Syrian groups close ranks.

Junblat and the NM were willing, in late December 1975, to abide by the cease-fire and withdraw from regions of Beirut which they occupied, in order to demonstrate their belief in a political solution to the crisis. In fact, the forces of the NM, and in particular, those of the PSP, and of the Independent Nasirites' Movement's militia (al-Murabitun), withdrew from the hotel district, on December 19, 1975, a move which coincided with the arrival of General Shihabi, the Syrian chief of staff, to meet the various Lebanese party leaders, and find a political solution to the conflict.

The year 1976 began with a qualitative change in the nature of the Civil War. The conservative parties had, in the past, refrained from attacking the Palestinian camps, and, in a way, the conflict had been, since May 1975, Lebanese in character. This was true despite the fact that the PRM had, from the outset, trained and supplied with arms the members of the various organizations of the NM. On January 4, 1976, the Phalangists and the Sham'unists began a food blockade of the Tal al-Za'tar camp, which reopened the Lebanese-Palestinian conflict. On January 14, the Phalangists' and Sham'un's partisans attacked and later occupied the Dubay Palestinian camp, a move that made Karami and other traditional Muslim leaders close rank with the NM. A Muslim summit conference was held in 'Aramun on January 16, 1976. The leaders who met there witnessed the bombardment, by the Lebanese Air Force, of areas close to 'Aramun, north of the besieged town of Damur. The PRM launched an attack against Jiyya, al-Na'ima, and Damur, in retaliation for the food blockade of Palestinian camps and the occupation of the Dubay camp. The Lebanese army and air force were ordered to intervene by President Franjiya and Sham'un, bypassing Prime Minister Karami, who, as minister of defense, was responsible for the armed forces. This was another example of the way President Franjiya defied the Sunni establishment. He made them feel by and large ignored in their demands for equal participation in major decision making. Although Karami, in fact, did try to order the army to stop fighting and withdraw its forces, it was of no avail.[53] The Muslim summit meeting issued a strong statement condemning the involvement of the Lebanese army in the conflict, and warned of the danger of dividing and undermining the army in the process.[54]

In comparison to earlier periods, the use of the army had increased since early January 1976, culminating in the Damur and al-Sa'diyyat battle, from January 16 to January 20, 1976. The reaction to the growing role of the army, which cooperated mainly with the conservative forces, led to the emergence of First Lieutenant Ahmad al-Khatib, in late January, as the commander of some Lebanese army forces in the Biqa' Valley. He later founded the Lebanon's Arab Army.[55] Al-Khatib represented the officers and soldiers in the Lebanese Army who resented the way it had been used against the PRM and the forces of the

NM. They believed that the ultimate control of the army was in the hands of partisan politicians like President Franjiya and Sham'un.[56] This was the first sign of the eventual disintegration of the Lebanese Army, a process that led to greater chaos and destruction and made it even more difficult to contain the Civil War.

The greater involvement of the Palestinians in the Civil War led to some tension between the NM, and especially Junblat, and the PRM. The attack on Damur and its environs was launched by the PRM, and especially by Fath forces, while the NM played only a secondary role. The manner in which the Palestinian forces and their allies occupied Damur, destroying and burning the houses, and forcing the population to flee, was criticized by Junblat. He attacked those who occupied Damur—that is, the PRM as well as some member organizations of the NM—for unjustifiably plundering and evicting its population. He added that slogans and ideologies were not sufficient. If ideological parties lacked self-discipline and ethical standards, they themselves became subversive elements.[57]

The tension that grew between Junblat and the PRM was rooted in the military superiority of the PRM. The sheer military power of the PRM, especially after the Yarmuk brigade of the Palestinian Liberation Army entered Lebanon from Syria on January 19, 1976, enabled it to have the last word in all military decisions. Moreover, because of the close ties the PRM had with the member organizations of the NM,[58] it managed to control and coordinate many of their other activities as well, as Junblat related in his memoirs on the Civil War.[59]

Disagreements arose frequently between the NM and the traditional Muslim leaders, especially Prime Minister Karami. Karami, in a way, represented both the Muslim establishment and the NM in the Cabinet. However, he was attacked and blamed by the NM whenever army troops intervened on the side of the conservative parties and when the political reforms that he proposed were not close enough to the reform program of the NM. Karami, like other Muslim leaders, was caught between the hammer and the anvil. If he did not support the popular demands that were put forward by the NM, his political base in the country would be much weaker. On the other hand, if he endorsed the reform program of the NM, he polarized his position vis-a-vis the conservative parties. Consequently, a compromise solution to the conflict might become very difficult to reach.[60]

It was not surprising that, when the fighting intensified in mid-January 1976, especially when the Phalangist party and Sham'un's party occupied the slum areas of Maslakh and Karantina, evicting all the inhabitants, Karami submitted his resignation, expressing his inability to influence events. Karami did not take back his resignation until a Syrian delegation mediated, forming 23 subcommittees to the Higher Military Committee, to supervise the cease-fire.

THE CONSTITUTIONAL DOCUMENT

The official visit by President Franjiya and Prime Minister Karami to Syria on February 7, 1976, was regarded as the culmination of Syria's effort to find a solution acceptable to the Conservative Front, the NM, and the traditional Muslim leaders. The outcome of this visit was the declaration of the Constitutional Document, on February 14, 1976, which marked the beginning of the fourth phase of the Civil War. The Constitutional Document clearly stated that "Lebanon is an Arab country, sovereign ... and independent."[61] This statement was directed to the NM and the traditional Muslim leaders who insisted on the Arabism of Lebanon. The conservative parties had been accused, by the NM and by some traditional Muslim leaders, of "isolationism" *(al-in 'izaliya)*, by which was meant that they did not regard Lebanon as an integral part of the Arab world (its membership in the Arab League notwithstanding) because they failed to give adequate support to Arab causes, and, in particular, to the Palestinians. To the conservative parties, Lebanon "had more in common with the Christian world than with the Arab Muslim world."[62] Consequently, the assertion in the Constitutional Document that Lebanon was Arab in character had a special significance to the NM and to the Muslim establishment.

The Constitutional Document had seventeen articles. The first article was the reaffirmation of the unwritten practice of allocating the three highest political posts in the country to particular sects. The president of the Republic was to continue to be a Maronite, the president of the Chamber of Deputies a Shi'ite, and the prime minister a Sunni Muslim. This was criticized by the NM and by some traditional Muslim leaders like Sa'ib Salam. They were willing to accept the continuation of the practice but not to have it set down in a written constitutional document.[63]

It was also proposed in the second major article that the distribution of the seats in the Chamber of Deputies be equally divided between Muslims and Christians, and that within each religious group there should be representation of each sect according to size. The traditional Muslim leaders were definitely in favor of this change. The Shi'ite traditional leaders immediately began demanding a share equal to that of the Sunnis. If this article pleased the Muslim establishment, whose communities had been represented by a proportion of five Muslim deputies to every six Christian deputies,* it was strongly criticized by the NM. The fundamental demand of the NM, the adoption of an electoral proportional representation system, had been completely ignored by this article.

---

*That is why all Lebanese parliaments, since 1943, had a total membership that was invariably a multiple of eleven.

It was true, on the other hand, that the Constitutional Document did stipulate that the electoral law would be amended "to secure a better representation of the electorate."[64] But the vagueness of the statement was not very reassuring to the NM. If the future effective political participation of the NM depended upon its ability to be represented in the Chamber of Deputies, then the changes proposed in the Constitutional Document were of no help to it, because the basic electoral list system, which favored sectarian traditional leadership, remained unchanged.

The third major article was the following: "The Chamber of Deputies will elect the prime minister by a majority vote. The prime minister will then begin parliamentary consultations to form his cabinet, and a list of the names of the cabinet members will be drawn up in agreement with the president of the Republic, whereupon decrees [of investiture] will be issued."[65] This article tended to strengthen the position of the prime minister vis-a-vis the president, but was not as strong as that proposed in the reform program of the NM.[66] The fact that the prime minister would be elected by the Chamber of Deputies, rather than appointed by the president, rendered his position more independent of the president. The joint selection, with the president, of the members of the cabinet, also insured, to some degree at least, equal participation in the process of selection.

The fifth and seventh articles made equal participation a real possibility. The fifth article stipulated that written provisions were to be made that would render the president, the prime minister, and all ministers responsible for their actions. The system had operated in such a way that effective power tended to be in the hands of the president, while the prime minister had to bear the responsibility. The seventh article stipulated that all decrees and laws would be issued with the agreement of both the president and the prime minister, and would carry both their signatures.[67]

One of the major grievances of the Muslim establishment and the traditional Sunni leadership had been that the position of the prime minister was weak in the Lebanese political system. The Muslims complained of the absence of genuine participation of the Muslims in governing. According to a group of Muslim leaders the premiership had become a position to make prime ministers fail in the eyes of the public and Parliament. A prime minister had to bear tremendous responsibilities for situations over which he had no real control.[68] In fact, the demand for equal partnership between the president and the prime minister was a fundamental one in the eyes of the traditional Muslim leaders. The lack of it had been one of the major complaints against President Franjiya since the resignation of Prime Minister Salam in April 1973. This was one of the major reasons for the disenchantment of the Muslim establishment with President Franjiya, even before the Civil War.

As the political system of Lebanon tended to favor the president of the Republic at the expense of the prime minister, it needed a particularly capable and politically sensitive president to keep balance and have an equal partnership with his prime minister. In fact, some presidents, at least for certain periods of time, did manage to maintain this equilibrium with their prime minister. For example, President Bishara al-Khuri's partnership with Riyad al-Sulh lasted, almost uninterrupted, from September 1943 to February 1951. President Fu'ad Shihab's relationship with Rashid Karami also lasted from September 1958 to March 1960, and from October 1961 to February 1964. President Franjiya had a good partnership with Sa'ib Salam, during the period from October 1970 to April 1973. Whenever the president of the Republic tried, as Franjiya did, from April 1973 to May 1975, to weaken the position of the prime minister, by periodically changing the person occupying the post, or by appointing a prime minister who had no popular base or support among the Sunnis, ominous signs warning of an impending crisis would begin to appear.[69] This happened toward the end of both al-Khuri's presidency and Sham'un's presidency, leading to the 1952 and 1958 crises, respectively. Those signs also appeared during Franjiya's presidency in the two years preceding the Civil War.

Thus, the Constitutional Document redressed the potential structural imbalance in the political system of Lebanon. It was therefore welcomed, on the whole, by the Sunni establishment. The attitude of the NM toward the Constitutional Document, however, was at first somewhat mixed. In an official memorandum issued by Junblat's PSP, on February 24, 1976, it accepted five articles of the Constitutional Document. It also rejected seven articles in toto, and either ignored or rejected in part the remaining five articles of the Constitutional Document.[70] The two major articles that were accepted by the NM were the ninth and the eleventh. The ninth article stated that the independence of the judiciary would be safeguarded and that a supreme constitutional court would be established to examine the constitutionality of laws and decrees. The eleventh article stipulated that the sectarian distribution of the posts in the civil service should be abolished and that recruitment should be based on the principle of merit, with the exception of the first category posts, which would continue to be filled on a sectarian basis.[71]

The major thrust of the PSP's memorandum was directed against the powers of the president. It rejected the political responsibility of the president of the Republic as expressed in the fifth article. It wanted to strengthen Parliament and the position of the prime minister in relation to the president. Its objective was to transform the predominantly presidential system of Lebanon into a parliamentary political system. The dissatisfaction of the NM with the Constitutional Document increased with the passage of time. The NM's demand for the revival of the National Dialogue Committee was indicative of their feelings toward the Constitutional Document, the reforms of which they found insufficient.[72]

Junblat urged Karami to send legislation to the Chamber of Deputies (after it was approved by the cabinet) concerning the five articles that the NM had accepted. However, he suggested that the other articles of the Constitutional Document be discussed in a reconvened NDC.* Junblat attacked Karami for trying to enforce law and order before finding a political solution to the crisis. However, he failed to revive the NDC.

After the declaration of the Constitutional Document, the Syrians had two plans to further improve the Lebanese situation. The first was to establish security (law and order) by means of the High Military Committee (HMC), composed of Lebanese, Syrian, and Palestinian officers, headed by the commander of the Lebanese army, General Hanna Sa‘id. The second was to form a new cabinet, or at least to expand Karami's six-man cabinet to make it more representative of all the parties concerned, and enable it to reconcile both sides of the conflict.

The NM had no intention of repeating the mistake it made when Karami's six-man cabinet was formed, in which it had no representative. Therefore the NM demanded that a cabinet be formed of at least 20 and preferably 24 members.[73] A large cabinet would increase the chances of its being represented. The NM also demanded that all those who fought in the Civil War, on both sides, participate in the cabinet. This was another effort to increase the NM's representation in the cabinet at the expense of the traditional Muslim leaders, who had not fought. On the other hand, both the conservative parties and the traditional Muslim leaders found themselves in agreement on the issue of the representation of the NM in the new cabinet, which they wanted to keep as low as possible.[74]

DIVISION IN THE ARMY:
THE EMERGENCE OF THE LAA

The most important problem that characterized the fourth phase of the Civil War was the disintegration and the divisions that bedeviled the Lebanese Army. Officers and soldiers were either not reporting to the barracks or were joining the movement (which became known as Lebanon's Arab Army, LAA *(Jaish Lubnan al-‘Arabi)*. It was reported that by February 21, 1976, about 900 soldiers had joined either First Lieutenant Ahmad al-Khatib in al-Biqa‘, or Major Ahmad al-Mi‘mari in the Sir and al-Danniya area, near Tripoli, or others still were being led by Major Salim Hamada in the al-Hirmil areas.[75] From March 8 to March 11, Lebanon's Arab Army forces gained new recruits and military barracks, especially in the South, the southern Biqa‘, and the North. This was

---

*Junblat proposed the expansion of the NDC's membership by including Sharbal Qassis, the head of the Lebanese Maronite Order of Monks, and Sa‘id ‘Aql, the famous poet and writer and the titular head of the Guardians of the Cedars. Both were well known for advocating secularization of the Lebanese polity and society.

done by attacking military positions, beginning with Arnun, the Rashaya citadel, then Marjicyun, al-Khiyam in the South, and 'Araman in al-Minya in the North.[76] The LAA met with little resistance in most cases as the majority of the soldiers and the officers in those areas supported Ahmad al-Khatib's movement. The commander of the army, General Sa'id, called for those soldiers and officers to return to the regular Lebanese Army and promised a general amnesty to all those who did. The commander of the air force, Colonel George Ghurayib, issued a statement putting the blame for the divisions in the army on those politicians who "sought their own interests at the expense of the public's interest."[77] However, it appears that President Franjiya refused to declare a general amnesty for the army officers and soldiers who had joined the LAA. He even wanted to change the higher command of the army for having been in favor of such a move. Prime Minister Karami, as minister of defense, refused to go along with President Franjiya.[78] These conflicts precipitated a serious crisis, and Karami declared his intention to resign. The Syrian mediators, Khaddam and Jamil, left Lebanon, tired of the wranglings among the Lebanese politicians and their inability to form a cabinet.

On March 11, 1976, the military commander of the Beirut District, Brigadier 'Aziz al-Ahdab, declared a temporary military rule over Lebanon and demanded the resignation of the president of the republic and the cabinet. He asked the Chamber of Deputies to convene within a week to elect a new president who then would form a new cabinet.[79] This marked the beginning of the fifth phase of the Civil War. Although it was a belated—and desperate—move to reunite the army, Ahdab's action immediately received wide support from among officers, soldiers, and even politicians. Ahdab was chosen by the army command because he hailed from a leading Sunni family of Tripoli, had an excellent military record, and was known for his Lebanese nationalist views, which had been expressed in his published works on historical and military subjects. The NM and the traditional Muslim leaders were all in favor of Ahdab's demand for the resignation of President Franjiya. Junblat, however, objected to the manner in which this demand was made, comparing it to a coup d'état. He argued that the declaration of martial law and the appointment of a military commander was the prerogative of the cabinet and not military officers. He believed that the military command ought to have put pressure on President Franjiya to resign in the same way that the army had done in the 1952 crisis, when President Bishara al-Khuri was forced to resign, and that they should not have occupied the television and radio stations and issued declarations on the air, as Ahdab had done.[80]

Ahdab's actions had two major objectives: to force President Franjiya to resign so that a new president could be elected and to reunite the already divided army. In spite of attempting to coordinate his effort with Khatib's LAA, Ahdab was unable to convince the LAA's commander to rejoin the regular Lebanese Army. A command council of 14 officers, headed by Brigadier Ahdab, was appointed on March 21, 1976, and included officers from most of the regional commands as well as the most prominent officers of the LAA: Ahmad al-Khatib, Ahmad al-Mi'mari, and Ahmad Butari.[81] However, Al-Khatib declined to join the command council of the army, as he considered the LAA the military wing of the NM. However, he was in full agreement with Ahdab on the issue of forcing Franjiya to resign.[82] Thus, an appearance of unity was maintained in the Lebanese Army, especially as Ahdab's movement had the support of a large number of officers, both Christian and Muslim. He also had wide support from various sections of the population, and for a brief moment the country's mood was optimistic as many believed that the solution to the conflict was in the making.

On the issue of the resignation of President Franjiya, Ahdab started a process which began with the signing of a petition by 66 deputies asking Franjiya to step down. Franjiya refused to accept the petition and resign on constitutional grounds, maintaining that the president of the republic would resign only if he were tried and found guilty of high treason. Franjiya was backed in this position by Sham'un, the Phalangists, Father Sharbal Qassis, and even the Maronite Patriarch Khuraish.[83]

THE NM'S MOUNTAIN OFFENSIVE

The NM and Syria during this fifth phase of the Civil War found themselves in opposite camps. While the NM demanded the unconditional resignation of Franjiya, Syria backed a compromise solution suggested by the conservative forces, making it possible to elect a new president while leaving the question of Franjiya's resignation open. The traditional Muslim leaders like Prime Minister Karami, Sa'ib Salam, and the President of the Chamber of Deputies Kamil al-As'ad, as well as Imam Musa al-Sadr went along with Syria on this compromise formula. The Chamber of Deputies voted unanimously on April 10, 1976, to amend Article 73 of the constitution, making it possible to elect a new president six months before the expiration of the term of the incumbent president, on September 22, 1976.[84]

The NM's differences with Syria came into the open in late March 1976, when Junblat mounted a successful military campaign in Mount Lebanon. Encouraged by the emergence of the LAA as a formidable force, he declared, on March 20, 1976, the formation of the Fakhr al-Din Army composed of the militias of the NM and the LAA. Junblat argued that resorting to the "military solution would prepare the ground for a political solutions."[85] The Holiday Inn Hotel, a stronghold of the Phalangist Party in the hotel district, was taken over by the NM on March 21, 1976. The fighting covered a wide area in Mount Lebanon: in Duhur al-Shuwayr, 'Aintura, Bulunya, Kafr-Shima, Ba'abdat, 'Alay, al-Kahhala, al-Mtain, Tarshish, Ra's al-Matn.[86] The presidential palace in B'abda was hit directly, and President Franjiya fled to Zuq Mikhail in Kisrawan. Syria's pressure on Junblat to stop the fighting produced no results. Junblat's position was that he was simply trying to lift the blockade imposed by the Phalangists and Sham'un's partisans on five villages in the northern Matn that were strongholds of the NM, and especially of the SSNP and the LCP.[87] Junblat tried, unsuccessfully, to convince Syrian President Asad to let the NM defeat the Conservative Front militarily, or at least allow them and the LAA to occupy key towns in the northern Matn and Kisrawan.

Pro-Syrian organizations in Lebanon began to denounce Junblat as the obstacle towards a political solution to the conflict and maintained that his military campaigns were leading to an eventual partition of the country. They shared this view with some of the Muslim traditional leaders, and in particular Prime Minister Karami and Imam Musa al-Sadr.

In the first half of April 1976, Syrian troops entered into eastern Lebanon at the request of Prime Minister Karami and with the support of some traditional Muslim leaders. By April 12, 1976, they had already reached Dahr al-Baydar in central Mount Lebanon. Junblat strongly criticized this Syrian military intervention and sent a cable to the secretary general of the Arab League, demanding that some action be taken with respect to what he described as "the occupation of Lebanon" by Syrian forces.[88] The PRM succeeded, however, in mediating between Syria and the NM, and in consequence the conflict subsided for a while.[89] The Palestinians also concluded an agreement with the Syrians on April 16, 1976, to revive the High Military Committee and to reaffirm the primacy of the Syrian initiative over the initiatives or mediation of all other parties.

THE ELECTION OF SARKIS

The election of a new president after Franjiya countersigned the amendment of Article 73 of the Lebanese constitution rekindled the conflict between Syria and the NM. There were two major candidates for the presidency, Ilyas Sarkis and Raymond Iddi. Sarkis, the governor of the Central Bank, who lost to Franjiya in 1970 by one vote, was the right-hand man of the late President Fu'ad Shihab. In 1970 he had the backing of the Shihabist officers in the army and the Nahjist (Shihabist) bloc in Parliament. Sarkis also had remained neutral, as had many other Shihabists in the Civil War. Junblat had maintained satisfactory relations with him. However, with the disintegration of the army, Sarkis ceased to have a solid power base, except for the support he got from Shihabist politicians who had not much political power of their own. In other words, in the eyes of Junblat, Sarkis would make a weak president if elected and would therefore have to rely ultimately on Syria. On the other hand, Iddi, Junblat's candidate, belonged to a distinguished Maronite family and had strong regional support in parts of Mount Lebanon, especially in Jublail.[90] Therefore he would be able to take a much more independent course of action, were he elected president. Iddi also had forged an alliance with Karami and Salam since early 1975, and was outspokenly critical of the conservative parties during the Civil War. Junblat preferred Iddi also because he had not been neutral in the Civil War and had opposed any kind of Syrian military intervention in Lebanon. Syria naturally supported Sarkis, as it did not want a Lebanese president like Iddi with strong and independent views. Ilyas Sarkis was eventually elected, on May 8, 1976, after tremendous Syrian pressure had been exerted on his behalf, and with a majority of 66 votes out of 69 (three abstained), in the second ballot.[91] At first the NM objected to the election of Sarkis, but gradually it resigned itself, accepted the election results, and began to establish contacts with the president-elect.

THE NM IN THE LAST PHASES OF THE CIVIL WAR

The sixth phase of the Civil War began in early June 1976, with the advance of the Syrian troops (some of which were already in Lebanon since April) into the 'Akkar, Biqa' and the central mountain areas of Sofar, and south towards Sidon. The NM called a general strike which was observed in Matn, Beirut and its suburbs, Tripoli, Sidon, Tyre, and Nabatiya. A United Military Central Command was formed for the NM, the PRM, and the LAA, on June 4, 1976. Some officers and soldiers of the Eastern and Northern command posts of the LAA, however, joined the Syrians instead.[92]

The NM was able, through its strong alliance with the PRM (except for the pro-Syrian Palestinian organization, al-Sa'iqa, headed by Zuhair Muhsin), to bolster up its position vis-a-vis the Syrians, and even some of the traditional Muslim leaders rallied behind it. The fact that PRM troops were pitted against Syrian troops enabled 'Arafat to convene an emergency session of Arab Foreign Ministers, on June 8, 1976. All the decisions taken at this meeting were not completely ineffective, because although fighting between Syrian troops and the United Command of the PRM, NM and LAA continued for weeks, they did slow down the Syrian advances. The tactic of the NM and the PRM was to get as much support as possible from major Arab countries, especially Saudi Arabia, Egypt, Libya, Iraq, and Algeria, to counterbalance Syria. However, the Arab League's decision to enforce a cease-fire between the Syrian troops and their adversaries was hardly put into effect. However, the Syrians did withdraw, on June 22, from the Beirut suburb of Khalda and the Beirut International Airport. The NM insisted on a total withdrawal, and the traditional Muslim leaders concurred. Even Karami, who had at first supported the Syrian intervention, now backed the decisions of the Arab League.[93]

The NM also tried to offset Syrian dominance over Lebanon by appealing to the Soviet Union and other communist countries, as well as to France, but, in general, their efforts were to no avail. The NM began to make contacts with some of the organizations of the Kufur Front and especially with the Phalangist Party, which feared the consequences of the Syrian military presence in Lebanon. Jallud, the Libyan Prime Minister, and some high-ranking PRM officials met with the leaders of the Phalangist Party to prepare the ground for a political dialogue among all the Lebanese parties to the conflict.

The dialogue never took place because of the military offensive by Sham'un partisans, who were later joined by the Phalangists and others, on the Palestinian camps of Tal al-Za'tar and Jisr al-Basha, on June 22, 1976, which forced the issue of the Palestinian armed presence in Lebanon to the fore again. The traditional Muslim leaders rallied behind the NM-PRM alliance. Salam criticized Syria for not withdrawing from Lebanon and continuing to attack Ba'albak, the Hirmil and the Biqa' areas.[94]

The National Union Front (NUF) was formed on July 11, 1976, of prominent politicians, including Karami,[95] Salam, al-Yafi and two other ex-prime ministers, Raymond Iddi, and pro-leftist politicians, both Muslim and Christian, thus uniting some of the traditional Muslim and Christian leaders and members of the NM. The NUF had three major objectives: the rejection of the partition of Lebanon, in any form, the ending of the Syrian intervention, and the implementation of the Cairo Agreement.[96] The formation of the NUF also was, in a way, a bridge between the already existing Muslim Bloc *(al-Tajammu' al-Islami)* and the NM.[97]

The NM launched a military offensive in Shakka and in the al-Kura area on July 5, 1976, to divert some of the conservative forces attacking the Tal al-Za'tar camp, but the offensive failed, and al-Kura, a stronghold of the SSNP, fell into the hands of the conservative parties.[98] The NM kept contacts with Syria, via its allies in the Muslim Bloc to ease the food blockade imposed on west Beirut and other areas under NM control.[99] The problem of food and fuel shortage, as well as other political considerations, led the NM to form the Central Political Council (CPC), *al Majlis al-Siyasi al-Markazi*, on July 22, 1976, involving twelve parties and six prominent politicians. Local councils were also formed in the South and in the city of Beirut. Junblat presided over the CPC, and four vice-presidents were elected: Deputy 'Abd al-Majid al-Rafi'i, a leader of the pro-Iraqi Ba'th, In'am Ra'd, the president of the SSNP, George Hawi, a prominent leader of the LCP, and Ibrahim Qulailat, the leader of the INM. It was argued that the formation of the CPC was an assertion of the NM's independence from the traditional Muslim leaders, in spite of their cooperation within the NUF.[100] The CPC also dealt with the everyday problems of the regions under the control of the NM, especially as these related to the food and fuel shortages. The establishment of the CPC created some tension between the NM and the LAA because the latter was not represented.[101]

By the end of the sixth phase of the Civil War there was an attempt to form a broad front including all the member organizations of the NM, as well as the traditional Muslim leaders. However, this did not materialize because some of the members of the Muslim bloc were not ready to go all the way against Syria by demanding the complete withdrawal of its troops from Lebanon. Salam had certain misgivings about cooperating with representatives of the LCP and OCA, and Karami's relations with Junblat remained tense.[102]

The NM's military and political reliance on the PRM became very clear during this sixth phase of the conflict. Indicative of this dominance of the PRM was the way it reached an agreement with Syria on July 29, 1976, without the participation of the NM. Junblat declared that this Syrian-Palestinian agreement was simply a device to gain time and would not succeed in putting an end to the conflict.[103]

By the beginning of the seventh phase, which started when President-elect Sarkis took office, on September 23, 1976, the NM had already mobilized its forces and refused to budge from its mountain strongholds unless a comprehensive political solution to the conflict was reached. The Shtura talks among Sarkis, 'Arafat, Syrian General Naji Jamil, and the Arab League representative Hasan Sabri al-Khuli were not fruitful, as 'Arafat fully endorsed the NM's position in not withdrawing PRM and NM troops from the central mountain areas. Thus, the Syrian attempt to separate the PRM from the NM was unsuccessful, too.

The second full-scale Syrian military offensive was launched on September 28, 1976, with the blessing of the conservative parties and Sarkis. The Syrians managed to reach 'Alay in the central region of Lebanon and the outskirts of Sidon in the South after more than three weeks of fighting.[104] Junblat, who was outside Lebanon, visited the major Arab countries, Saudi Arabia, Egypt, Iraq, Libya, and Algeria, and France, asking them to intervene or put pressure on Syria to stop its military offensive. 'Arafat's cables to the leaders of the Arab world, coupled with Junblat's lobbying, led to the convening of a summit meeting in Riyad between Syria's Asad, Sarkis, Prince Sabah of Kuwait, Egypt's Sadat, and King Khalid of Saudi Arabia.[105] The Arab rulers at the Riyad summit called for a cease-fire to be enforced on October 21, 1976, and established the Arab Deterrent Force (ADF), composed mainly of Syrian troops, as well as troops from other Arab countries. It proposed a timetable for the withdrawal of Lebanese and Palestinian militias from the various regions of Lebanon and their replacement by ADF troops. In effect the resolutions of the Riyad summit eventually put an end to the military dimension of the Civil War in Lebanon.

The NM was neither represented nor in any way involved in the Riyad summit. However, it accepted the cease-fire and eventually cooperated with the newly organized Arab Deterrent Force, which was at first under the command of a Lebanese colonel, Ahmad al-Hajj. By the end of the seventh and last phase of the Civil War, that is, by November 1976, the PRM's reconciliation with Syria was already underway, accelerated by the fighting which broke out between the local conservative militias backed by Israel, on the one side, and the forces of the PRM, NM, and LAA, on the other, in southern Lebanon. The NM followed suit in its reconciliation with Syria and its gradual acceptance of the new regime of President Sarkis. As the ADF entered the various regions under the command of the PRM and NM, the military confrontation with the conservative parties ended (except for southern Lebanon), and the NM sought a political and peaceful solution to the conflict.

NOTES

1. For a good study of the feudal period in Lebanon see Iliya F. Harik, *Politics and Change in a Traditional Lebanon Society, 1711-1845* (Princeton, New Jersey: Princeton University Press, 1968); an excellent work on the most important Maronite feudal ('Muqata'ji) family is Mary-Jane Anhoury Deeb, "The Khazin Family: A Case Study of the Effect of Social Change on Traditional Roles," M.A. thesis, American University in Cairo, 1972; an excellent study on urban notables is Albert Hourani's "Ottoman Reform and the Politics of Notables," in William R. Polk and Richard L. Chambers, *Beginnings of Modernization in the Middle East, the Nineteenth Century* (Chicago: The University of Chicago Press, 1968).

2. Marius Deeb, "Muhadarat fi 'Ilm al-Ijtima' al-Siyasi: Lubnan wa al-Bilad al-'Arabiya," mimeographed (Beirut: Faculty of Law and Political Science, The Lebanese University, May 1973), pp. 64-65; Iliya F. Harik, *Man Tahkum Lubnan* (Beirut: Dar al-Nahar, 1972), p. 23.

3. See, for example, the reasons for forming the Tripartite Alliance as put forward by a leading figure in the Phalangist Party, *Al-Qiwa al-Siyasiya*, p. 28.

4. Munazzamat al-Ishtirakiyyin al-Lubnaniyyin, *Limadha Munazzamat al-Ishtirakiyyin al-Lubnaniyyin? Harakat al-Qawmiyyin al-'Arab min al-Fashiya ila al-Nasiriya* (Beirut: Dar al-Tali'a, 1970), pp. 31-85.

5. Ibid., *passim*.

6. See the publication on the twenty-fifth anniversary of the PSP's foundation. Kamal Junblat, *Rub' Qarn min al-Nidal* (Beirut: PSP Publications, n.d.).

7. Sami Dhubyan, *Al-Haraka al-Wataniya al-Lubnaniyya* (Beirut: Dar al-Masira, 1977), p. 136.

8. See Khalil Ahmad Khalil, "Al-Hizb al-Taqaddumi al-Ishtiraki," in *Al-Qiwa al-Siyasiya*.

9. *Al-Hawadith* 1004, February 6, 1976, p. 35; for the views of a leading member of the INM, see the interview with Dr. Ziyad al-Hafiz in ibid. 1043, November 5, 1976, pp. 42-43.

10. See Muhammad Dakrub, *Judhur al-Sindiyana al-Hamra': Hikayat Nushu' al-Hizb al-Shuyu'i al-Lubnani 1924-1931* (Beirut: Dar al-Farabi, 1974), pp. 33, 92-94; S. Ayyub (Sami al-Khuri), *Al-Hizb al-Shuyu'i fi Suriya wa Lubnan 1927-1958* (Beirut: Dar al-Hurriya, 1959), pp. 127-29; al-Hizb al-Shuyu'i al-Lubnani, *Nidal al-Hizb al-Shuyu'i al-Lubnani min khilal Watha'iqihi*, vol. 1 (Beirut: Matabi' al-Amal Press, n.d.), pp. 130-31.

11. Niqula al-Shawi, *Katabat wa Dirasat* (Beirut: Dar al-Farabi, n.d.), pp. 304-06, 377-84.

12. Al-Hizb al-Shuyu'i al-Lubnani, *Al-Shuyu'iyyun al-Lubnaniyyun wa Muhimmat al-Marhala al-Muqbila* (Beirut: Matabi' al-Amal Press, n.d.), pp. 51-52.

13. Dhubyan, op. cit., p. 219.

14. Ibid., p. 223.

15. Roger Owen, ed., *Essays on the Crisis in Lebanon* (London: Ithaca Press, 1976), p. 64; for the increase in the membership of the LCP in the late 1960s and early 1970s, see *Al-Shuyu'iyyun al-Lubnaniyyun*, op. cit., pp. 224, 286, 324–25.

16. See, for example, Albert H. Hourani, *Syria and Lebanon: A Political Essay* (London: Oxford University Press, 1946), p. 197; idem, *Arabic Thought in the Liberal Age* (London: Oxford University Press, 1962), pp. 317–18; Stephen Hensley Longrigg, *Syria and Lebanon under French Mandate* (London: Oxford University Press, 1958), pp. 225–26; Yamak Labib Zuwiyya, *The Syrian Social Nationalist Party* (Cambridge, Mass.: Harvard University Press, 1966); Jubran Jurayj, *Ma'a Antur Sa'ada* (n.p., n.d.). For the development of leftist tendencies in the SSNP, see Joseph Shuwairi's introduction to the Arabic translation of Zuwiyya's book on the SSNP. Yanak Labib Zuwiyya, *Al-Hizb al-Qawmi al-Ijtima'i: Tahil wa Taqyim* (Beirut: Dar Ibn Khaldun, 1973), pp. 10–67.

17. Quoted from In'am Ra'd's address, in *Al-Qiwa al-Siyasiya*, op. cit., p. 323.

18. Niqula al-Firizli, "Hizb al-Ba'th al-'Arabi al-Ishtiraki," in ibid.

19. See Dhubyan, op. cit., pp. 280–83, 293–97; for the ideology and policies pursued by the UFWP, see *Dirasat Nasiriya No. 2 Mawaqif Qawmiya* (n.p.: UFWP Publications, 1971).

20. Dhubyan, op. cit., pp. 276–79; see also the interview with Mustafa Sa'd in *al-Hawadith* 1008, March 5, 1976, pp. 52–53.

21. Dhubyan, op. cit., pp. 225–31.

22. Another important organization, which was in Tripoli and based and operated mainly in northern Lebanon, was Faruq al-Muqaddam's 24th of October Democratic Socialist Movement. Its origins go back to October 24, 1969, when it was founded. Prior to the Civil War it had had several clashes with the Lebanese authorities. For its history, ideology, and role in the Civil War, see ibid., pp. 251–67, and the interview with its leader in *al-Hawadith* 1009, March 12, 1976, pp. 56–57.

23. *Al-Nahar*, May 24, 1975, p. 10.

24. Fu'ad Matar, *Suqut al-Imbraturiya al-Lubnaniyya*, vol. 1; *Al-Sharara* (Beirut: Dar al-Qadaya, 1976).

25. Ibid., p. 60.

26. *Al-Anwar*, January 1, 1976, p. 3.

27. Deeb, "Muhadarat fi 'Ilm al-Ijtima' al-Siyasi," op. cit., pp. 64, 90, 96.

28. Dhubyan, op. cit., pp. 369–81.

29. Ibid., pp. 274–81.

30. *Al-Nahar*, September 2, 1975, p. 2.

31. Ibid., September 9, 1975, p. 2.

32. Matar, op. cit., p. 111.

33. Ibid., p. 114.

34. Ibid., p. 119.

35. Antoine Khuwairi, *Hawadith Lubnan 1975*, vol. 1 (Junya: Al-Bulusiya Press, 1976), pp. 199–200; Kanal S. Salibi, *Crossroads to Civil War* (London: Ithaca Press, 1976), pp. 125–27.

36. *Al-Nahar*, September 25, 1975, p. 1.

37. Ibid., p. 3.

38. Ibid., October 14, 1975, p. 2.

39. Matar, op. cit., p. 165.

40. Ibid.

41. Ibid., p. 169.

42. *Al-Anwar*, November 12, 1975, pp. 1, 6.

43. Ibid., November 14, 1975, p. 2.

44. Ibid., November 25, 1975, p. 3.

45. Ibid.

46. Ibid., December 19, 1975, pp. 3–4.

47. Ibid., December 15, 1975, p. 2.

48. *Al-Nahar*, December 10, 1975, p. 3.

49. Ibid., p. 2.

50. For the point of view of the Phalangist Party as given by Amin Jumayil, see *Al-Anwar*, December 19, 1975, p. 3; for the point of view of the OCA, see the interview with Fawwaz Tarabulsi in *al-Hawadith* 998, December 26, 1975, p. 43.

51. For the point of view of the PSP, see *al-Anwar*, December 19, 1975, p. 3.

52. Matar, op. cit., vol. 2, pp. 27-28.

53. Ibid., p. 75.

54. Ibid., pp. 75-76.

55. *Al-Anwar*, January 30, 1976, p. 6.

56. See the interview with Ahmad al-Khatib, *al-Hawadith* 1005, February 13, 1976, pp. 48-49.

57. Matar, op. cit., pp. 105-06.

58. See above in this chapter.

59. See Junblat's memoirs, serialized in *al-Watan al-'Arabi* 66, May 18-24, 1978, p. 39.

60. Marius Deeb, "Some Major Causes of the Lebanese Crisis" (Paper delivered at the Ninth Annual Meeting of the Middle East Studies Association of North America, Louisville, Kentucky, November 1975), p. 6.

61. *Al-Nahar*, February 15, 1976, p. 1.

62. Salibi, *Crossroads to Civil War*, op. cit., p. 160.

63. *Al-Nahar*, February 13, 1976, p. 2.

64. Ibid., February 15, 1976, p. 8.

65. Ibid.

66. Dhubyan, op. cit., pp. 375-77.

67. *Al-Nahar*, February 1976, p. 8; Antoine Khuwairi, *Al-Harb fi Lubnan 1976*, vol. 1 (Junya: Al-Bulusiya Press, 1977), p. 172.

68. *Al-Nahar*, March 12, 1975, p. 4.

69. Deeb, "Some Major Causes of the Lebanese Crisis," op. cit., p. 2.

70. *Al-Anwar*, February 25, 1976, p. 3.

71. *Al-Nahar*, February 15, 1976, p. 8.

72. *Al-Anwar*, February 25, 1976, p. 3.

73. Khuwairi, *Al-Harb fi Lubnan*, op. cit., pp. 238-39.

74. *Al-Anwar*, March 4, 1976, p. 2.

75. Khuwairi, *Al-Harb fi Lubnan*, op. cit., p. 265; *Al-Anwar*, February 22, 1976, p. 10.

76. Khuwairi, *Al-Harb fi Lubnan*, op. cit., pp. 264-66, 270-73; *Al-Anwar*, March 10, 1976, p. 8; ibid., March 11, 1976.

77. Khuwairi, *Al-Harb fi Lubnan*, op. cit., p. 278.

78. *Al-Anwar*, March 20, 1976, p. 2.

79. *Al-Nahar*, March 12, 1976, pp. 1, 8.

80. Khuwairi, *Al-Harb fi Lubnan*, op. cit., pp. 307-08.

81. *Al-Anwar*, March 22, 1976, p. 1.

82. Matar, op. cit., vol. 3, p. 272.

83. *Al-Nahar*, March 16, 1976, p. 1.

84. Ibid., April 11, 1976, p. 3.

85. *Al-Anwar*, March 21, 1976, p. 2.

86. Ibid., March 25, 1976, p. 6; ibid., March 26, 1976, p. 4; ibid., March 27, 1976, p. 6. See also Khuwairi, *Al-Harb fi Lubnan*, op. cit., pp. 411-13, 425-26.

87. *Al-Anwar*, March 28, 1976, p. 6.

88. *Al-Nahar*, April 13, 1976, p. 4.

89. *Al-Sayyad* 1647, April 15, 1976, pp. 10–11.

90. See above, this chapter.

91. *Al-Nahar*, May 9, 1976, p. 3.

92. Khuwairi, *Al-Harb fi Lubnan*, op. cit., vol. 2, pp. 298–300; for the ideology and program of Khatib's LAA, which was spelled out on June 5, 1976, see ibid., pp. 327–29.

93. *Al-Nahar*, June 17, 1976, pp. 2, 6. When the Mufti Hasan Khalid supported the view of gradual withdrawal of Syrian troops to al-Biqa' valley, he was taken to task by Sa'ib Salam, the prominent Sunni traditional leader. Khuwairi, *Al-Harb fi Lubnan*, op. cit., pp. 420–21. Only the Shi'ite spiritual leader Musa al-Sadr and Kamil al-As'ad, the speaker of the House and traditional Shi'ite leader, wholeheartedly supported the Syrian position.

94. *Al-Nahar*, June 30, 1976, p. 2.

95. Franjiya dismissed Philippe Taqla, the foreign minister, and replaced him with Sham'un, who was also appointed deputy prime minister on June 16, 1976. This made Karami move closer to the NM and the PRM. Ibid., June 17, 1976, p. 1. See also above, this chapter.

96. Khuwairi, *Al-Harb fi Lubnan*, op. cit., p. 650.

97. Ibid., pp. 658–60; *Al-Nahar*, July 21, 1976, p. 2.

98. For the point of view of the SSNP, see Khuwairi, *Al-Harb fi Lubnan*, op. cit., pp. 629–30; for the point of view of the Phalangist Party and the local conservative militias, see ibid., pp. 627–32.

99. *Al-Nahar*, July 21, 1976, p. 3.

100. Ibid., July 23, 1976, pp. 2, 4; *Al-Sayyad* 1658, July 29, 1976, pp. 24–25; ibid. 1659, August 4, 1976, pp. 21–23.

101. For the views of Ahmad al-Khatib, the commander of the LAA, see the interview in *al-Sayyad* 1661, August 19, 1976, pp. 42–45.

102. The fragmentation of the traditional Muslim leadership and their growing differences with the NM were manifested in the formation of a Shi'ite-Sunni National Islamic Front *(al-Jabha al-Wataniya al-Islamiya)* on September 3, 1976, led by Shaikh Subhi Salih and Shaikh 'Abd al-Hamid al-Hur, and fully backed by some prominent officers of the LAA. Khuwairi, *Al-Harb fi Lubnan*, op. cit., vol. 3, pp. 280–81. See also *al-Sayyad* 1664, September 9, 1976, pp. 16–17, 52–53.

103. Ibid. 1661, August 19, 1976, p. 10. Junblat became even more critical of the Constitutional Document which he described as "unconstitutional" on September 8, 1976, and spared neither the Syrians nor the traditional Muslim leaders in his polemics. Khuwairi, *Al-Harb fi Lubnan*, op. cit., pp. 325–27.

104. The Syrian advance was slow, and the fighting was intermittent between the Syrian troops and those of the PRM and the NM. See ibid., pp. 498–501, 514–18, 525–26, 535–38, 646–47, 652–53, 658–60.

105. See below, Chapter Four.

4

THE PALESTINIAN ROLE
IN THE CIVIL WAR

With the establishment of the Palestine Liberation Organization *(Munaz-zammat al-Tahrir al-Filastiniyya)* in May 1964, the Arab countries changed their policy of the previous decade and a half by recognizing a separate Palestinian entity *(Kiyan)*. King Husain of Jordan supported the creation of the PLO and its army in spite of its potential threat to his own kingdom, in which two-thirds of the citizens were Palestinian. The PLO leadership was given to Ahmad Shuqayri, a traditional politician, who was Egypt's nominee and served 'Abd al-Nasir's interests in his rivalry with Jordan. At the time of its establishment, the PLO did not espouse armed struggle, and it was dominated primarily by traditional Palestinian leaders. Some Arab cynics at the time regarded the creation of the PLO "as a device to enable the Arab governments to pass the responsibility of confronting Israel to the Palestinians, and thereby avoid shouldering it themselves."[1]

In fact, some Palestinians were beginning to think that Palestinians should take the initiative and responsibility in the struggle against Israel. They were encouraged by the success of Algeria's FLN in 1962 against the French to adopt the idea of armed struggle to achieve their objectives. Prior to this, another group had emerged, composed of educated Palestinians mainly from a petit bourgeois background: the Palestinian National Liberation Movement *(Harakat al-Tahrir al-Watani al-Filastini)*. Their organization was known as *Fath*.* However, Fath's first guerrilla operation against Israel took place only on January 1, 1965. From early 1965 until the Arab-Israeli war of June 1967, three other guerrilla organizations emerged, two of which, the Vengeance Youth *(Shabab al-Tha'ir)* and

---

*"Fath" is the acronym formed from the Arabic name of the Palestinian Liberation Movement read in reverse. Literally, it means "conquest."

Heroes of the Return *(Abtal al-'Awdat)*, were connected to the Arab Nationalist Movement, led by George Habash. The third group, the Palestinian Liberation Front *(Jabhat al-Tahrir al-Filastini)* was formed by Palestinian officers trained in the Syrian Army, such as Ahmad Jabril and 'Abd al-Latif Shruru.[2]

Fath and the three other guerrilla groups (which later merged into the Popular Front for the Liberation of Palestine under George Habash) constituted the base of what came to be known since late 1967 as the Palestinian Resistance Movement, the PRM *(Harakat al-Muqawama al-Filastiniya)*, or the Palestinian Revolution *(al-Thawra al-Filastiniya)*. Both names referred to all the Palestinian groups involved in the armed struggle against Israel. The popularity of the PRM, particularly among the Palestinians but also among the Arab masses in general, rose, not surprisingly, after the disastrous defeat of the regular Arab armies of Egypt, Syria, and Jordan in June 1967.

Led by a closely knit group and headed by Yasir 'Arafat, a Palestinian who hailed originally from Jerusalem, studied engineering at Cairo University, and worked in Kuwait, Fath emerged as the major guerrilla force. 'Arafat had been a political activist from an early age. His closest associates in Fath were Salah Khalaf (Abu Iyad), representing the left wing of Fath, Khalil al-Wazir (Abu-Jihad), the soft-spoken organizer, and the politically conservative al-Hasan brothers, Khalid and Hani.[3] Fath's ideology consisted of four basic principles. First, the Palestinians should have an independent political movement and take the initiative in their struggle for the liberation of Palestine. This implied that the PRM had to safeguard its independence with respect to attempts by some Arab governments to control it. Second, the PRM was not to interfere in the internal affairs of any Arab country and therefore was not to promote or assist movements or parties the avowed objectives of which were the overthrow of existing Arab regimes. Third, the struggle against Israel was to be first and foremost an armed struggle. Fourth, at this early stage of the Palestinian Revolution, "national unity" was to be emphasized; consequently, a social ideology that could antagonize certain Palestinian classes and groups from the PRM was best avoided.[4]

In practice, Fath did not always adhere to these principles. When King Husain cracked down on the PRM in September 1970, and eventually put an end, in July 1971, to the PRM's military presence in Jordan, Fath called for the overthrow of the Jordanian regime and for the unity of Palestinians and East Bank Jordanians. Moreover, the support Fath received from Arab as well as non-Arab leaders of revolutionary and leftist parties and organizations affected, at least to some extent, its character and image. However, some Fath leaders did keep close ties with the more conservative regimes in the Arab world and especially with Saudi Arabia and the Arab states of the Gulf.

We dealt in Chapter Three with the divisions in the Arab Nationalist Movement (ANM) from the June War of 1967. It was typical of the post-June 1967 period that the leader of the ANM chose to lead primarily the Palestinian branch of this movement, which united with three guerrilla organizations to form the Popular Front for the Liberation of Palestine (PFLP) in December 1967. This decision was indicative of George Habash's priorities, and the Palestinian priority came first. However, by early 1969, the PFLP had split twice. The first split, in late 1968, resulted in the formation of the PFLP-General Command, led by Ahmad Jabril. At first, the PFLP-GC was non-ideological and had strong ties with Syria as well as Libya after its 1969 revolution. Gradually, however, the PFLP-GC became more leftist, as could be seen in the editorials of its organ, *Ila al-Amam* (whose editor and ideologue, Fadil Shruru, is a leading PFLP-GC member). The second split took place in February 1969, and eventually resulted in the Popular Democratic Front for the Liberation of Palestine (PDFLP), led by Nayif Hawatmeh, a former leading member of the Arab Nationalist Movement.[5] Both the PFLP and the PDFLP professed a Marxist-Leninist ideology but with no formal ties to either Moscow or Peking. They took the Cuban and Vietnamese revolutions as models, although they insisted that they never lost sight of their own indigenous and independent revolutionary policies. The PDFLP was instrumental in putting forward the idea of a democratic, nonsectarian state for Palestinians in which Jews, Muslims, and Christians would enjoy equal rights. This idea became a slogan and was adopted by almost all the guerrilla organizations, including Fath.[6] Although the PFLP and PDFLP differed in tactics as well as in emphasis on certain objectives, their views were similar with respect to two fundamental issues. First, they regarded their struggle as part of an overall struggle taking place in the Arab world to "liberate" each Arab state and establish a revolutionary society instead. Thus, they did not adhere to the principle of noninterference in the internal affairs of the Arab countries. However, the PRM, they believed, "is not expected to substitute for the national liberation movement in the Arab countries, but it is expected to openly criticize the stands adopted by the Arab governments towards the Palestine problem and put the blame on those responsible for the defeat [of 1967]."[7] Second, the PFLP and the PDFLP criticized the fourth principle of the strategy put forward by Fath (and others) of "Palestinian National Unity," on the grounds that the leadership of the PRM would eventually be dominated by members of the Palestinian bourgeoisie and petite bourgeoisie. They believed that true "national unity" was that of classes under the leadership of the workers and the peasants.[8]

There were two other major guerrilla organizations that belonged to the PRM. First there was the Syrian-sponsored and backed Vanguard of the Popular Liberation War *(Tala'i' Harb al-Tahrir al-Sh'biya)*, better known after its militia, the *Sa'iqa* (Thunderbolt). It was led by Zuhair Muhsin and was a direct instrument of the Syrian regime. The second organization was much smaller and was made up of pro-Iraqi Palestinian Ba'thists, called the Arab Liberation Front *(Jabhat al-Tahrir al-'Arabiya)*. The ALF followed the directions of the Iraqi Ba'thist regime.

By early 1969 the guerrilla organizations had managed to wrest the PLO from the traditional leadership that had dominated it since its inception. 'Arafat became president of the Executive Committee of the PLO, and most of the guerrilla organizations were represented in the Executive Committee.

After the June 1967 war, the PRM operated much more frequently across the Jordanian and Lebanese borders than from the Syrian border with Israel. The upsurge in guerrilla bases and activities in Jordan during the 1968-70 period was not surprising, as it was the country with the largest concentration of displaced Palestinians. Simultaneously, PRM activities increased in Lebanon, which had the second largest Palestinian population. The Palestinian refugees in Lebanon were distributed in 15 major camps. It was no accident that most of these camps were situated near major urban centers; this way, refugees could seek employment in the cities and be utilized as somewhat cheaper labor for Lebanese industries and enterprises.[9] In fact, of the six Palestinian camps in southern Lebanon, three were near Tyre, two in the Saida area, and one in Nabatiya town. In the Muhafaza of Biqa' there was one camp at the entrance of Ba'albak. The two camps in northern Lebanon were three and seventeen kilometers, respectively, from Tripoli. The rest of the camps were either in Beirut itself or close to its suburbs. Mar Ilyas Burj al-Barajna and the Shatila-Sabra camps were in Beirut; Jisr al-Basha, Tal al-Za'tar, and Dubay were very close to its outskirts. These camps were populated by Palestinian refugees who either had fled or been evicted from the northern part of Mandatory Palestine in 1948, that is, mostly from Acre and Upper Galilee. The total number of refugees after the Arab-Israeli war of 1948-49 was 141,000, and it augmented by the mid-1970s to approximately 350,000.[10] During the period 1948-67, there had been political activism in these camps, and many joined the various political parties of the time, namely the ANM, the Ba'th, and the SSNP. However, the Palestinian refugees in Lebanon were under surveillance by the Lebanese authorities. The rise of the PRM after June 1967 transformed the camps into strongholds of the guerrilla organizations, and already by April 1969, clashes began taking place between Palestinian demonstrators and the Lebanese security forces. In October of that year, fighting broke out between the Lebanese army and the PRM forces in the various parts of the country and eventually led to the signing of the agreement between the Lebanese authorities, represented by the commander of the army, General Emile Bustani, and PLO leader Yasir 'Arafat in Cairo on November 3, 1969. The Cairo Agreement legitimized the military presence of the Palestinians in the 'Arqub area in southern Lebanon. It also allowed the Palestinians resident in Lebanon to participate in the PRM, although their armed struggle was to remain, in the rather general terms of the agreement, within "the principles of Lebanon's sovereignty and security."[11] The Cairo Agreement was accepted by the Lebanese cabinet as well as by the parliament. Sham'un and Jumayil were also among those who accepted it. Professor Kamal Salibi argues that Emile Bustani in particular, and perhaps other Maronites as well who aspired to the presidency (elections for which were to be held in August 1970), signed or approved of the Cairo Agreement in order to enlist Muslim support for their candidacy.[12]

The Cairo Agreement thus gave the PRM a foothold in Lebanon and control of the Palestinian camps and the 'Arqub area. Lebanon became even more important to the Palestinians after the eviction of the PRM from Jordan by late 1971. All the guerrilla leaders as well as the rank and file consequently moved from Jordan not only to Syria, but especially to Lebanon because of the greater freedom of action given to them there under the Cairo Agreement and the importance of Beirut as a media and information center, while in Syria the strong Syrian army kept the PRM under strict surveillance and control.

Once the Cairo Agreement was signed, no major clashes took place between the PRM and the Lebanese authorities until the events of May 1973. These events were triggered by an Israeli raid on Beirut on April 10, 1973, which led to the killing of three prominent leaders of the PRM. Prime Minister Salam resigned after he tried unsuccessfully to dismiss the commander of the Lebanese Army, General Iskandar Ghanim, because of his failure to repulse the Israeli attack. Tensions between the Lebanese Army and the PRM increased and led to fighting between May 2 and May 18, 1973. Palestinian camps, especially those on the outskirts of Beirut, were bombarded, and the Lebanese Army posts were attacked. Meetings were then held between the Lebanese Army and the PRM, which were successful in stopping the fighting and in getting both sides to reach an agreement known as the Milkart Agreement or Protocol, which was attached as an appendix to the Cairo Agreement. It was a detailed agreement which aimed at lessening the chances of conflict between the army and the PRM. It explicitly defined the number of men and the kind of arms permitted in the Palestinian camps. It also restricted the areas from which the PRM forces were to be allowed to operate in the border areas and the 'Arqub region.[13]

The clashes of May 1973 had a tremendous impact on the attitude of the PRM in Lebanon. During 1973-75, the PRM tried to avoid conflict with the Lebanese authorities, but at the same time it was preparing itself to defend its "acquired" status in Lebanon dating from the Cairo Agreement of 1969. The PRM's suspicions, however, were increasing as reports of consignments of arms and ammunition being distributed to the conservative parties with the full knowledge of the Lebanese authorities reached them.[14]

It was perhaps more than symbolic that the Civil War in Lebanon had been sparked by the ambushing of a bus in 'Ain al-Rummana, on April 13, 1975, by the Phalangists, which resulted in the killing of 26 persons and the wounding of 20 more, most of them Palestinians (although some had been Lebanese) who had been attending a Palestinian rally and were on their way back to Tal al-Za'tar. According to the Palestinians, the attack had not been a surprise. The crisis had been building up from the beginning of 1975, when more arms were being brought in for the Phalangists' and Sham'un's militias and when demands began to be made by the Phalangists for a plebiscite on the armed Palestinian presence and on whether the Cairo Agreement ought to be upheld.[15]

According to Salah Khalaf (Abu Iyad), the prominent leader of the Fath organization, the PRM had had more than its share of accusations from the organ of the Phalangist Party, *Al-'Amal*, for the last three years. Despite all the provocation by the Phalangist Party, the PRM had tried to maintain a dialogue with them. Negotiations to sign a document between the Phalangist Party and the various organizations of the PRM were held. The document eventually signed was supposed to define the role of the PRM in Lebanon. However, it was not issued because the Phalangists objected to the phrase denying a causal relationship between Israeli incursions in southern Lebanon and the armed presence of the PRM in that region. The reaction of the PRM to the 'Ain al-Rummana incident was to blame the Phalangist Party for it, while emphasizing that its relationship with the Lebanese authorities was good.[16]

Hawatmeh, the leader of the PDFLP, accused the Phalangist Party of provoking the 'Ain al-Rummana incident and maintained that the Phalangists were trying to push the PRM into a large-scale armed conflict, which could eventually lead Lebanon into a kind of civil war.[17] Salah Khalaf expressed the viewpoint of the PRM: they regarded Lebanon only as a temporary location and had no other objectives in the country. Its importance to them, he continued, was primarily political and not military, for Beirut was an important media and information center from which the PRM benefited. The PRM, he added, was interested in dealing with a strong government in Lebanon, because only such a government could reach an agreement with the PRM and ensure the enforcement of its decisions.[18] In other words, the PRM tried to reassure the conservative parties of its good intentions in Lebanon and allay their fears concerning the PRM's interest in interfering in the internal affairs of Lebanon, in order to prevent a military confrontation between the two sides.

The Arab Front in Support of the Palestinian Revolution held a conference on April 25–26, 1975, and passed a resolution condemning the Phalangist Party for the 'Ain al-Rummana incident, calling for its isolation and boycott in Lebanon and the Arab world. Kamal Junblat was behind this move, but the PRM had obviously supported the action. The PRM thus inadvertently involved itself in Lebanese political affairs by espousing Junblat's stand toward the Phalangist Party. However, the PRM considered doing so an act of self-defense against the provocations of the Phalangists. The PFLP also issued a statement, dated April 25, 1975, condemning the Phalangist Party on the grounds that it was trying to push the Lebanese authorities and the Lebanese Army to fight the PRM. It also accused the Phalangist Party of attempting to sow the seeds of discord within the PRM itself and trying to pit the leaders of the PLO against those of the Rejection Front.[19]

A meeting was held on June 23, 1975, between 'Arafat, the PLO leader, and President Franjiya, in the presence of Salah Khalaf, Professor Walid Khalidi, a leading Palestinian academician, Hasib al-Sabbagh, a Palestinian businessman, and the Saudi and Egyptian ambassadors to Lebanon, to discuss the various aspects of Lebanese-Palestinian relations. Salah Khalaf had paved the way for the meeting by declaring that the Palestinians were keen on having frank and open relations with Christian organizations, be they the Phalangist Party or the Lebanese Order of Monks, if those parties and organizations were not set against the very presence of the Palestinians in Lebanon.[20] The meeting resulted in 'Arafat's message to the Lebanese, televised on June 23, 1975. 'Arafat declared in his statement that the PRM was not an actor on the Lebanese internal political scene, and that it was neither a sect *(Ta'ifa)*, nor in alliance with or an appendage of one. He also stated that the PRM had no opinion on the kind of political or economic system Lebanon chose to have. He also reiterated the Palestinian position concerning its respect without any reservation for Lebanon's sovereignty. He asked the Lebanese to recognize the right of the PRM to exist on their territory, within the framework of the agreement reached between the PRM and the Lebanese authorities.[21]

'Arafat's statement of June 23, 1975, which preceded the formation of Karami's six-member cabinet on July 1, 1975, represented the mainstream elements of the PRM, but did not necessarily represent the views of the PFLP and other members of the Rejection Front. Although the PFLP was not interested in getting involved in "side-battles" in Lebanon at the expense of its struggle against Israel, its Lebanese counterpart, the Arab Socialist Action Party (ASAP), regarded the struggle in Lebanon as a class struggle and had strong views about Lebanon's political and economic system.[22]

On the other hand, as the fighting escalated in mid-September 1975, around 600 soldiers of the Palestine Liberation Army (PLA) and the Sa'iqa entered Lebanon from Syria, at the request of Prime Minister Karami, to keep law and order in Tripoli. Later, on September 19, the PLA forces returned to Syria, at the request of the Lebanese authorities, while elements from Fath and the Sa'iqa maintained order in Tripoli.[23] In Beirut, too, the PRM was joined by representatives of the conservative parties and created a security committee with a 400-man force, including members from the various guerrilla organizations, the Rejection Front among them, under the command of Abu Hasan ('Ali Hasan Salama),[24] to establish security in Beirut and elsewhere.

The formation of the National Dialogue Committee (NDC) on September 24, 1975, marked the beginning of the third phase of the Lebanese Civil War. It was praised by the Palestinian leadership, who saw it as a step forward in finding a solution to the conflict. According to them it could establish the foundations for security and peace by replacing armed conflict with democratic dialogue.[25]

'Arafat submitted a memorandum on October 17, 1975, drafted by the PLO executive committee, to the NDC, concerning Palestinian-Lebanese relations. The memorandum asserted once again that Palestinians would never be

interested in settling permanently in Lebanon: "Our people will reject any substitute citizenship or political identity" other than a Palestinian one and would
reject any pressure to integrate in or be absorbed by any other Arab society.[26]
This reaffirmation of the PRM's good intentions was important in allaying the
fears of the conservative parties, which viewed with suspicion the settling of the
Palestinians in Lebanon and the fact that they were fast becoming an integral
part of the political scene. The memorandum also reiterated that it would abide
by the agreements signed between the PLO and the Lebanese authorities. Fath
urged the various parties to the conflict to avoid resorting to force in order to
provide a suitable atmosphere for strengthening Lebanese-Palestinian relations.[27]
The PRM was not interested in prolonging the fighting in Lebanon and actually
participated in most committees designed to keep law and order in the country.

The PLO and the Syrians boycotted the emergency session of Arab foreign
ministers held in Cairo on October 15, 1975, which had been convened at the
request of the state of Juwait. On the other hand, a Palestinian delegation was
sent, at the same time, to Kuwait, Bahrain, and the United Arab Emirates to
explain the Palestinian point of view in the light of the events in Lebanon, as
well as in relation to the signing of the second Sinai Agreement between Egypt
and Israel.[28] The basic attitude of Syria and the PLO was that the conflict in
Lebanon could be contained and eventually stopped by the parties themselves
with Syrian help and mediation. They saw no need for "Arabizing" the conflict
and involving other Arab countries in finding a solution to it. On October 23,
1975, the Arab Front in Support of the Palestinian Revolution (AFSPR) convened a meeting in Damascus, where they endorsed a series of resolutions in
favor of the PRM and the NM and accused the conservative parties of fomenting
trouble in Lebanon and prolonging the fighting.[29]

President Franjiya complained on December 17, 1975, that the PRM was
not abiding by its agreements with the Lebanese authorities, despite the PLO
memorandum submitted to the NDC, and that it was arming some elements of
the NM as well (see Chapter Two above). The PRM was caught in a dilemma. On
one hand, the PRM (including the PFLP and the other members of the Rejection
Front) did not want to be drawn into the fighting and conflict in Lebanon. On
the other, since its expulsion from Jordan, it feared that another attempt was
being made to oust its military forces from Lebanon as well. Consequently, it
was prepared to fight to retain its "status" in Lebanon. Thus the line of demar-
cation between its non-involvement in the internal affairs of Lebanon and the
defense of its threatened position in the country became rather blurred and even
disappeared completely at times.

The PFLP criticized openly the "defense" strategy of the PLO in fighting
the conservative parties. They believed that only an aggressive and decisive
victory over those forces would undermine their power sufficiently to ensure
that the presence of the Palestinians would no longer be threatened in Lebanon.
Otherwise, they argued, fighting in stages would only give time to the conserva-

tive forces to rally their supporters and mobilize them by playing on their national and sectarian feelings in order to fight a long, drawn-out war, which would exhaust the impoverished masses (the bulk of their and the NM's supporters) economically and weaken the Palestinians' position in Lebanon.[30]

Thus, we see that by the end of 1975 there were two major views held by the members of the PRM. The first was held by a minority, represented by the PFLP and the Rejection Front, who, though they denied that the conflict was one between the Lebanese and the Palestinians, believed that they ought to remain allies of the NM and that consequently they could not remain neutral in the conflict.[31] The Fath and the Sa'iqa had no particular demands as such, and were ready for a cease-fire at any time, which would lead to permanent peace. Zuhair Muhsin, the leader of the Sa'iqa, related in an internal circular in early October 1975 how the PRM leaders, 'Arafat, Khalaf, and Hawatmeh met prime minister Karami and expressed their desire to stop the fighting for good. They wished to have pressure exerted on the Lebanese National Movement to freeze its demands and to limit its struggle to more democratic means, naturally, if the conservative parties were willing to do likewise and accept an end to the fighting.[32]

The Fath and the Sa'iqa's aim, as well as that of their allies in the PRM at the time, was to protect the PRM military presence in Lebanon, as legitimized by the Cairo Agreement, with the least possible confrontation or fighting. Consequently, they were unwilling to endorse fully the demands of the NM. By the end of 1975 there were clear differences between the stands and views of the NM and those of the majority of the organizations in the PRM with respect to their objectives. Faruq Qaddumi, the PLO leader in charge of foreign affairs, maintained that Franjiya's accusations that the PRM was not abiding by the Cairo Agreement reinforced the intentions of the conservative forces to continue threatening its presence in Lebanon. He insisted that the PRM was keen on not being involved in the conflict and that a civil war in Lebanon was in the interest neither of Lebanon nor of the Palestinians.[33] 'Arafat and his allies in the PRM were not only ready to soften the demands of the NM but also to bridge the gap separating the NM and the traditional Muslim leaders, as they had tried to do by participating in the Muslim summit meeting of December 30, 1975.[34]

The Rejection Front, and the PFLP in particular, were more willing to uphold NM demands. They proposed a decisive military attack to paralyze the forces of the conservative parties and end the Civil War. Nevertheless, the objective of such a policy was to enable the PRM to pursue its struggle against Israel rather than involve itself in side-battles in Lebanon or elsewhere.

However, by early January 1976 the situation changed drastically for the PRM, when a food blockade was imposed by the Phalangists on the Tal al-Za'tar Palestinian camp.[35] The High Coordination Committee, composed of representatives of the various parties and groups, was unable to solve the blockade issue as fighting intensified. The Phalangist Party and NLP militias also began a siege on the Palestinian camp of Dubay on January 11, 1976, on the eve of the UN Security Council discussion of the Palestinian problem. Two days later, while the battle over the Dubay camp was raging, a Maronite summit was held in Ba'abda, and a statement was issued in which the conflict in Lebanon was described as one between the Lebanese and the Palestinians. The camp of Dubay then fell into the hands of the conservative parties on January 14, 1976, and subsequently 'Arafat sent cables to Arab states claiming the the Lebanese Army had assisted the conservative parties in overrunning the camp.[36]

The response of the Arab countries to the cables and messages sent by 'Arafat was prompt. From Saudi Arabia, Kuwait, the Arab Yemenite Republic, and Tunisia, as well as other Arab countries, support for the Palestinians was strongly expressed.[37] The Arab ambassadors and diplomats in Lebanon met with Karami and later with Franjiya to avert the imminent collision between the PRM and the Lebanese Army after the food blockade on Tal al-Za'tar and Dubay had been imposed.

The attack on the Karantina-Maslakh areas was not directed against the PRM, for the vast majority of the residents of this slum area were Lebanese, mostly Shi'ites, coming from Ba'albak, al-Hirmil, and other Biqa' regions.[38] The Phalangist and NLP militias overran the area on January 19, 1976, evicted its residents, and completely leveled the houses with bulldozers. The Karantina was situated between the Beirut River and the port in the eastern part of Beirut, which was dominated by the conservative forces. Some residents of the Karantina had been armed and supported the NM. The PRM regarded the overrunning and eventual destruction of that slum area as another step taken by the conservative parties toward the partition of Lebanon.[39]

'Arafat's reaction was to attack the strategically situated town of Damur, south of Beirut, to prevent the blockade of the vital Beirut-Sidon road by the militias supporting Sham'un.[40] The Yarmuk Brigade of the Palestine Liberation Army (PLA) was ordered by the leaders of the PRM to cross the border into Lebanon from Syria on January 19, 1976. The reasons for the Yarmuk Brigade's entry was to relieve the forces engaged in the fighting in Damur, Jiyya, and al-Sa'diyyat. As Zuhair Muhsin, the leader of the Sa'iqa, explained, it was only after the Phalangists had attacked the Karantina-Maslakh slum areas and after the Lebanese Army and Air Force had been ordered to assist Sham'un and his supporters, who were being besieged in al-Sa'diyyat, that the PRM had decided to order the PLA Yarmuk Brigade to joint the PRM forces in Lebanon.[41]

The offensive against Damur was led by the Fath commander in southern Lebanon, Abu Musa. The purpose of this offensive was to prevent the Phalangists, the NLP, and their allies from surrounding Beirut. In the North the conservative forces had already taken over Dubay and cleared the Karantina-Maslakh area. On the eastern side they had blockaded Tal al-Za'tar. The PRM feared, according to Abu Musa, that the next step would be to occupy Khalda and 'Aramun from the south and then, using the Lebanese Army in Ba'abda and various military barricades, to enter by force the Burj al-Barajna and Shatila-Sabra Palestinian camps and completely surround western Beirut. From the Palestinian point of view the operation was basically military in nature.[42] The Damur and al-Saʻdiyyat battles lasted a week, and on January 22, 1976, Shamʻun's palace in al-Saʻdiyyat was occupied by the forces led by the commander of the Saʻiqa in southern Lebanon, Mustafa Saʻd al-Din, who was wounded in the battle. Both the Fath and the Saʻiqa commanders admitted that some plundering and burning of houses had taken place after the battles, while the PFLP strongly criticized these actions, especially the indiscriminate shootings in Damur.[43]

The prompt arrival of the Syrian delegation, headed by Foreign Minister 'Abd al-Halim Khaddam, on January 21, 1976, raised the hopes for a settlement to the conflict. After several meetings were held with all concerned parties, the Syrian proposed the formation of a High Military Committee (HMC) to supervise the cease-fire over all Lebanese territory. The HMC was formed on January 22, 1976, and it included six high-ranking officers, two representing the Lebanese Army, two Syrian officers, and two members of the PRM.[44] The HMC was supposed to form provincial committees in the five muhafazat of Lebanon. The Palestinians were represented on these provincial committees as well as on the branch committees to be formed in the various districts of the cities. From late January 1976, the mainstream of the PRM played a peace-keeping role through the HMC. The PRM reaffirmed in late January 1976 its stand against sectarianism and against sectarian conflict. It also reaffirmed its respect for Lebanese sovereignty and territorial integrity and stated that it regarded its presence in Lebanon as temporary. Finally, it declared its willingness to abide completely by the agreements reached between it and the Lebanese authorities.[45]

Although the PRM did not get involved in the political efforts to form a new cabinet or expand Karami's existing cabinet, it did express its support for the NM. The reason for this, according to Salah Khalaf, was that the PRM had been under attack by some of the conservative elements in the Lebanese political establishment since the crisis of May 1973, and especially since the beginning of the Civil War. He added that although the Palestinians had no wish to extend their influence beyond their camps, they would be forced to go outside their camps if obliged to defend themselves or the NM.[46] In a similar vein, the organ of the PRM, Filastin al-Thawra, stated that it regarded the relationship between the PRM and the NM as "organic," as they shared common political and socioeconomic objectives.[47]

With Ahdab's coup in mid-March 1976, the situation changed once again for the PRM, especially when he demanded the resignation of President Franjiya and the election of a new president.[48] The PRM tried from then onwards to prevent full-scale fighting and to reconcile the views of Junblat and of the Syrian regime. A delegation, headed by 'Arafat and including Salah Khalaf, Zuhair Muhsin, and Nayif Hawatmeh as members, met with President Asad on March 17, and reached an agreement not to resort to arms to force the resignation of President Franjiya but to let the changes follow constitutional procedures.[49] The PRM also exerted tremendous pressure on Junblat and his allies not to opt for a military solution to achieve their objectives. Simultaneously, the Palestinian news agency, *Wafa*, issued a statement declaring that the PRM supported the NM and would stand by it under any circumstances,[50] perhaps as a kind of reassurance to the NM that the PRM was not siding with the Syrians against it. However, the Sa'iqa, which represented the Syrians in the PRM, took Junblat to task and accused him of rekindling tensions by launching the offensive in Mount Lebanon in late March 1976, and trying to enlist the support of the PRM forces in the fighting.[51]

On the other hand, Fath was still trying to play the role of mediator by the end of April 1976, between Syria and the NM. The PRM cooperated with other elements in the HMC to ensure the safety of the members of parliament who met on April 10, 1976, to amend Article 73 of the constitution in preparation for the election of a new president.[52]

Fath was optimistic about bridging the gap between the NM and Syria. In fact, a Syrian-Palestinian agreement was reached on April 16, 1976, declaring a complete cease-fire and the revival of the HMC to enforce it in preparation for the presidential election. The agreement also repealed all proposals for an Arab or an international involvement or mediation in the Lebanese Civil War.[53] Although Junblat did not respond positively to the agreement, he was willing to postpone a confrontation with Syria until after the election of a new president. When, however, the NM reluctantly endorsed the Syrian-Palestinian Agreement of April 16, 1976, it emphasized in its statement the "independence" of the NM and its right to demand support from other Arab countries.[54]

Salah Khalaf, in an interview with *Monday Morning*, the Lebanese weekly in the English language, on April 11, 1976, maintained that the Lebanese Civil War was in its last stage and that the solution was to be a Lebanese one, which would take into consideration five "wills": the NM, the conservative parties, the PRM, the Syrians, and the "silent majority" of the Lebanese people. He also asserted that the PRM would refuse any kind of "tutelage" by any Arab regime, an indirect reference to the Syrians. He also pointed to the confusion in the role of the Sa'iqa, which he claimed was both an integral part of the PRM and a part of the ruling Ba'th Party in Syria. The confusion, he added, would eventually "bring harm to the Sa'iqa itself," a veiled threat to the Sa'iqa for being so acquiescent to the Syrians.[55] Salah Khalaf was thus voicing the growing reservations among the Palestinians about the role of the Sa'iqa and criticizing the Syrians for attempting to control the other organizations of the PRM.

By late April 1976, the PLA was asked to establish law and order in Beirut, especially in the commercial areas, and in some of the suburbs. The HMC held meetings to implement a cease-fire and prepare for the presidential elections to be held in 'Usaili Palace in Beirut. The PRM officially backed no one candidate for the presidency, but it did not conceal its preference for Raymond Iddi, the

National Bloc leader. However, in the words of Salah Khalaf, any Maronite leader would do as a new president as long as he was neutral and had not actually been involved in the fighting on the side of the conservative parties.[56]

By the time of the presidential elections, held on May 8, the NM had criticized publicly Syria's interference in the electoral process and the sending of its troops into Lebanon in mid-April 1976. The PRM was still trying to mend the bridges between the two sides, although it had begun to regard itself as fighting alongside the NM.

On May 9, 1976, Fath openly supported the NM's military campaign in Mount Lebanon, accusing the conservative parties of breaking the cease-fire in direct contradiction to the Syrian-Palestinian Agreement of April 16. Faruq Qaddumi, chairman of the political department of the PLO, informed the Arab diplomats in Beirut that the PRM would prevent the conservative parties from gaining any victories in Mount Lebanon and would safeguard the continued existence of the PRM in Lebanon.[57]

As the rift between Syria and the Fath became apparent and the PRM itself split between the pro-Syrian Sa'iqa and the Fath, the latter moved closer to the Rejection Front's position, headed by the PFLP. In a speech delivered on May 22, 1976, Salah Khalaf explained why the PRM had decided to fight with the NM in Mount Lebanon. The PRM had felt threatened by Syria and other Arab countries, he said. He added that the road to Palestine had to pass through 'Uyun al-Siman, 'Aintura, and even Junya itself to prevent any further threat to the Palestinian presence in Lebanon.[58] Thus, the decision to fight side by side with the NM and to challenge Syria made Fath's stand almost identical with that of the Rejection Front. On May 25, 1976, when 'Arafat, the leader of the PLO, decided to visit Syria, he was refused entry into the country.

The PRM accused Syria of fomenting trouble in the 'Akkar region in order to give itself a pretext for intervening militarily in Lebanon. Salah Khalaf, the second man in Fath, accused Ahmad al-Mi'mari, the commander of Lebanon's Arab Army in northern Lebanon, of bombarding al-Qibbiyat, a Christian town in 'Akkar, without the knowledge of the NM or the PRM, when it was supposed to coordinate its activities with these two organizations. The suspicion was that this had been done in preparation for a Syrian military intervention. Similarly, the PRM maintained that the conservative parties were escalating the fighting to show that without external intervention there could be no security or stability in Lebanon.[59]

With the Syrian military intervention on June 1, 1976, which marked the beginning of the seventh phase of the Civil War, it was clear that the PRM, with the exception of the pro-Syrian Sa'iqa, was going to oppose it. Was the confrontation between Syria and the PRM unavoidable? From the PRM's point of view, it acted upon three major considerations. First, since the early 1970s Junblat and his allies had cooperated with the PRM, and during the Civil War the NM had fought with the PRM. In turn, the PRM had, to a large extent, armed and trained the fighters of the NM.[60] Consequently, when the PRM had been asked by Syria to remain neutral in the confrontation between Syria and the NM, it had refused, because a weakened NM would have undermined its Lebanese popular base and in the long run could have endangered its very presence in Lebanon. Second, in spite of its "strategic relations" with Syria since the mid-1960s, the Fath had, in fact, greater freedom to operate in Lebanon. This was even more true for the members of the Rejection Front, especially the PFLP and the ALF, who were not allowed to operate at all in Syria. After the PRM's expulsion from Jordan in 1971, Lebanon was the only other country in which they could operate relatively freely. The third consideration was the PRM's objections to two basic policies pursued by the Syrians, especially after the October War of 1973. Syria had developed excellent relations with King Husain, whom the Palestinians considered an arch-enemy after their expulsion from Jordan in 1971, and the September 1970 massacre. Also, under Asad, Syria was eager for a peaceful settlement of the Arab-Israeli conflict in accordance with the UN Resolution 242 of November 1967. These two policies had roused the suspicions of the leaders of the PRM concerning Syria's long-term intentions. They therefore saw Syria's military intervention in Lebanon as a prelude to their liquidation, in the manner of Jordan's King Husain. So it was not surprising that the PRM chose to close ranks with the NM and form a united command for both. The PRM espoused the NM's call for a purely Lebanese settlement of the conflict and for the reform of the political system.[61]

On the Arab level, it called for an emergency meeting of the foreign ministers of the Arab League members, which in fact convened on June 8, 1976. Since the Ribat summit of 1974, the PLO had increased its political clout in the Arab world. The Palestinian cause undoubtedly enjoyed tremendous popular support in the Arab countries, and no Arab government could ignore 'Arafat's call for support when the PRM forces were under military attack by Syria. The actual support given to the PRM varied from mere moral support from one country to financial and even military support from another. The absence of a permanent base for the PRM forced its leadership to develop ties with all the major Arab countries, whether conservative or "progressive." The rivalries and differences among the various Arab countries could affect the PRM inadvertently, because the movement could always be used in inter-Arab squabbles. The best illustration of this possibility was the way the AFL and the Sa'iqa had become instruments in the hands of the Iraqi and the Syrian regimes. Other major Arab countries, such as Saudi Arabia, Egypt, Libya, and Algeria, were constantly trying to influence the PRM or some of its organizations. However, the PRM was, in turn, often able to obtain what it wanted by playing on rivalries between the Arab countries.

In the light of this background, one can analyze how the PRM and its ally, the NM, tried to offset the Syrian military intervention by means of other Arab countries. The first Arab countries to act were those which wanted to avert, for their own sake, a PRM-Syrian conflict. 'Abd al-Salam Jallud, the prime minister of Libya, and the Algerian minister of education, 'Abd al-Qasim Ben Mahmud, arrived in Damascus on June 5, 1976, to mediate between the two sides. Libya in particular did not want to weaken the anti-Egyptian front, which had emerged after the signing of the Second Sinai Agreement of September 1975, and of which both the Syrians and the PRM had been amongst its foremost critics. Therefore, it was of vital importance for Libya to reconcile the PRM and Syria. Egypt was at odds with Syria and the PRM, exploited the Syrian military intervention to support the PRM and the NM, and, as a gesture, reopened the Voice of Palestine, the Palestinian broadcasting station in Cairo, which had been closed in September 1975. Iraq, which was ruled by a rival Ba'th Party of the Syrian Ba'th, moved some of its troops close to the Syrian borders as a kind of pressure on the Syrians. Even before the emergency meeting of the foreign ministers of the Arab League members was convened, Libyan and Algerian mediators had negotiated a cease-fire agreement on June 7, which, however, was not observed by the Syrians.[62]

Domestically, the Fath, in cooperation with other organizations of the PRM and the NM, took over the offices and arrested some of the leaders of pro-Syrian organizations in Lebanon, such as the Sa'iqa, the Nasirite Union of the Forces of Working People, led by Shatila, and the Qunzizah branch of the SSNP. The Sa'iqa, in turn, openly accused the Fath of aiming at the partition of Lebanon and of fomenting trouble in the Arab countries.[63]

The Arab foreign ministers' extraordinary conference, held in Cairo on June 8-9, 1976, was attended by 'Arafat himself, who asked the Arab countries not to shirk their responsibility with respect to the Palestinian people.[64] The decisions of the Arab League represented a position halfway between what the PLO wanted and Syria's stand. The very fact that the Arab countries were willing to take some action through the Arab League was favorable to the PRM. The second and third points on which the conference members agreed—an immediate cease-fire and the formation of a token Arab Security Force to establish security and stability in Lebanon and replace the Syrian forces[65]—satisfied the PRM, to a certain extent. However, Syrian forces were, in fact, to be included within this Arab Security Force. Similarly, there was no explicit decision calling for the withdrawal of Syrian troops from Lebanese territory.

Immediately after the Arab League's extraordinary meeting in Cairo, 'Arafat went to Libya, Algeria, Abu Dhabi, Qatar, and Iraq to gather support for the implementation of the Arab League resolutions. On June 18, he complained that the Arab Security Force arrived in Lebanon only ten days after the resolution had been taken.[66] Meanwhile, shelling and artillery fighting continued between the Syrian forces and the Sa'iqa, on the one hand, and the PRM and the NM, on the other, in the southern suburbs of Beirut, in the central mountain area, and near Saida in the south of Lebanon.[67]

On June 21, 1976, the first 1,000 men of the Arab Security Force, half of whom were Syrian and the other half Libyan, arrived in Beirut. An agreement had been reached by Jallud, the Libyan prime minister, that the Arab Security Force would separate the Syrian troops from those of the PRM and the NM in the Saida and Zahrani areas in the South, in the districts south of Beirut, and close to Khalda and the Beirut International Airport. Part of the agreement had also been the release of the leaders of the pro-Syrian organizations arrested by the PRM and of the pro-Syrian ex-commander of the PLA, Misbah al-Budairi.[68]

As the first limited withdrawal of the Syrians began and the Arab Security Forces replaced them, Sham'un launched his military offensive against the Tal al-Za'tar and Jisr al-Basha Palestinian camps, on June 22, 1976. Sham'un, as we noted above, timed his attack with the Syrian withdrawal to prevent, among other things, any reconciliation between the PRM and the Syrians (see Chapter Two). The reaction of the PRM was to accuse the Syrian regime of being in collusion with Sham'un and his allies in their attack on Tal al-Za'tar, especially as Syrian troops were pushing against the PRM and the NM in the Biqa' and the Sanin areas in Mount Lebanon at the time when Tal al-Za'tar was under attack. The PRM argued that it was because the Syrians fought the forces of the NM and the PRM on various fronts and managed to divert them that the conservative parties were able to concentrate their forces and escalate their attacks on Jisr al-Basha and Tal al-Za'tar camps.[69] The PRM also complained of the inaction of many Arab countries and their delay in sending the troops for the Arab Security Forces. The Arab League members were called for another extraordinary meeting, held on June 30, 1976, to discuss the deteriorating and critical situation in Lebanon. The meeting's urgency was emphasized by the fall of Jisr al-Basha, on June 29, 1976, into the hands of the conservative forces.

The Arab League meeting of foreign ministers (which both 'Arafat and Khaddam attended) passed resolutions, first, to expedite the sending of Arab Security Force troops to Lebanon (which, in fact, arrived in Beirut on July 1, 1976) consisting of Sudanese and Saudi troops and, second, to form an Arab Committee, to be headed by the secretary-general of the Arab League, Mahmud Riyad, and with the foreign ministers of Tunisia and Bahrain as members. The committee's objective was to supervise a cease-fire after a meeting with all the parties concerned.[70]

The PRM set conditions for a cease-fire which included the end of the military attack on Tal al-Za'tar and the return of Jisr al-Basha to the Palestinians. The Arab League's emissary, Sabri al-Khuli, tried to hold a meeting of representatives of all concerned parties, including Khaddam and 'Arafat, in Sofar, in Mount Lebanon, on July 5, 1976. The failure to reach a cease-fire agreement in Tal al-Za'tar and the military offensive launched by the NM and the PRM in Kura and Batrun contributed to the collapse of the meeting, which prompted the secretary-general of the Arab League to call for another extraordinary meeting of foreign ministers, to be held in Cairo on July 12, 1976.[71]

In the meantime the members of the conservative parties launched a successful counterattack in Shakka and al-Kura and other areas, occupying the whole region, and defeating the NM and the PRM forces. Syrian forces in the South shelled the oil refineries in al-Zahrani and Saida. 'Arafat cabled President Sadat describing the desperate situation in Tal al-Za'tar and asking for Arab Security Forces to take positions around the camp and stop the Syrians from shelling Palestinian camps near Saida and in Beirut. 'Arafat was hoping to move Sadat to action against his Syrian rival, Asad. Sadat, on the other hand, by supporting the PRM, hoped to improve his tarnished image after the signing of the Second Sinai Agreement of September 1975. On July 12, 1976, in an Arab League meeting, the Palestinian delegation accused the Syrians of complete political and military coordination with the conservative parties and demanded a timetable for the withdrawal of Syrian troops from Lebanon and their replacement by the Arab Security Force.[72] The meeting of July 12, 1976, did not produce any tangible result, and the resolutions expressed only the Arab states' wish that relations between the PLO and the Syrians be normalized. The Arab ministers, however, gave the secretary-general of the league the authority to control the implementation of the decisions taken by the Arab League since June 10, 1976, and reaffirmed their support for the Arab Security Force and its peace-keeping mission in Lebanon.[73] The three-member committee formed by the Arab League and headed by the secretary-general, Mahmud Riyad, submitted its report to the Arab ministers. The report recommended convening an Arab summit meeting to resolve the Lebanese crisis.[74]

The PRM and especially Fath, the PDFLP, and the PFLP-GC, had shown flexibility in mending their differences with Syria with the mediation of Jallud. The PRM also arranged meetings with the Phalangist Party to solve the problems of supplying food and fuel to the two sections of Beirut. The relationship the Fath leader, Abu Hasan, had maintained with Alexander Jumayil, a Phalangist leader, had kept the dialogue going. The three meetings held between the PRM and the Phalangists between the 19th and the 21st of July, 1976, contributed to the lessening of the conflict and to the establishment of a neutral zone between the eastern and western sections of Beirut, near the museum area, where some of the Arab Security forces were posted.[75]

Mainly due to Jallud's efforts as well as to those of the Arab League, a Palestinian delegation headed by the chairman of the political department of the PLO, Faruq al-Qaddumi, and representing the Fath, the PDFLP, and the PFLP-GC arrived in Damascus on July 21, 1976, to negotiate an agreement with the Syrians and put an end to the Syrian-Palestinian confrontation. After more than a week of negotiations with the Syrians, headed by Foreign Minister 'Abd al-Halim Khaddam, an agreement was reached and signed on July 29, 1976. The Syrian-Palestinian Agreement reasserted the PRM's right to operate in Lebanon, in accordance to the Cairo Agreement and its appendixes and the Constitutional Document of February 1976. However, there was no mention of withdrawing

Syrian troops from Lebanon. In fact, the agreement stated that the Palestinians had praised the Syrians' stand with respect to the Palestinian cause and for "the support which Syria had given the PRM in its struggle against the Zionist enemy."[76] The Syrian-Palestinian Agreement proposed the immediate formation of a Lebanese-Syrian-Palestinian Committee, to be chaired by a representative of the Arab League, to implement a cease-fire and establish law and order. The reaction of the Rejection Front to this agreement of July 29 was negative. It charged that it legitimized the Syrian occupation of al-Biqa', the North, Jizzin, and other parts of Lebanon. The Rejection Front refused to enter into negotiations with Syria unless it withdrew all its troops and broke off its relationship with the conservative parties.

The Syrian-Palestinian negotiations for the implementation of the agreement of July 29 were under way in early August 1976, while the battle of Tal al-Za'tar was still raging. The PRM was able to get a great deal of sympathy for the civilians, especially the women, children, and wounded, besieged in the camp. Efforts to evacuate the wounded were only partially successful. A large number of civilians, on the other hand, remained in the camp because, according to the International Red Cross, the conservative forces were blocking their evacuation. Even the call for mercy by the secretary-general of the United Nations and Pope Paul VI went unheeded.[77] Tal al-Za'tar, which eventually fell into the hands of the conservative Lebanese forces on August 12, 1976, after a siege of 52 days, remained in the eyes of the Palestinians the symbol of their resistance and of martyrdom, the memory of which was to be cherished by all Palestinian guerrilla fighters.

In an emotional letter to the kings and presidents of the Arab countries, 'Arafat spoke of the suffering of the people of Tal al-Za'tar, who included not only Palestinians but also Lebanese rural emigrants who had fought with the Palestinians. It was reported that 2,000 had died in Tal al-Za'tar and several thousand had been wounded.[78] The fall of Tal al-Za'tar made any reconciliation between the PRM and the Syrians very difficult indeed. 'Arafat, Khalaf, and others put the blame for the fall of Tal al-Za'tar first and foremost on the Syrian regime and then on those "silent Arab regimes" who had allowed it to take place.[79] Khalaf criticized the inaction of certain major Arab countries, such as Algeria and Saudi Arabia. The only advice those Arab countries had given the PRM had been to reach "an understanding with the Syrians," he protested.[80]

The Saudi reaction to the fall of Tal al-Za'tar was to urge Arab leaders to convene a meeting on any level to stop the bloodshed in Lebanon. On his way back from the non-alignment conference in Colombo, Sri Lanka, President Sadat stopped in Saudi Arabia on August 17, and met with King Khalid to discuss the conflict in Lebanon. Kuwait proposed, in agreement with Saudi Arabia, the convening of an Arab summit conference. Eight Arab countries and the PLO agreed to the Kuwait-Saudi proposal, and on August 19, 1976, the secretary-general of the Arab League called for an Arab summit conference, to be convened as soon as possible. On September 4, the Arab foreign ministers met in Cairo and decided to convene an Arab summit conference in the third week of October 1976, with the main objective being to find a solution to the Lebanese crisis.[81]

The basic attitude of the PRM (excluding the Rejection Front) was a willingness to discuss matters, particularly with the Phalangist Party. Meetings were held between the PRM and the Phalangists under the auspices of the Arab League and the Arab Security Forces on August 21, 25, 28, and September 4, which aimed at finding a solution to the conflict. The discussions were not fruitful, however, because the Phalangist Party insisted on the withdrawal of the PRM and the NM forces from Mount Lebanon as an initial step to the negotiations, while the PRM regarded this matter as part and parcel of a total and comprehensive solution to the Lebanese conflict. The PRM insisted on a comprehensive solution before withdrawing from Mount Lebanon because it did not trust the intentions of the conservative parties, and did not wish to give up its strong card before even beginning the negotiations. In addition, it did not want to leave its ally, the NM, in the lurch. The PRM's position with respect to the conservative parties' demand for the implementation of the Cairo Agreement (which would have amounted to their withdrawal to the camps in the southern regions of Lebanon) was to refuse to abide by it until the Civil War came to an end and until a "legitimate authority," representing the whole of Lebanon and not merely the interests of one side or another, took power. Salah Khalaf maintained that if the "legitimate" Lebanese authorities asked the PRM to observe the Cairo Agreement they could implement it in "two hours." No Palestinian guerrilla, he added, was happy patrolling the streets of Beirut to keep law and order because this was not his function.[82] In an effort to defend the PRM's position concerning the controversy over the Cairo Agreement, Khalaf gave the *Nahar* newspaper a copy of the agreement, which hitherto supposedly had been top secret. The complete text of this agreement was made public for the first time when it was printed by the *Nahar* on September 5, 1976.[83]

With Franjiya's term coming to an end, the PRM became interested in developing good relations with the new president, Sarkis, who in their eyes represented "legitimacy" in Lebanon. Arab and Lebanese mediators who visited Damascus in early September 1976 were able to convene two important meetings between Sarkis, 'Arafat, and General Naji Jamil, the Syrian air force commander and vice defense minister, in the presence of Hasan Sabri al-Khuli of the Arab League, in Shtura, on September 17 and 19, 1976. In a way this meeting was a convening of the four-sided committee (Lebanese-Syrian-Palestinian-Arab League) that had been stipulated in the Syrian-Palestinian Agreement of July 29, 1976. The second meeting was disappointing to the PRM because they had wanted to withdraw their forces from Mount Lebanon only as part and parcel of a comprehensive solution to the conflict. 'Arafat was willing to begin implementing the clauses of the Cairo Agreement immediately if the Syrian troops began to withdraw simultaneously from Lebanon, in accordance with a "peace agreement" proposed by the commander of the Arab Security Force. However, according to what transpired from the meeting, General Jamil categorically refused to link Syrian withdrawal to the implementation of Palestinian-Lebanese agreements because, he maintained, Syrian withdrawal was a matter to be settled directly between the Syrian and the Lebanese authorities.[84] Sarkis tended to side with Syria on this issue and was closer in his views to those of the conservative parties on the question of the Palestinian presence in Lebanon, and especially in Mount Lebanon. Also, as Sarkis had no army of his own, he had to rely on Syrian troops to establish law and order in Lebanon.

On September 23, 1976, on the very day that Sarkis took over the presidency, 'Arafat sent him a letter reiterating the position of the PRM and its willingness to abide by the Cairo Agreement and repeating his previous claim that the PRM regarded its presence in Lebanon as temporary. He declared a unilateral cease-fire as an expression of good-will to be observed by the PRM and the NM.[85]

Five days after Sarkis was inaugurated, Syrian troops suddenly mounted an offensive on the PRM and the NM forces in Qurnayil, 'Aintura, and Sanin in Mount Lebanon. 'Arafat immediately sent cables to the Arab kings and presidents depicting the PRM as the victim of aggression, especially after negotiations with the Lebanese and the Syrians were underway.[86]

The battle raged for four days. The Syrians advanced toward Bhamdun and the villages of the 'Alay district but were met with fierce resistance from PRM and NM forces.[87] The Syrian offensive was halted on October 2, 1976, because of Arab pressure, especially that of Saudi Arabia, which implicitly criticized Syria's resort to arms instead of negotiation to settle the Lebanese conflict. The four-sided committee was able to reconvene on October 9 and 11, in Shtura, and the Arab League representative was optimistic that the working paper for putting an end to the Civil War would be accepted by all parties concerned. The Palestinians agreed on a timetable for withdrawing from Mount Lebanon. The Lebanese and the Syrian sides were concerned about a deterrent force to enable the Lebanese authorities to establish law and order in the country. The PRM's view was to expand the Arab Security Force so that it could play that role, and those decisions would then be endorsed by an Arab summit meeting.[88]

On the eve of the third Shtura meeting, which was to be held on September 13, 1976, the Syrian troops attacked the PRM and the NM forces in the Jizzin area and later in the Bhamdun-'Alay areas. 'Arafat reacted immediately by sending cables to the Arab kings and presidents accusing Syria of wanting to present the other Arab countries in the proposed Arab summit meeting with the *fait accompli* of its advances in Mount Lebanon.[89] 'Arafat also complained personally to King Khalid of Saudi Arabia and the leaders of Egypt, Libya, Algeria, and Iraq.

On October 15, 1976, the Saudi Royal Cabinet called for a six-member Arab summit meeting, to be held on the next day, in Riyadh. The idea of this small summit had been in the air since late September 1976, and with the renewed Syrian offensive, Saudi and Kuwaiti opinions that it should be held prevailed. Consequently, the leaders of Saudi Arabia, Egypt, Kuwait, Syria, Lebanon, and the PLO met in Riyadh on October 16, 1976.

The decisions of the Riyadh summit were not a setback to the PRM. After all they did endorse the Ribat Summit decision that the PLO was the sole representative of the Palestinian people. It also endorsed the Cairo Agreement, which had "legitimized" the PRM's status in Lebanon, and demanded that the PRM withdraw to the camps within 90 days. The Arab Security Forces were renamed the Arab Deterrent Forces, and the Syrian troops within it were to constitute the vast majority. The ADF would be under the command of the Lebanese president and would be expanded to 30,000 men.

In a way the PRM was able to keep its independence. Its ties to the various Arab regimes and rulers helped it to do so. If Syria's intention had been to transform the PRM into a pliant tool, subservient to its own interests, it did not succeed. Taking advantage of Arab rivalries and squabbles, the PLO's leadership was able to survive the storm it encountered during the Lebanese Civil War.

NOTES

1. Malcolm H. Kerr, *The Arab Cold War, Gamal 'Abd al-Nasir and his Rivals 1958-1970*, 3rd ed. (London: Oxford University Press, 1971), p. 115.

2. Al-Habha al-Sha'biya li-Tahrir Filastin, *'Ala Tariq al-Thawra al-Filastiniya* (Beirut: Dar al-Tali'a, 1970), pp. 136–37; William B. Quandt et al., *The Politics of Palestinian Nationalism* (Berkeley: University of California Press, 1973), pp. 60, 87.

3. One of the best sources in English on the background of Fath leaders is Quandt, *The Politics of Palestinian Nationalism*, op. cit., pp. 83–84.

4. Kamal 'Adwan, *Fath: al-Milad wal-Masira* (Beirut: al-Ra'y al-Jadid Press, 1974), pp. 45–47.

5. For the views of the PDFLP, see al-Jabha al-Sha'biya al-Dimuqratiya li-Tahrir Filastin, *Hawl Azmat Haraka al-Muqawama al-Filastiniya* (Beirut: Dar al-Tali'a, 1970). For the views of the PFLP, see al-Habha al-Sha'biya li-Tahrir Filastin, *Al-Jabha wa Qadiyat al-Inshiqaq* (Beirut, 1970).

6. Al-Jabha al-Sha'biya al-Dimuqratiya li-Tahrir Filastin, *Harakat al-Muqawama al-Filastiniya fi Waqi'iha al-Rahin* (Beirut: Dar al-Tali'a, 1969), pp. 163–67.

7. From PFLP's, "The August Program and a Democratic Solution," cited in Tareq Y. Ismael, *The Arab Left* (Syracuse, N.Y.: Syracuse University Press, 1976), p. 169.

8. Ibid., pp. 170–71.

9. As Henri Iddi, the former Minister of Public Works, stated in an interview on a French radio station. *Journal of Palestine Studies* 5 (Autumn 1975–Winter 1976): 221.

10. Mu'in Ahmad Mahmud, *Al-Filastiniyun fi Lubnan: al-Waqi' al-Ijtima'i* (Beirut: Ibn Khaldun Press, 1973), pp. 15, 26–33.

11. See the text of the Cairo Agreement as given by Abu Iyad *(Salah Khalaf)* to *al-Nahar* newspaper and printed on September 5, 1976. Antoine Khuwairi, *Al-Harb fi Lubnan 1976*, vol. 3 (Junya: Al-Bulusiya Press, 1977), pp. 296–97.

12. Kamal S. Salibi, *Crossroads to Civil War* (London: Ithaca Press, 1976), pp. 43–44.

13. For the Milkart Agreement or Protocol, see the appendix in Sham'un, *Azmat fi Lubnan*, op. cit., pp. 148–56.

14. Salibi, *Crossroads to Civil War*, p. 70.

15. *Al-Hadaf* 300, April 26, 1975, 10–11.

16. Antoine Khuwairi, *Hawadith Lubnan 1975* (Junya: Al-Bulusiya Press, 1976), pp. 23–24.

17. Ibid., p. 24.

18. Ibid., p. 58.

19. *Al-Hadaf* 301, May 3, 1975, p. 5.

20. Fu'ad Matar, *Suqut al-Inbraturiya al-Lubnaniyya*, vol. 1: *Al-Sharara* (Beirut: Dar al-Qadaya, 1976), pp. 64–65.

21. Ibid., pp. 232–34.

22. *Al-Hadaf* 301, May 3, 1975, p. 32; ibid. 318, August 30, 1975, pp. 13–14.

23. Khuwairi, *Hawadith Lubnan*, op. cit., pp. 203–04, 208, 242.

24. Ibid., pp. 217, 219.

25. Ibid., p. 253.

26. Matar, op. cit., pp. 156–57.

27. Ibid., p. 157.

28. Khuwairi, *Hawadith Lubnan*, op. cit., pp. 314–15.

29. Ibid., pp. 326–27.

30. *Al-Hadaf* 325, November 8, 1975, p. 8.

31. Ibid. 331, December 20, 1975, p. 15.

32. Zuhair Muhsin, *Mawqifuna fi al-Azmat al-Lubnaniyya* (Damascus: al-Qiyada al-Qawmiya Press, 1977), p. 59.

33. *Al-Anwar*, December 23, 1975, p. 1.

34. Ibid., December 31, 1975, p. 1.

35. See Chapter Two above.

36. Matar, op. cit., vol. 2: *Al-Makhad*, p. 71; *Al-Nahar*, January 15, 1976, pp. 1, 6.

37. Matar, op. cit., pp. 71–72.

38. *Al-Hawadith* 1003, January 30, 1976, p. 45; *Al-Nahar*, January 20, 1976, p. 3.

39. Ibid.

40. Matar, op. cit., p. 73.

41. Muhsin, op. cit., pp. 64–65.

42. *Filastin al-Thawra* 176, February 1, 1976, pp. 6–7.

43. For the role of the Sa'iqa, see *Al-Hawadith* 1003, January 30, 1976, p. 39. For the PFLP's attitude, see *Al-Hadaf* 340, February 28, 1976, p. 15.

44. The representatives of the PRM were Zuhair Muhsin and Colonel Sa'd Sayil, a Fath military commander. Khuwairi, *al-Harb fi Lubnan*, vol. 1, op. cit., p. 84.

45. Ibid., p. 99.

46. *Filastin al-Thawra* 178, February 15, 1976, p. 7.

47. Ibid., pp. 26–27.

48. According to the Sa'iqa leader, Zuhair Muhsin, Junblat and the Fath in particular participated in the preparation and execution of Ahdab's coup. Muhsin, op. cit., p. 83. According to Ghassan Tuwaini, who was a member of the cabinet at the time, Fath could not prevent Ahdab from going ahead to the TV broadcasting station without antagonizing him and his officers who engineered and backed his coup. Interview with Ambassador Ghassan Tuwaini, March 12, 1979.

49. Khuwairi, *Al-Harb fi Lubnan*, op. cit., pp. 372, 431.

50. Ibid., p. 388.

51. Ibid., p. 416.

52. Ibid., pp. 542–43.

53. Ibid., pp. 596–98.

54. Ibid., pp. 610–11.

55. Ibid., pp. 565–66.

56. Ibid., p. 566.

57. Idem, *al-Harb fi Lubnan*, op. cit., vol. 2, pp. 75–76.

58. Ibid., pp. 195–96.

59. Ibid., pp. 239, 261–62.

60. See the statement made by Ibrahim Qulailat, the leader of the INM, in *Al-Hawadith* 1004, February 8, 1976, pp. 34–35.

61. Khuwairi, *Al-Harb fi Lubnan*, op. cit., vol. 2, p. 273; see also *Filastin al-Thawra* 203, October 10, 1976, pp. 4–5.

62. Khuwairi, *Al-Harb fi Lubnan*, op. cit., pp. 342–43.

63. Ibid., p. 348.

64. *Al-Nahar*, June 9, 1976, pp. 1, 4.

65. Ibid., June 10, 1976, p. 1.

66. Khuwairi, *Al-Harb fi Lubnan*, op. cit., p. 417.

67. Layla Badi' 'Itani et al., *Harb Lubnan* (Beirut: Dar al-Masira, 1977), pp. 242–43.

68. Khuwairi, *Al-Harb fi Lubnan*, op. cit., pp. 500, 508–09, 516–17.

69. Ibid., p. 572.

70. Ibid., p. 584.

71. Ibid., pp. 619–20.

72. Ibid., pp. 664–65.

73. Ibid., pp. 663–64.

74. Ibid., p. 677.

75. Ibid., pp. 698, 707, 729–30. Father Yuwakim Mubarak attended some of these meetings, and tried to create an understanding between the Phalangist Party and the PRM.

76. Ibid., pp. 797–98.

77. Ibid., vol. 3, pp. 83–84.

78. Ibid., pp. 96–97.

79. Ibid., pp. 142–43.

80. Ibid., p. 178.

81. Ibid., pp. 114–15, 129, 154–55, 192, 285–86.

82. Ibid., pp. 302–04.

83. Ibid., pp. 387–89, 400–01.

84. Ibid., pp. 402–03, 503.

85. Ibid., pp. 466–68.

86. Ibid., p. 507.

87. See *Filastin al-Thawra* 202, October 3, 1976, pp. 15–19, 22–27.

88. Ibid. 203, October 10, 1976, pp. 6, 35–36; ibid. 204, October 17, 1976, pp. 10–19, 37.

89. Ibid., pp. 6–7, 20–26.

5

THE SYRIAN ROLE
IN THE CIVIL WAR

Syria has always had close ties with Lebanon. Prior to the establishment of the "Grand Liban" in 1920, a large section of Lebanon, excluding Mount Lebanon and some coastal areas, was part of Syria. Traditional Muslim leaders, especially the Sunni leaders, had had close ties with Syrian politicians, especially during the French Mandate period, and some maintained those ties even after independence in 1943. Arab nationalists and those who believed in the unity of the Fertile Crescent (Greater Syria) looked beyond the Lebanese borders for support and the fulfillment of their visions. The close relationship between Syria and Lebanon was symbolized by the lack of formal diplomatic relations, whereby an exchange of ambassadors or even envoys was considered unnecessary. It was often pointed out that Beirut, the Lebanese capital, was only 60 miles away from the Syrian capital, Damascus.

Inevitably, any event that took place in Syria affected Lebanon, and vice-versa. Syria was plagued by political instability ever since the first coup three years after the evacuation of French troops in April 1946. In the following two decades, Syria was central in Arab politics, mainly as a bone of contention among the major Arab powers: Iraq, Egypt, and, to a lesser extent, Saudi Arabia.[1]

The 1970s, however, were a major turning point for Syria, especially with respect to its new role in the Arab world as a whole and in Lebanon in particular. The emergence of Hafiz Asad, the former minister of defense and air force commander, as the strong man in Syria after a November 1970 coup d'état against his former leftist Ba'thist colleague, Salah Jadid, was a very important factor in Syria's changing role. After Asad was elected president in April 1971, he formed a political front with other progressive groups and parties, including the Syrian Communist Party. President Asad also acquired some charismatic popularity among the Syrian masses which was greatly enhanced by the success of the Syrian forces in the early stages of the October War of 1973. Asad pursued a foreign policy of non-alignment with the East or West. However, he relied on the Soviet Union for arms and economic aid, although he also developed sound relations with the Federal Republic of Germany and France. Unlike his predecessors, Salah Jadid and Nur al-Din al-Atasi, he was interested in a peaceful settlement of the Arab-Israeli conflict on the basis of UN Security Council Resolution 242 of November 1976. He also responded positively to U.S. overtures in both the political and economic spheres. A disengagement agreement was reached on the Golan Heights in May 1974 between Israeli and Syrian forces thanks to the shuttle diplomacy of Henry Kissinger. Consequently, diplomatic relations with the United States were resumed in June 1974.

Syria also kept ties with both the more "radical" regimes of the Arab world, such as Libya, Algeria, and the PLO, and the "conservative" regimes of Saudi Arabia and the Arab states of the Gulf. It managed to secure financial and political support from both sides. By then it had also built the second or third strongest army (after Iraq) in the Arab world. Thus, Syria under Asad was no longer a bone of contention between Iraq and Egypt or between Egypt and Saudi Arabia. It had become a major Arab power in its own right.

The repercussions on Lebanon of the growing power of Syria were tremendous. Never before had Lebanon had such a powerful regime installed in Syria, a regime which by 1975 had already been in power longer than any other regime since the end of the French Mandate. Yet another factor affected this relationship between Lebanon and Syria. Since 1958, Nasir of Egypt had been a dominant influence among the Sunni establishment and the Arab nationalists in Lebanon up until his death in September 1970. However, as Egypt, under Sadat, entered a new phase of "isolationism" and was no longer actively involved in the affairs of the Arab East, Syria became the Arab country with the greatest influence over Lebanon, an influence expressed in various ways prior to the Civil War. When fighting broke out between the Lebanese Army and the PRM in May 1973, Syria closed its border with Lebanon in support of the PRM. Gradually, a close relationship was built between President Franjiya and President Asad. It was reported that Toni Franjiya, the president's son, had business dealings with President Asad's brother, Rif'at, who held the important post of the commander of the special forces, an equivalent to a pretorian guard in the Syrian Army. Syria also cultivated good relations with Nasirite groups in Lebanon, and in particular with the Beirut-based Union of the Forces of the Working People (UFWP), a Nasirite organization which managed to elect one of its leading members, Najah Wakim, to Parliament, representing the third constituency of Beirut. Kamal Shatila, the secretary-general of the UFWP, stood by the Syrian regime throughout the various phases of the Civil War. The direct instrument of the Syrian regime in Lebanese politics on the party level was the Organization of the Ba'th Party (OBP), led by 'Asim Qansu. On the Palestinian level, there was also the Sa'iqa, which was under the complete control of Syria, while its secretary-general, Zuhir Muhsin, was the chairman of the military department of the PLO.

During the third phase of the Civil War, the pro-Syrian parties in Lebanon began to organize themselves into what they later called the Nationalist Front (al-Jabha al-Qawmiya), which included Qansu's OBP, Shatila's UFWP, a section of the Syrian Social Nationalist Party, led by Qunaizah, and, at times, Imam Musa al-Sadr's Movement of the Disinherited, as well.

The Syrian involvement in Lebanon began in the first few weeks of the Civil War, when President Franjiya appointed a military cabinet on May 23, 1975. The traditional Muslim leaders expressed strong opposition to this move, as did the NM and the PRM. On the very next day President Asad sent his foreign minister, 'Abd al-Halim Khaddam, and his vice defense minister, Naji Jamil, to mediate in the political crisis. The Syrian mediators were successful in convincing President Franjiya to give up the military cabinet experiment and to accept as prime minister Rashid Karami, who was the candidate of the Sunni establishment and who also had the support of the majority of the members of Parliament.[2] Karami, however, was unable to form his six-member cabinet without Syrian mediation and support. In fact, Khaddam, accompanied by the Syrian chief of staff, General Hikmat Shihabi, made two visits to Lebanon during the month of June for that purpose. The first visit was on June 16–17, and the second, which was crucial in obtaining the support of Junblat and the NM for the appointment of Prince Majid Arslan, a traditional Druze leader and a rival of Junblat in Karami's cabinet, was on June 29, 1975. Syria acted decisively, because on the very same day, June 29, Iraq, which was ruled by its rival Ba'th Party, called for an extraordinary meeting of the foreign ministers of the Arab League to discuss the situation in Lebanon.[3]

Whenever the conflict passed through a critical stage, Syria intervened to mediate. After the relative calm of the months of July and August, fighting flared up again in early September 1975, immediately after the signing of the Second Sinai Agreement between the Israelis and the Egyptians. The intensity of the fighting reached such a level that the Lebanese authorities asked President Asad to come to the help of Lebanon. Khaddam, the Syrian foreign minister, was sent to Lebanon on September 19, and met with Franjiya, Patriarch Khuraish, the leaders of the conservative parties, and the leaders of the PRM and the NM. At this meeting, Franjiya accused the Syrian-backed parties in Lebanon of starting the fighting. He also implied that Syria was trying to take advantage of the situation to conclude political and military agreements with the Lebanese similar to those recently concluded with Jordan. Franjiya even appeared to have threatened to resort to the Arab League or to some other major Arab countries for assistance.[4] The "Arabization" of the conflict was anathema to Syria. Consequently, it did not take long for Khaddam to clear up the misunderstanding between himself and Franjiya and make a determined effort to find a solution to the crisis. Khaddam actually negotiated a cease-fire as well as the formation of the National Dialogue Committee (NDC) to propose reforms and lead the various groups and parties to a national reconciliation.

Syria's position until this point had been almost identical to that of the PRM. It had wanted to put an end to the conflict as quickly as possible because it feared the conflict might be exploited by Israel, Egypt, or any other power for their own ends. In other words, Syria did not see a prolonging of the fighting as serving its own best interests.

Syria backed Karami in his attempt at national reconciliation and at avoiding expansion of the conflict by finding a political solution that would include some of the reforms demanded by the NM and the traditional Muslim leaders.[5] Syria continued to object to the involvement of any other Arab power in the conflict. When an extraordinary meeting of the Arab foreign ministers of the Arab League was held in Cairo on October 15, 1975, both Syria and the PLO boycotted it. Qansu, the secretary-general of the pro-Syrian OBP in Lebanon, decided that no Arab country had "the right to discuss the security and stability of Lebanon except Syria."[6]

According to Zuhair Muhsin, Syria realized that the agreement for a cease-fire was being broken primarily by the conservative parties and that the fighting was escalating during the month of November 1975. Subsequently, Syria was convinced by some Lebanese politicians that although the Phalangist Party was basically more moderate than the other conservative parties and that therefore it would be more amenable to compromise and more ready to find a solution acceptable to all parties in the conflict, the isolation and boycott imposed on the Phalangist Party by the NM had led it to harden its position. Consequently, Zuhair Muhsin himself helped in laying the ground for the visit of the leader of the Phalangist Party, Pierre Jumayil, and a delegation of members of his party to Syria on December 6, 1975. The visit was only a partial success. Although Jumayil expressed to the Syrians his willingness to introduce certain moderate reforms in the political and social system of Lebanon and to stop political mobilization against the Palestinians,[7] among his supporters, his visit was marred by the events of what became known as "Black Saturday."

On the very day of his visit to Damascus, about 200 persons, mostly innocent civilians, were massacred by the militias of the conservative parties. These events and the inability of the Lebanese authorities to enforce a cease-fire made Syria realize that not only was a cease-fire necessary but also that steps had to be taken to find a political solution based on reforms, some of which had already been proposed by the NM in the National Dialogue Committee. By mid-December 1975, Syria took the initiative and invited traditional Muslim leaders and Junblat to Damascus to allay their fears concerning the visit of the Phalangist leader and to discuss a way to put an end to the conflict. The Syrian chief of staff, General Hikmat al-Shihabi, was sent to Lebanon on December 19, to sound out the Maronite leaders on how far they were willing to go in accepting political reforms. He was trying to find common denominators between the two sides to help draw up a plan for reform. The Syrian emissary also asked the opinion of the various leaders on specific reform proposals, such as political sectarianism, electoral laws, and the power of both the president and the prime minister. He was optimistic, as some Maronite leaders like Jumayil had expressed their willingness to find a solution to the conflict in all its aspects.[8]

Syria actively pursued the course of finding a solution to the conflict after Shihabi's visit to Lebanon on December 19, a process which took almost two months and which culminated in the Constitutional Document of February 14, 1976. To begin with, Syrian officials worked with Karami and the leaders of the NM on certain specific reform proposals, which were then submitted to President Franjiya in late December 1975.[9] The conservative parties' reaction to the Syrian-sponsored proposals was not favorable. Both Sham'un and Qasis criticized them.[10] Jumayil was not enthusiastic either. He expressed the view that, although both Muslims and Christians rejected the idea of partition, under a *force majeure*, or when it was realized that both sides could not go on living in the same political community, partition would then be seen as a "natural" solution.[11] Khaddam retorted that Syria would never accept the partition of Lebanon. The Lebanese, he maintained, had two alternatives: either they could live together within the existing Lebanese state as a unified and independent nation or else, if the country was partitioned, Syria would intervene immediately and reincorporate the whole of Lebanon (including Mount Lebanon) into Syria.[12]

It was hard for President Franjiya to convince the leaders of the conservative parties to view the Syrian proposals for reform favorably. It took him three weeks to give the Syrians a reply.[13] By that time, however, it was obvious that circumstances had changed, as a blockade of food and other supplies had been imposed on Tal al-Za'tar on January 3, 1976, by the conservative militias, which later overran the Palestinian camp of Dubay and occupied the Karantina-Maslakh slum areas, evicting their inhabitants. The NM and the PRM, in turn, overran Jiyya, Damur, whose inhabitants were also evicted, and al-Sa'diyyat, where Sham'un resided. Faced with these new conditions, Syria sent, on January 16, its Chief of Staff, Hikmat Shihabi, to mediate. However, due to the critical military situation, this was not a propitious moment for mediation, and Shihabi returned to Damascus on the very same day.[14] The PRM had already mobilized the PLA forces, which were stationed in Syria, to come and assist them in Lebanon, if necessary, and on January 19, the PLA forces did enter Lebanon.

Perhaps Syria was waiting for a clear military victory by the PRM and the NM in Jiyya, Damur, and al-Sa'diyyat before attempting to find a solution. The conservative parties then might have been more willing to discuss seriously reform proposals acceptable to both sides that could constitute a basis for national reconciliation. On January 21, 1976, a Syrian delegation, consisting of Khaddam, Jamil, and Shihabi arrived in Lebanon to mediate the conflict. The urgency of the Syrian delegation's mission was particularly evident as some of the fiercest battles of the Civil War had just taken place, and, on the very same day of the Syrian delegation's arrival, the secretary-general of the Arab League had called for an extraordinary Arab summit conference to be held before the end of the month.[15] Syria acted quickly to settle the conflict before other Arab countries became involved in the mediation. Although Saudi Arabia, whose King Khalid had visited Damascus in late December 1975, supported the Syrian efforts, it also wanted more Arab involvement and therefore had proposed an Arab summit of the Arab League members, or at least of some of the members of the major Arab countries. Syria was particularly wary of its major rivals, Iraq and Egypt, which could, in an Arab summit, weaken its preponderant position in Lebanese affairs. Consequently, it convinced Lebanon to decline the Arab League offer to mediate in favor of the continuation of Syria's role in the conflict.

As Syria had been preparing the ground for an agreement since the last week of December, it was not difficult for the Syrian delegation, headed by Khaddam, to reach both a military agreement with a permanent cease-fire and a comprehensive political settlement dealing with all aspects of the crisis. The Syrians were instrumental in the formation of the High Military Committee (HMC) on January 22, 1976, composed of high-ranking Lebanese, Syrians, and Palestinian officers. The HMC met on the very same day and declared a cease-fire and then began making the arrangements needed to remove barricades and militias from the fronts in the various regions of the country. On the political level, the major parts of the settlement later became included in the Constitutional Document of February 14, 1976. The members of the Syrian delegation remained in Lebanon from January 21 to February 5, 1976, meeting with all sides, and discussing the political reforms and steps to be taken after the acceptance of these reforms. The food blockade, imposed by the Phalangists on Tal al-Za'tar, was lifted, and conservative militias were withdrawn from the Palestinian camp of Dubay on January 21, 1976.[16] The Syrian delegation met with various Christian representatives, such as the Greek Orthodox, Greek Catholic, and Protestant. It tried to allay the fears of conservative parties' leaders, especially of Sham'un, who was at first reluctant to accept the Syrian mediatory role.[17] President Asad himself gave directions to Khaddam to meet all sides to reassure them that Syria was working for the interests of all the Lebanese and was not in favor of one or the other side. Thus until January 22, Syria was basically allied to the PRM and the NM, but after that date it began to attempt a more balanced relationship with all parties concerned: the PRM, the NM, the traditional Muslim leaders, the conservative parties, and Franjiya.[18] The Syrians assured Jumayil and Sham'un, as well as the other members of the conservative parties, that they would guarantee that the Palestinians would abide by their agreements with the Lebanese authorities. In this way they were able to convince even Sham'un of their honest intentions. The Syrian delegation headed by Khaddam prepared the ground for President Franjiya's official visit to Damascus on February 7, 1976. This visit and the Constitutional Document, which was announced publicly by President Franjiya a week later, constituted the culmination of the

Syrian efforts to find a political solution to the Civil War. On the military level, the HMC and its subcommittees were generally effective all over the country. There were few incidents, and life slowly returned to normal.

The communique issued at the end of President Franjiya's one-day visit to Damascus was general. It referred to the reforms to be implemented to strengthen national unity and, more specifically, to the guarantees of the Syrian government that the PLO would abide by the Cairo Agreement. It also praised the Syrian role in Lebanon and its efforts to put an end to the Civil War.[19]

On the very same day the Constitutional Document was officially announced by President Franjiya, the Syrian mediators, Khaddam, Jamil, and Shihabi, arrived in Lebanon to help him overcome the last objections to its declaration. A compromise was difficult to reach, however, among the conservative parties, the traditional Muslim leaders, and the NM on whether to mention in the Constitutional Document that the highest political offices were to be reserved for certain sects.[20] The Syrians put pressure on the NM and the traditional Muslim leaders to accept a formula that would allay the fears of the Maronites. The Syrians were trying hard to show the Maronite leaders of the conservative parties that they were not partisans. On the other hand, the fact that the Constitutional Document perpetuated the tradition, which had been followed since 1943, of reserving the presidency of the republic to the Maronites, the premiership to the Sunnis, and the presidency of the Chamber of Deputies to the Shi'ites, did not endear the Syrians to most of the traditional Muslim leaders, let alone the NM.

Almost immediately after the Constitutional Document was read by President Franjiya on February 14, 1976, and televised to the Lebanese people, various politicians began expressing their reservations to or outright criticisms of the Document, and these were far more numerous than those who supported it. Almost all were grateful to the Syrians for the cease-fire but were critical or even disapproved of some part of the Constitutional Document. It is no wonder that the Syrian mediators immediately engaged in discussions with the various groups to get them to temper their criticism and even give their support for the document. They also wished to have support for the steps that were to follow the implementation of the Constitutional Document, namely, national reconciliation and the formation of a new cabinet or the expansion of the existing one. The Syrian mediators feared that political differences could easily lead to more violence which could, in turn, rekindle the conflict.

The Syrian mediators managed to minimize the criticism of the Constitutional Document and pacify the various parties involved. This was particularly true with respect to the traditional Muslim leaders and the NM. As a second step, after the declaration of the Constitutional Document, the Syrian delegation actively pursued the formation of a new cabinet or the expansion of the existing one. President Asad himself asked Khaddam and his colleagues to stay in Lebanon to assist in the formation of a "national reconciliation cabinet." The Syrian plan consisted of three steps: first, to change or expand the cabinet, second, to implement the Cairo Agreement, and, third, to put into effect the reform program of the Constitutional Document.[21] At first, Junblat appeared dissatisfied with the proposed reforms and called for the revival of the National Dialogue Committee to discuss such issues as secularism and proportional representation. By February 24, however, Junblat had become more flexible and willing to accept to participate in a new cabinet. Inflexibility, on the other hand, was shown by the Phalangist Party and by Sham'un's National Liberal Party, which were against any changes in the cabinet. The adamancy of these two parties made Khaddam and his colleagues leave Lebanon after a stay of almost two weeks; they laid the blame for their inability to form a new cabinet primarily on Jumayil and Sham'un and left this task to Franjiya to achieve.[22]

The Syrian initiative, which had reached an impasse by the end of February 1976, was renewed on March 9, when Khaddam, Jamil, and Shihabi returned to Lebanon. By that time they had to face new developments caused by the increasing popularity of Ahmad al-Khatib's LAA, which had been successful in taking over a number of military barracks. The question of the formation of a new cabinet receded into the background as the question of what to do with the LAA officers and soldiers occupied the Syrian mediators. The commander of the army, Hanna Sa'id, the commander of the air force, and other top-ranking officers were ready to reorganize the army, and establish a new military command to satisfy the demands of Khatib's LAA. But Sham'un and Franjiya adamantly refused. Instead, Franjiya asked Karami to dismiss some of the top officers in command of the army, which the latter refused to do, and virtually resigned in protest, blaming the adamancy of Franjiya.[23] The Syrians, who backed Karami on this issue, were not able to change Franjiya's mind. Dissatisfied with the situation and probably aware of Ahdab's imminent coup, the Syrian mediators and the Syrian members of the HMC returned to Syria a few hours before Ahdab's appearance on television, when he declared his "reformist" intentions and demanded the resignation of President Franjiya.[24] Thus, the hopes which Syria had entertained that the Civil War would come to an end after the declaration of the Constitutional Document faltered.

These later developments had placed Franjiya, the foremost Maronite supporter of the Syrian mediation, essentially at loggerheads with the Syrians. Syria also became concerned about the situation in Lebanon, and President Asad postponed his scheduled visit to France. In the fifth phase of the Civil War, that is, since the start of Ahdab's movement, the Syrians kept in contact with the various parties and politicians in Lebanon by telephone and invited many of them to visit Damascus, among them a Phalangist delegation, some traditional Muslim leaders like Kamil al-As'ad, Karami, and Sa'ib Salam, and the spiritual leaders of these Muslim sects, Mufti Khalid, Imam al-Sadr, and Shaykh 'Aql Abu Shaqra, as well as Palestinian leaders, such as 'Arafat and Salah Khalaf. All flocked to Damascus to revive the Syrian initiative.

Syria was strongly against any attempt to settle the conflict militarily or to use force to oblige President Franjiya to step down. The idea of a military solution, which Junblat was entertaining, was regarded by Syria as an unnecessary one which could only worsen the situation. The Syrians wanted to revive Karami's cabinet and the HMC and also proposed the election of a new president of the republic, with the necessary constitutional amendment. They also proposed to pass a decree showing clemency and pardoning the officers and the soldiers who had joined Khatib's LAA in order to reunify the Lebanese Army.[25]

In the meantime, in mid-March the NM under Junblat launched an offensive in the Beirut hotel district and Mount Lebanon, an offensive Syria strongly disapproved of and regarded as an obstacle to a political solution to the conflict. Syria was not willing to let Junblat gain a military victory over the conservative parties, as that would have alienated the Christians and particularly the Maronites, who, in turn, would have sought foreign intervention or opted for the partition of Lebanon. President Asad, in a speech on April 12, 1976, accused the NM of conducting a sectarian war in Mount Lebanon and thus alienating the Christians.[26] When the Syrian peace efforts had been accepted by all sides in Lebanon, Muhsin wrote, this had been "a historical opportunity for the Christians of Lebanon (and in particular the Maronites) to begin to look Eastward, and ask for protection from the Arab countries, instead of seeking (as they had hitherto), protection from Western powers."[27] He implied that now the NM was forcing them to look once again to foreign powers in the West for aid.

From mid-March and particularly from April 10, 1976, when Article 73 of the Constitution was amended to enable the Lebanese Chamber of Deputies to elect a new president, the Syrians viewed Junblat's escalation of the fighting as completely unnecessary, as otherwise, they believed, the crisis could have ended. Therefore, on April 10, Syrian troops entered the eastern part of Lebanon. The Syrians justified this act by maintaining that since the Lebanese Army had disintegrated, Syria was faced with one of two choices: either give up its initiative at solving the conflict or else intervene. It had opted for the latter, and the Syrian troops had entered into Lebanon to put pressure on the two sides to stop the fighting.[28]

The Syrians were unhappy with the attitude and activities of Junblat, and in spite of the PRM's efforts to mediate between them, the rift between Junblat and Syria had become even greater by late May 1976. On the other hand, the Syrians had regained the confidence of Franjiya and the Phalangists, especially because they found a constitutional way out for President Franjiya and for the election of a new president.

Syrian troops were already in Lebanon when the Chamber of Deputies met on May 8, 1976, to elect a new president. The very presence of Syrian troops in the country, as well as the direct pressure exerted by Syria on some reluctant deputies to vote for Ilyas Sarkis, affected the final outcome of the elections. Sarkis was favored by Syria over its long-time critic Raymond Iddi, the leader of the National Bloc Party. On the eve of the elections, the official spokesman of the pro-Syrian National Command of the Ba'th, Suhail Sukkariyya, issued a statement attacking Junblat and Raymond Iddi and praising Ilyas Sarkis for his political views and especially for his endorsement of the Constitutional Document.[29]

By the time the Syrian troops intervened militarily in Lebanon on June 1, 1976, Syria had managed to rally wide support for its intervention. On the Lebanese level, the conservative parties and President Franjiya welcomed its military intervention. A few, like Sham'un, had been apprehensive at first but had had their apprehensions dispelled later. Traditional Muslim leaders, like Imam al-Sadr, Kamil al-As'ad, Karami, and even the Sunni Mufti Hasan Khalid (a notable exception was Sa'ib Salam) supported Syria. Two major LAA commanders, Ibrahim Shahin of the eastern region of Lebanon, and Ahmad al-Mi'mari, of the northern region, defected to the Syrian side in June 1976. The LAA was not a particularly disciplined army and suffered such losses among both its leaders and its rank and file throughout the summer of 1976. Thus, those left who did oppose the Syrian intervention were the NM and the PRM, as well as Raymond Iddi.

On the international level there were four major foreign powers interested in Lebanon. First, there was Israel, who realized that Syria was intervening, in effect, on the side of the Maronite conservative parties and was on a collision course with the PRM and the NM. It was consequently too pleased to interfere, as long as Syrian troops did not move into the southern regions of Lebanon, that is, the area adjacent to Israel's northern border.

Second, there was France, which traditionally had had close ties with Lebanon, especially with the Maronites, and who supported the Syrian intervention. Khaddam, the Syrian foreign minister, had been dispatched to France on June 2 to meet his French counterpart, and both had agreed on the importance of safeguarding Lebanon's sovereignty and territorial integrity.[30] To neutralize France at least or get its tacit approval of Syria's intervention was very important. On May 22, 1976, during his visit to the United States, President Giscard d'Estaing had proposed sending French troops to Lebanon in a peacekeeping capacity, to reestablish law and order with the approval of President-elect Ilyas Sarkis and the parties concerned. It was therefore vital for Syria that France approve of its role in Lebanon and not intervene in the conflict. President Asad visited France on June 17–19, 1976, a visit which had been scheduled previously for mid-March but had been postponed because of the Lebanese crisis. He explained to the French government that Syria's military intentions were limited to reestablishing law and order in the country and to creating the necessary atmosphere for a political settlement. When this was achieved, he assured the French, the Syrian troops would withdraw.[31]

Third, there was the Soviet Union, which had no choice but to support Syria's military intervention because it had already lost Egypt from its sphere of influence in the Middle East and could not afford to lose Syria as well, since it was a strategically important country in the Arab world. Significantly, Syria chose to intervene in Lebanon on the very day when Kosygin was on an official visit to Syria, leaving the Soviet Union with no other choice but to support the Syrians.

The fourth country with an interest in the situation in Lebanon was the United States. The U.S. attitude toward the Syrian military intervention, was one of tacit approval. King Husain on his visit to the United States in late March 1976 had convinced the Ford administration that Syrian intervention would prevent a leftist takeover of Lebanon and would put an end to the conflict and that, after this was achieved, Syrian troops would withdraw from Lebanon.[32] The U.S. envoy, L. Dean Brown, who arrived in Lebanon on March 31, and stayed there until after the election of Sarkis in May, reported to U.S. Secretary of State Henry Kissinger that the role of Syria was constructive and that Lebanon was not in any danger of becoming a Syrian satellite.[33] Brown's report and the fact that Syria was in fact intervening in support of the conservative forces and in opposition to the NM and the PRM (although the intervention was declared publicly to be nonpartisan) convinced the United States to accept this intervention.

On the Arab level, Syria was bound to find strong opposition among its rivals. First, there was Iraq, which was ruled by a rival Ba'th Party and with which it had been in conflict for years. It was not difficult for Iraq to accuse Syria of betraying the Palestine cause and of no longer being a progressive country when the Syrian troops were fighting against those of the PRM and the NM. However, Iraq, although a major Arab power, was relatively isolated and not a confrontation state with Israel; therefore it did not need to match its words with deeds. Iraq did, on the other hand, move some of its troops to its common borders with Syria as a form of pressure.[34] Syria, however, knew only too well that Iraq would not intervene militarily, although it did send a few thousand Iraqi military volunteers to Lebanon to fight on the side of the NM and the PRM.

Syria's other rival was Egypt. Egypt was opposed to Syria since the latter had criticized Egypt for signing the Second Sinai Agreement with Israel. Since the beginning of the Civil War, Egypt's role in Lebanon had been minimal, consisting mainly of verbal denunciations of Syria. Egypt, however, was in favor of some Arab action but preferred such action to be taken through the Arab League. Nothing had come of that proposal from September 1975 to May 1976. Egypt's ineffective role in Lebanon during the Civil War could be contrasted to its role in Lebanon during the heyday of Nasirism between 1961 and 1970, when it overshadowed Syria, irrespective of which Syrian regime was in power. When Syria intervened militarily, however, Egypt began to play a more active role with respect to the Lebanese crisis, trying to appear as a supporter of the PRM and the NM. It did so mainly in order to improve its image in the Arab world as the defender of the Palestinian cause; since the signing of the Second Sinai Agreement, its image had been tarnished and its relations with the PRM rather strained. Nevertheless, Egypt had concentrated its activities since June 1976 through the Arab League, hoping that the Arab Security Forces would replace the Syrian troops after their withdrawal. Egypt was not willing to intervene militarily or send troops even as part of the Arab Security Forces (although the commander of the Arab Security Forces was an Egyptian, General Muhammad Hasan Ghunaim). Egypt expressed a policy of "hands off Lebanon" and believed that it was the Lebanese who had to resolve their conflict among themselves and with the Palestinians:[35]

Other major Arab countries, like Morocco, either were not interested in the Lebanese conflict or else had ties with both the Syrians and the PRM and consequently did not wish to take sides. Libya and, to a lesser extent, Algeria were in that position and therefore were trying to prevent a rift between Syria and the PRM. Libya, in particular, was worried about a weakening of the anti-Egyptian front, in which Syria and the PRM had been the major forces against the U.S.-sponsored, step-by-step, peaceful settlement of the Arab-Israeli conflict. Saudi Arabia and Kuwait, on the one hand, could not afford to go against the PRM because of their internal politics and, on the other, were trying to get Syria and Egypt to join in a united Arab front for Geneva-type peace talks with Israel.

Syria was thus in a unique position in the Arab world: on good terms with both the conservative and progressive regimes. Due to its prestige in the Arab world since the 1973 October War, and being the second major Arab confrontation state (after Egypt) with Israel, it could not be ignored by the major Arab powers. This, in part, explains why Syria was able to intervene militarily in Lebanon without creating an uproar among the ruling elements of the Arab world.

Syria's continued interest and important role in Lebanon had preceded the Civil War of 1975-76. It had played a similar role at the end of May 1973, when the Lebanese Army and the PRM had clashed. Moreover, the Syrians had been a major external mediator and actor on the Lebanese scene since the beginning of the Civil War. It had been indefatigable in trying to put an end to the fighting and conflict in Lebanon. Thus, the Syrian role as major arbiter in the conflict was acceptable to all the principal Arab countries and to some foreign powers as well.

Syria, on the one hand, continued to support the goal of the PRM for armed struggle and so on, and, on the other, criticized it for being bogged down in the internal affairs of Lebanon. It wanted to convince the leaders of the PRM to change their policies rather than to crack down on the PRM. Hitherto, no other Arab country had had a closer relationship with the PRM than Syria from the beginning of their armed struggle in the mid-1960s. After their eviction from Jordan, Syria and Lebanon remained the only two countries with Palestinian guerrillas still active politically and militarily. Perhaps it was easy to condemn Syria for its confrontation with the PRM in Lebanon, but, in fact, no other Arab country was willing or able to play the same role as Syria had played with respect to the PRM since the mid-1960s. After Jordan, none of the Arab countries had a significant or compact Palestinian population, a necessary precondition for the PRM to recruit and operate from, except Lebanon and Syria. Kuwait was perhaps the exception, but due to its geographical position it could not be used by the PRM for its operations. Therefore, it was not surprising that the Arab countries viewed the Syrian-Palestinian conflict as only temporary and believed that the two sides inevitably would be reconciled. Syria had realized that the PRM would not survive without it and that sooner or later the PRM would have to come to terms with Syria. It is doubtful, however, as some have claimed, that Syria had any serious intention of transforming the PRM into a pliant tool to serve its own interests, like the Sa'iqa was, or that it really wanted to replace 'Arafat by Zuhair Muhsin. As Muhsin himself argued, he could not become the chairman of the Executive Committee of the PLO because he was a party man, and a leading member of the pro-Syrian Ba'th and therefore would not have been able to establish what he called "balanced relations" with all the Arab regimes, as an independent (nonpartisan) leader, as could 'Arafat.[36]

Taking all these elements into consideration, it was not difficult for Syria to intervene militarily in Lebanon and achieve its objectives. President Asad, a master of political tactics, made his moves with superb timing. As we have noted above, the Syrian military intervention coincided with Kosygin's official visit to Syria. Later, when the Arab League foreign ministers met in Cairo on June 8 and 9, Syria participated and showed its willingness to compromise and accept the Arab League resolutions and peace initiatives as complementary to its own. On the eve of the conference of the prime ministers of Saudi Arabia, Egypt, Syria, and Kuwait in Riyadh on June 23, Syria withdrew some of its troops from the southern suburbs of Beirut, a move designed to show its good intentions to other Arab countries. The Riyadh Conference emphasized the need for reconciling Egypt and Syria and endorsed the decisions of the Arab League taken on June 9, 1976. President Asad also tried to explain his viewpoint to some non-aligned nations and visited President Tito of Yugoslavia between June 25 and 27. He also visited Rumania, the only Communist country which had kept its diplomatic relations with Israel after 1967, on June 27 and 28 to transmit his non-belligerent intentions to Israel and allay any fear it may have had concerning its own security.[37]

Syria's ability to combine its efforts with those of the Arab League was shown in the fact that the first contingent of the Arab Security Force was half Syrian. The Arab Security Force had never been envisaged by the Arab League as matching the troops of the Syrian Army in Lebanon in size; it was to remain only as a token peace-keeping force. When the Tal al-Za'tar battle erupted in late June 1976, Syria doubled its efforts to explain its viewpoint to Arab and foreign powers. Khaddam visited the Soviet Union on July 5-8, 1976, and President Asad sent messengers to some of the leaders of the Arab world, such as Northern and Southern Yemen, Somalia, and the North African countries, to explain his views. In a very important speech on July 20, 1976, President Asad put the blame on the PRM for deviating from their principal goals by involving themselves in the internal affairs of Lebanon. He accused them of being ungrateful to Syria, which consistently had supported them and provided them with arms and even Syrian soldiers to fight to protect their camps in Lebanon against Israeli raids. Leaving room for compromise, he pointed out that Syria had neither used its air force nor its full military capabilities to fight the PRM and the NM. On the contrary, he maintained, the Syrian troops had been trying to advance with the minimum of casualties inflicted on the other side because they still hoped that the PRM would stop fighting the Syrian Army. He also attacked some of the reform programs of the NM, which were not included in the Constitutional Document, especially those which dealt with secularism, which, Asad maintained, were unacceptable to the Muslim 'Ulama', and to most of the traditional Muslim leaders in Lebanon.[38] Syria did not want a confrontation with the PRM, but it wanted the PRM to cooperate with its forces rather than demand their withdrawal. On July 21, 1976, leading members of the PRM went to Damascus accompanied by Libyan Prime Minister Jallud to start talks with Syrian officials. The Syrian-Palestinian Agreement of July 29, 1976, which resulted from these talks, was basically a victory for the Syrians, because neither the withdrawal of Syrian troops from Lebanon nor the battle raging against the camp of Tal al-Za'tar was mentioned. Concerning the latter, Syria believed that had it not been for the rift between Syria and the PRM, Sham'un and his allies would never have dared to attack the Palestinian camps of Tal al-Za'tar and Jisr al-Basha.[39]

The fall of the camp of Tal al-Za'tar on August 12, 1976, affected the prospects for a Syrian-Palestinian rapprochement as embodied in the agreement of July 29, 1976. On the Arab level, the Saudi and Kuwaiti reaction to the fall of the camp was an urgent demand for an Arab summit conference and an emphasis on the need for Arab solidarity and for a reconciliation between Egypt and Syria as a necessary precondition of ending the Civil War in Lebanon. The Syrian attitude toward an Arab summit conference was cool. It was reported that while attending the non-alignment conference in Colombo, Sri Lanka, in mid-August 1976, Khaddam, the Syrian foreign minister, had stated that "Syria had not consulted anyone when it entered Lebanon, and would not consult anyone when it decided to withdraw from Lebanon."[40] Nevertheless, Syria eventually agreed at the Arab League council meeting of September 4, to attend an Arab summit conference to be held in Cairo during the third week of October 1976.[41] Most Arab countries (including Saudi Arabia, Kuwait, Tunisia, and Libya), called for a Syrian-Palestinian reconciliation and demanded the implementation of the July 29 Syrian-Palestinian agreement, which served that purpose.[42] On August 23, Saudi Arabia indirectly endorsed Syria's policy in

Lebanon by criticizing Junblat's attitude towards a Palestinian-Phalangist agreement, which was regarded by Saudi Arabia as necessary for the solution of the Lebanese crisis.[43] President Sadat, on the eve of Sarkis' taking office as president of Lebanon, expressed his full support for the new president, who had visited Cairo on September 18, 1976. Sadat also proposed a six-leader summit conference of Egypt, Saudi Arabia, Syria, Kuwait, Lebanon, and the PLO, to put an end to the Lebanese conflict.[44]

In the meantime, the Soviet Union's attitude had changed somewhat. It called for the ending of external intervention in Lebanon and the withdrawal of the Syrian troops. However, it also asked for a Syrian-Palestinian reconciliation and strongly criticized what it called the "extreme leftist" element in the PRM and the NM.[45] Thus, the Soviet Union had become verbally critical of the Syrian military intervention, although in effect it did nothing about it and tried not to alienate Syria too much.

From the Syrian point of view, as long as the PRM was insisting on the withdrawal of Syrian troops from Lebanon simultaneously with the withdrawal of their own forces from Mount Lebanon and linked this withdrawal to a comprehensive solution to the Lebanese crisis, there was no hope for the implementation of the Syrian-Palestinian Agreement of July 29, 1976. The Syrian Vice-Defense Minister, Naji Jamil, made this quite clear to 'Arafat in the presence of Sabri al-Khuli in the Shtura meeting on September 19, 1976.

Syria waited for Sarkis to take office on September 23, 1976, and then launched a military offensive in Mount Lebanon and Jizzin. Syria opted for a military offensive, first, because it believed that further roundtable talks among the various factions would lead nowhere, as hard-liners on both sides refused to compromise. Second, Syria felt politically stronger with Sarkis in power, whose legitimacy was accepted by most Lebanese factions as well as by all Arab countries and major foreign powers. Third, Syria had only three weeks before the proposed Arab summit conference was convened and wanted to create facts to strengthen its bargaining position at that conference.

However, Syria was faced with strong criticism from Egypt and Iraq and more significantly from Saudi Arabia, which strongly disapproved of resorting to military force. Consequently, and as a sign of its disapproval, Saudi Arabia withdrew its troops from the Syrian-Israeli front.[46] Syria suddenly stopped its advances on October 2, 1976, outside 'Alay in Mount Lebanon, to the disappointment of the conservative parties, which wanted it to continue its offensive against the NM and the PRM. A Syrian official explained that Syria, unlike the conservative parties, could not ignore Arab or international considerations.[47] Egypt, Saudi Arabia, and Kuwait exerted special efforts to convene an Arab summit to include Syria, Lebanon, and the PLO. Syria, on the other hand, wanted either to exclude both the PLO and Lebanon or else to include Jordan as well. Simultaneously, it resumed talks with the Palestinians at Shtura on October 9 and 11, but no agreement was reached. The resumption of the fighting by the Syrians in the Jizzin and Bhamdun areas on October 12-13 prompted Saudi Arabia to call officially on October 15 for a summit conference of the leaders of Saudi Arabia, Egypt, Syria, Kuwait, Lebanon, and the PLO to be held in Riyadh the next day to put an end to the war.

The decisions of the Riyadh summit conference were crucial in ending the Civil War. It transformed the Arab Security Force into an Arab Deterrent Force (ADF), increased its size to about 30,000 men, and put it under the command of the president of Lebanon, Ilyas Sarkis. The decisions of the Riyadh summit, however, did not refer at all to the withdrawal of Syrian troops from Lebanon, and, in fact, the Syrian troops already in Lebanon were to constitute more than two-thirds of the Arab Deterrent Force itself. The Riyadh summit also called for the return to the status quo ante bellum, that is, to the period prior to April 13, 1975. It urged the PLO to abide by the Cairo Agreement, which was to be implemented under the supervision of a four-member committee representing Saudi Arabia, Egypt, Syria, and Kuwait. The Riyadh summit also led to a Syrian-Palestinian and Syrian-Egyptian reconciliation and urged that a dialogue begin among the Lebanese factions for a national reconciliation. It also legitimized the Syrian military presence via the ADF, and Syria became unquestionably the preponderant Arab power in Lebanon. Not even Nasir at the peak of his power could boast of such influence on the internal affairs of Lebanon.

NOTES

1. For the period up till 1958, in which Syria played a crucial role in inter-Arab politics, see Patrick Seale, *The Struggle for Syria: A Study of Post-War Arab Politics 1945-1958* (London: Oxford University Press, 1965).

2. Fu'ad Matar, *Suqut al-Imbratuyiya al-Lubnaniyya*, vol. 1: *Al-Sharara* (Beirut: Dar al-Qadaya, 1976), p. 30.

3. Ibid., pp. 57-58, 79-80, 84-85; *Al-Nahar*, July 2, 1975, p. 8.

4. Antoine Khuwairi, *Hawadith Lubnan 1975* (Junya: Al-Bulusiya Press, 1976), pp. 219-22; and *Al-Hawadith* 985, September 26, 1975, pp. 18-19.

5. Khuwairi, *Hawadith Lubnan*, op. cit., pp. 291-92.

6. Ibid., p. 304.

7. Zuhayr Muhsin, *Mawqifuna fi al-Azma al-Lubnaniyya* (Damascus: Mataba'at al-Qiyada al-Qawmiya, 1977), pp. 59-61.

8. Khuwairi, *Hawadith Lubnan*, op. cit., pp. 546-47.

9. Matar, op. cit., vol. 2: *Al-Makhad*, pp. 34-35; Muhsin, op. cit., pp. 62-63.

10. *Al-Anwar*, December 23, 1975, pp. 1, 2, 3, 6.

11. Matar, op. cit., pp. 38, 39.

12. *Al-Nahar*, January 8, 1976, p. 1.

13. Muhsin, op. cit., p. 63.

14. Antoine Khuwairi, *Al-Harb fi Lubnan 1976*, vol. 1 (Junya: Al-Bulusiya Press, 1977), pp. 51-52.

15. Ibid., p. 80.

16. Ibid., p. 84.

17. Ibid., pp. 86-87.

18. Muhsin, op. cit., p. 86.

19. Khuwairi, *Al-Harb fi Lubnan*, op. cit., pp. 139–40, 169–70; Matar, op. cit., pp. 128–29.

20. *Al-Nahar*, February 15, 1976, pp. 2, 8.

21. Khuwairi, *Al-Harb fi Lubnan*, op. cit., pp. 196–98.

22. Ibid., pp. 219–20; see also Camile Sham'un, *Azmat fi Lubnan* (Beirut: Al-Fikr al-Hurr Press, 1977), pp. 54–56.

23. Khuwairi, *Al-Harb fi Lubnan*, op. cit., pp. 286–87.

24. Ibid., pp. 496–97.

25. Ibid., pp. 404–05.

26. Ibid., pp. 574–75.

27. Muhsin, op. cit., p. 94.

28. Ibid., p. 100.

29. Khuwairi, *Al-Harb fi Lubnan*, op. cit., vol. 2, pp. 47–48.

30. Ibid., p. 303.

31. Ibid., p. 497.

32. *Al-Anwar*, April 2, 1976, p. 4.

33. See L. Dean Brown's press interview, in *Al-Nahar*, May 12, 1976, p. 1.

34. Khuwairi, *Al-Harb fi Lubnan*, op. cit., vol. 3, pp. 917–18.

35. Ibid., vol. 2, pp. 429–30.

36. Muhsin, op. cit., pp. 115–16.

37. *Al-Nahar*, June 27, 1976, pp. 1, 4; ibid., June 29, 1976, pp. 1, 4.

38. Ibid., July 21, 1976.

39. Muhsin, op. cit., pp. 109–11. Muhsin claimed that the Sa'iqa members in Tal al-Za'tar fought with the other PRM organizations throughout the 52 days of the siege by the conservative parties.

40. Khuwairi, *Al-Harb fi Lubnan*, op. cit., vol. 3, p. 154.

41. Ibid., pp. 284–86.

42. See the attitudes of Kuwait and Tunisia, in ibid., p. 368.

43. Ibid., p. 189.

44. Ibid., pp. 443–46.

45. Ibid., pp. 145, 224, 334.

46. Ibid., pp. 542–43, 585. The Saudi troops had been in Syria since the October War of 1973.

47. Ibid., p. 552.

6

CONCLUSION

Whenever the politically dominant leadership among the Maronites—and especially the president of the republic himself—espouses a narrow conception of Lebanese nationalism, whether manifested in the pursuit of foreign policies at odds with the mainstream of the Arab hinterland or alienating the leadership of the Muslim communities (especially that of the urban Muslim masses), the precarious balance of the Lebanese political system is upset, and a crisis situation develops. Is it accidental that Lebanon enjoyed greater stability under a Maronite leadership which, when in power, pursued foreign policies compatible with those of the major powers of the Arab hinterland and chose to have a close partnership with the dominant Muslim leadership? This was the case in particular during the terms of President Bishara al-Khuri (1943-52) and President Fu'ad Shihab (1958-64). Prior to and during the Civil War of 1975-76, the dominant Maronite leadership viewed the Palestinian armed presence in Lebanon as a threat, much as Sham'un when he was president in the late 1950s perceived the rise of Nasirism. In both cases, the Maronite leadership was able to mobilize the Maronite community against that threat, and violence erupted, leading to a civil war. In the case of the 1975-76 Civil War the threat seemed even more real to the Maronites because it was a physical presence encountered in everyday life. Moreover, unlike 1958, there was no alternative Christian leadership (Raymond Iddi and Khuraish notwithstanding) to create a balance and have a moderating effect on the political conceptions of the Maronite community.

On the other hand, the motley array of parties and organizations forming the National Movement under Junblat's leadership were united only in their desire for a greater share of political power and in their support for the Palestinian Resistance Movement. The National Movement had to steer a difficult course between the Scylla of the traditional Muslim leaders, who were still dominant on the "official" political level, and the Charybdis of the Palestinian

Resistance Movement, whose military and even political power at the grass roots was at times almost overwhelming. As Junblat admitted in his memoirs, the Lebanese situation was still unripe for the kind of reform the National Movement demanded. At best this was a precocious and ill-timed "revolutionary" movement, unacceptable to both Lebanon and the rest of the Arab world.

For their part, the traditional Muslim leaders were in a real dilemma. On the one hand, they had become alienated by the president of the republic and the dominant Maronite leadership during the Civil War; and on the other, they had lost popular support among the masses to the National Movement and the PRM, a process which had begun prior to the events but which culminated during the Civil War. Finally, they had become completely dependent militarily on the NM and the PRM. It was not surprising, therefore, that when Syria intervened in the conflict some rallied to its side. It is still to be seen whether they will eventually reconcile themselves to the fact that their power has waned and accept reforms that would give a greater say to the new leadership among the rural and urban masses, who were among the main backers of the National Movement.

Although the Palestinian Resistance Movement did not want a civil war in Lebanon, its very presence, which was perceived by the conservative parties as a threat, made it a catalyst in the conflict. Unless some political changes take place in areas where the Palestinian population is concentrated, for instance, Jordan, the West Bank, and Gaza, the fate of the Palestinians as a political and military force will remain tied to Lebanon. Thus, the role of the Palestinians, both as a separate "national" movement and a revolutionary vanguard in the Arab world will continue to be linked inextricably to Lebanon in the foreseeable future.

Finally, Syria, finding itself abandoned after the signing of the Second Sinai Agreement between Israel and Egypt and faced with a rival Ba'th regime in Iraq, tried successfully to fill the political vacuum left by Sadat's "isolationism" in the Arab world. The preponderant influence of Syria over Lebanese politics is destined to continue, and it is doubtful when any other major regional power will be able to replace it or counterbalance its influence in Lebanon.

Although the Civil War in Lebanon has ended in military terms, the problems that caused it or were aggravated by it remain. It is perhaps in these concluding remarks that we should look back and view those issues that led to the Civil War of 1975–76 and the problems which are left unresolved today.

There is, first, the problem of the sovereignty of the Lebanese state (*Siyadat al Dawla*), which is regarded by the parties of the conservative Lebanese front as the major cause of the Civil War. They maintain that the armed presence of the Palestinians in Lebanon is tantamount to the existence of a state within a state and therefore an infringement on the sovereignty of Lebanon.

A derivative of this problem of sovereignty is the extent to which the Lebanese state has, in Trotsky's terms, "a monopoly over organized violence." The ineffectiveness of the state to control the growth of the private militias of both the Lebanese Front and the National Movement during the Civil War, further weakened the state's authority.

The *disintegration of the regular Lebanese Army* during the Civil War compounded this problem of sovereignty and rendered the state completely ineffective in imposing its authority over all its territory. The newly organized Lebanese Army today is less than one-third its size prior to the Civil War. The Arab Deterrent Force (composed mainly of Syrian troops) has taken the regular army's place as the major force keeping some form of law and order in the country. The question here is to what extent is it under the control of the state?

A further erosion of the sovereignty of the state has been *Lebanon's growing dependence on Syria* throughout the Civil War. Most significantly has been the almost total reliance of President Sarkis himself on Damascus in making his major foreign and domestic political decisions.

Thus, the question remains, to what extent can Lebanon resolve its problem of sovereignty, and to what extent is it necessary for it to do so before other problems can be resolved?

The second problem is that of *political reform, al-Islah al-Siyasi*. This was, in the eyes of the National Movement's leftist and progressive parties, their major objective in the Civil War. They saw political reform as the precondition for social and economic reform. Basically, theirs were class (petit bourgeois) demands couched in political terms.

What was meant by political reform? First, it meant eliminating the structural imbalance between the presidency on the one hand and the premiership and the parliament on the other, with all the attendant sectarian implications. Second, it meant widening political participation by adopting a system of proportional representation of political parties and groups on a nonsectarian basis, in the Lebanese polity.

The parties of the Lebanese Front were not in favor of those political reforms for three main reasons. First, the proposed reforms would weaken the very powerful presidency, which in the eyes of both the Phalangists and Sham'un had been a guarantee against the growing numerical majority of the Muslim communities. Second, if a proportional representation system were adopted, then the power basis of Sham'un and other traditional Christian *and* Muslim leaders would be weakened. Third, if representation was widened on a nonsectarian basis, then not only would the traditional Christian and Muslim leaders suffer but the Phalangist Party would as well, because its appeal is based on sectarianism.

Nevertheless, an important step was taken toward political reform during the Civil War with the declaration of the Syrian-sponsored Constitutional Document, which strengthened the position of the prime minister vis-a-vis the president and changed the ratio of five Muslim deputies for every six Christian deputies in Parliament to an equal proportion of one to one. The Document also abolished the recruitment of civil servants on a sectarian basis except for the highest ranking posts. This Constitutional Document, however, has not yet been put into effect. Even if this Constitutional Document were adopted as a reform program, would social and economic reform ensue?

The third major problem is that of the *Lebanese national identity*—a problem which both sides to the conflict have had to face and for which they have provided various solutions.

⌐ The Lebanese Front (the Phalangists, Sham'unists, and others) tended during the Civil War to emphasize their distinctness from the Arab world as Maronite Christians with a different history, centered around their church, and geographically confined to Mount Lebanon. On this basis they were able to justify, at times, the idea of the partition of Lebanon. However, they had to face the problems of the common cultural and linguistic heritage they shared with the Arab world, as well as the difficulty of incorporating all other non-Maronite Christians of Lebanon in their framework. Perhaps their greatest fear lay in the awareness of their declining number in relation to the Muslim communities and their inevitable decline in power as well. ⌐

To the traditional Muslim leaders and the National Movement, including the leftist and progressive parties, the crisis of identity centered around the problem of how to reconcile the Arab identity to which they adhered and their own loyalty and allegiance to Lebanon. The solution to this problem varied from one party or organization to another. On the whole, however, the attachment of Junblat as well as that of the traditional Muslim leaders appeared to be moving gradually toward an independent Lebanese entity as expressed in their demands for a political system that was both democratic and parliamentary and which they contrasted to the systems prevalent in the rest of the Arab world. Their common resistance to Syrian military intervention in the later stages of the Civil War was also demonstrative of this attitude. They neither seemed to want to isolate themselves from the Arab world nor wish to be incorporated into the Arab hinterland.

If the unwritten National Pact of 1943 described Lebanon as having "an Arab face" ("un visage Arabe"), the Syrian-sponsored Constitutional Document of February 1976 unequivocally described Lebanon as an Arab country, "un pays Arabe," although still independent and sovereign. Can this then form the basis for a national identity agreeable to all sides? Perhaps the very dominant Syrian role in Lebanon, which tied it to the Arab hinterland more than ever, will produce, paradoxically, a clearer and better defined Lebanese national identity.

SELECTED BIBLIOGRAPHY

BOOKS AND ARTICLES

Annuaire des Sociétés Libanaises par Actions. Beirut: MECICO, 1969.

Ashqar, Joseph. *Pierre al-Jumayyil fi Khidmat Lubnan*. Beirut: Dar al-Tiba'a wal-Nashr al-Lubnaniyya, 1950.

'Atiyya, Najla. *Lubnan al-Mushkila wal-Ma'sat*. Beirut, 1977.

Ayyub, S. [Al-Khuri, Sami]. *Al-Hizb al-Shuyu'i fi Suriya wa Lubnan 1922-1958*. Beirut: Dar al-Hurriya lil-Tiba'a wal-Nashr, 1959.

Binder, Leonard, ed. *Politics in Lebanon*. New York: John Wiley and Sons, 1966.

Bulaybil, Edmond. *Taqwim Bikfaya al-Kubra wa Tarikh Usariha*. Bikfaya: Matba'at al-'Ara'is, 1935.

——. *Crise au Moyen Orient*. Paris: Gallimard, 1963.

Courbage, Youssef, and Phillippe Fargues. *La Situation Demographique au Liban*, vol. 2: *Analyses des Données*. Beirut: The Catholic Press, 1974.

Crow, Ralph E. "Religious Sectarianism in the Lebanese Political System." *Journal of Politics* 24 (August 1962): 489–520.

Dahir, Mas'ud. *Tarikh Lubnan al-Ijtima'i 1914-1926*. Beirut: Dar al-Farabi, 1974.

Dakrub, Muhammad. *Judhur al-Sindyana al-Hamra': Hikayat Nushu' al-Hizb al-Shuyu'i al-Lebanon, 1924-1931*. Beirut: Dar al-Farabi, 1974.

Deeb, Marius. "Muhadarat fi 'Ilm al-Ijtima' al-Siyasi: Lubnan wal Bilad al-'Arabiya." Mimeographed. Beirut: Faculty of Law and Political Science, The Lebanese University, May 1973.

——. "Some Major Causes of the Lebanese Crisis." Paper delivered at the Middle East Studies Association of North America, Ninth Annual Meeting, November 1975, Louisville, Kentucky.

Deeb, Mary-Jane Anhoury. "The Khazin Family: A Case Study of the Effect of Social Change on Traditional Roles." M.A. thesis, The American University in Cairo, 1972.

Dhubyan, Sami. *Al-Haraka al-Wataniya al-Lubnaniyya*. Beirut: Dar al-Masira, 1977.

Entelis, John P. *Pluralism and Party Transformation in Lebanon: Al-Kata'ib, 1936-1970*. Leiden: E. J. Brill, 1974.

Farraj, 'Afif. *Kamal Junblat Jadaliyat al-Mithali wal-Waqa'i*. Beirut: Dar Ibn Khaldun, 1977.

Gemayel, Pierre. *The Kataeb and the Current Events*. Beirut: The Kataeb Party, 1969.

al-Hakim, Yusif. *Bayrut wa Lubnan fi 'Ahd al-'Uthman*. Beirut: The Catholic Press, 1964.

Harik, Iliya F. "The Ethnic Revolution and Political Integration in the Middle East." *International Journal of Middle East Studies* 3 (July 1972): 303-23.

―――. "The Iqta' System in Lebanon: A Comparative Political View." *Middle East Journal* 19 (Autumn 1965): 405-20.

―――. *Man Yahkum Lubnan*. Beirut: Dar al-Nahar, 1972.

―――. *Politics and Change in a Traditional Society: Lebanon, 1711-1845*. Princeton, N.J.: Princeton University Press, 1968.

al-Hashim, Joseph. *Sawt Lubnan fi Harb al-Sanatayn*. Beirut: Manshurat Idha'at Sawt Lubnan, 1977.

Hess, Clyde G., Jr., and Herbert L. Bodman, Jr. "Confessionalism and Feudality in Lebanese Politics." *Middle East Journal* 8 (Winter 1954): 10-26.

Hitti, Philip K. *Lebanon in History*. London: Macmillan, 1957.

al-Hizb al-Shuyu'i al-Lubnani. *Nidal al-Hizb al-Shuyu'i al-Lubnani min Khilal Watha'iqihi*. Vol. 1. Beirut: Matabi' al-Amal Press, n.d.

―――. *Al-Qadiya al-Zira'iya fi Lubnan fi Daw' al-Marksiya*. Beirut: Matabi' al-Amal Press, n.d.

―――. *Al-Shuyu'iyyun al-Lubnaniyyun wa Muhimmat al-Marhala al-Muqbila: Al-Mu'tamar al-Thalith lil-Hizb al-Shuyu'i al-Lubnani*. Beirut: Matabi' al-Amal Press, n.d.

al-Hizb al-Suri al-Qawmi al-Ijtima'i. *Al-Hizb Thawra Mutasa'ida, al-Mukhayyim*. Beirut: 'Umdat al-Thaqafa Publications, 1971.

Hottinger, Arnold. "Zu'ama' and Parties in the Lebanese Crisis of 1958." *Middle East Journal* 15 (Spring 1961): 127-40.

Hournai, Albert H. *Arabic Thought in the Liberal Age*. London: Oxford University Press, 1962.

―――. "Lebanon from Feudalism to the Modern State." *Middle Eastern Studies* 2 (April 1966): 256-63.

————. *Minorities in the Arab World*. London: Oxford University Press, 1947.

————. *Syria and Lebanon: A Political Essay*. London: Oxford University Press, 1946.

————. "Ottoman Reform and the Politics of Notables." In William R. Polk and Richard L. Chambers, *Beginnings of Modernization in the Middle East, the Nineteenth Century*. Chicago: University of Chicago Press, 1968.

Hudson, Michael C. "The Electoral Process and Political Development in Lebanon." *Middle East Journal* 20 (Spring 1966): 173–86.

————. "The Palestinian Factor in the Lebanese Civil War." *Middle East Journal* 32 (Summer 1978): 261–78.

————. *The Precarious Republic: Political Modernization in Lebanon*. New York: Random House, 1968.

————. "The Precarious Republic Revisited: Reflections on the Collapse of Pluralist Politics in Lebanon." Seminar Paper No. 2. Published by the Institute of Arab Development Center for Contemporary Arab Studies, Georgetown University, Washington, D.C.

Ismael, Tareq Y. *The Arab Left*. Syracuse, N.Y.: Syracuse University Press, 1976.

Issawi, Charles. "Economic Development and Liberalism in Lebanon." *Middle East Journal* 18 (Summer 1964): 279–92.

'Itani, Layla Badi', et al. *Harb Lubnan*. Beirut: Dar al-Masira, 1977.

Junblat, Kamal. *Al-Dimuqratiya al-Jadida*. n.p.: Lajna Turath al-Qa'id al-Shahid Kamal Junblat, 1978.

————. *Fi Majra al-Siyasa al-Lubnaniyya Awda' wa Takhtit*. Beirut: Dar al-Tali'a, n.d.

————. *Haqiqat al-Thawra al-Lubnaniyya*. Beirut: Dar al-Nashr al-'Arabiya, 1959.

————. *Mukhtarat fi Dhikra Miladihi al-Sittin*. n.p., n.d.

————. *Rub' Qarn min al-Nidal*. Beirut: Al-Hizb al-Taqaddumi al-Ishtiraki Publications, n.d.

Jurayj, Jubran. *Ma'a Antun Sa'ada*. n.p., n.d.

Karami, Nadya, and Nawwaf Karami. *Waqi' al-Thawra al-Lubnaniyya*. Beirut: Matba'at Karam, 1959.

Al-Kata'ib al-Lubnaniyya. *Gayan Kata'ibi Khatir fi Kitab Maftuh*. Beirut, 1956.

Kerr, Malcolm H. *The Arab Cold War, Gamal 'Abd al-Nasir and His Rivals 1958-1970*. 3rd ed. London: Oxford University Press, 1971.

Khalaf, Samir, and Per Kongstadt. *Hamra of Beirut: A Case of Rapid Urbanization*. Leiden: E. J. Brill, 1973.

————. "Primordial Ties and Politics in Lebanon." *Middle Eastern Studies* 4 (April 1968): 243–69.

Khalid, Hasan. *Al-Muslimun fi Lubanan Wal-Harb al-Ahliya*. Beirut: Dar al-Kindi, 1978.

Khalil, Khalil Ahmad. *Lubnan Yasaran*. Beirut: Dar al-Farabi, 1972.

al-Khuri, Bishara. *Haqa'iq Lubnaniyya*. 3 vols. Harissa: Matba'at Bsil Ikhwan, 1960–61.

Khuwairi, Antoine. *Al-Harb fi Lubnan 1976*. 3 vols. Junya: Al-Bulusiya Press, 1977.

————. *Hawadith Lubnan 1975*. Junya: Al-Bulusiya Press, 1976.

Kishli, Muhammad. *Al-Azma al-Lubaniyya wal-Wujud al-Filastini*. Beirut: Dar Ibn-Khaldun, 1975.

Longrigg, Stephen Hensley. *Syria and Lebanon Under French Mandate*. London: Oxford University Press, 1958.

Lubnan al-Akhar. *Mu'tamar Hawl al-'Almana wal-Hawiya al-'Arabiya*. Beirut: Matabi' Dar Sadir, 1976.

Malha, Jean. *Majmu'at al-Bayanat al-Wizariya al-Lubnaniyya*. Beirut: Maktabat Khayyat, n.d.

Malone, Joe, and Lois Malone. "Conversations in Lebanon—May 1977." Mimeographed.

Ma'luf, Jean, and Joseph Abi Farhat. *Al-Mawsu'a al-Intikhabiyya al-Musawwara fi Lubnan 1861–1972*. Beirut: Dar al-Tali'a al-Lubnaniyya, 1972.

Matar, Fu'ad. *Suqut al-Imbraturiya al-Lubnaniyya*. Vol. 1: *Al-Sharara*. [Beirut]: Dar al-Qadaya, 1976.

————. *Suqut al-Imbraturiyya al-Lubnaniyya*. Vol. 2: *Al-Makhad*. [Beirut]: Dar al-Qadaya, 1976.

————. *Suqut al-Imbraturiyya al-Lubnaniyya*. Vol. 3: *Al-Inqisam*. [Beirut]: Dar al-Qadaya, 1976.

Muhsin, Zuhair. *Mawqifuna fi al-Azma al-Lubnaniyya*. Damascus: al-Qiyada al-Qawmiya Press, 1977.

Munazzamat al-Ishtirakiyyin al-Lubnaniyyin. *Limadha Munazamat al-Ishtirakiyyin al-Lubnaniyyin? Harakat al-Qawmiyyin al-'Arab min al-Fashiya ila al-Nasiriya*. Beirut: Dar al-Tali'a, 1970.

Munazzamat al-Tahrir al-Filastiniya, Markaz al-Takhtit. *Yawmiyat al-Harb al-Lubnaniyya*. 2 vols. Beirut, 1977.

Al-Nadi al-Thaqafi al-'Arabi. *Al-Qiwa al-Siyasiya fi Lubnan*. Beirut: Dar al-Tali'a, 1970.

Al-Nahar. *Harb al-Sanatayn*. [Beirut]: Dar al-Nahar, [1977].

Nasr, J. A. *Mihnat Lubnan fi Thawrat al-Yasar*. [Beirut]: Dar al-'Amal, 1977.

Owen, Roger, ed. *Essays on the Crisis in Lebanon*. London: Ithaca Press, 1976.

Polk, William R. *The Opening of South Lebanon, 1788-1840: A Study of the Impact of the West on the Middle East*. Cambridge, Mass.: Harvard University Press, 1963.

Quandt, William B., et al. *The Politics of Palestinian Nationalism*. Berkeley: University of California Press, 1973.

Qubain, Fahim I. *Crisis in Lebanon*. Washington, D.C.: The Middle East Institute, 1961.

al-Riyashi, Iskandar. *Al-Ayam al-Lubnaniyya*. Beirut: Sharikat al-Tabi' wal-Nashr al-Lubnaniyya, n.d.

———. *Qabl wa Ba'd 1918 ila 1941*. n.p., n.d.

Sa'ada, George 'Arij. *Tarikh al-Intikhabat fi Lubnan min Sadr al-Tarikh hatta al-Yawm*. Beirut: Dar Wikalat al-Nashr al-'Arabiya, 1964.

Salem, Elie. "Cabinet Politics in Lebanon." *Middle East Journal* 21 (Autumn 1967): 488-502.

———. *Modernization Without Revolution: Lebanon's Experience*. Bloomington: Indiana University Press, 1973.

Salibi, Kamal S. *Crossroads to Civil War: Lebanon 1958-1976*. London: Ithaca Press, 1976.

———. "Lebanon Since the Crisis of 1958." *The World Today* 17 (January 1961): 32-42.

———. "Lebanon under Fuad Chehab 1958-1964." *Middle Eastern Studies* 2 (April 1966): 211-26.

———. *The Modern History of Lebanon*. London: Widenfeld and Nicholson, 1965.

Seale, Patrick. *The Struggle for Syria: A Study of Post-War Arab Politics 1945-1958*. London: Oxford University Press, 1965.

Sham'un, Camile. *Azmat fi Lubnan*. Beirut: Al-Fikr al-Hurr Press, 1977.

Sharara, Waddah. *Fi Usul Lubnan al-Ta'ifi Khat al-Yamin al-Jamahiri*. Beirut: Dar al-Tali'a, 1975.

al-Shawi, Niqula. *Kitabat wa Dirasat*. Beirut: Dar al-Farabi, n.d.

Smock, David R., and Audrey C. Smock. *The Politics of Pluralism: A Comparative Study of Lebanon and Ghana*. New York: Elsevier, 1975.

Stoakes, Frank. "The Civil War in Lebanon." *The World Today* (January 1976): 8-17.

———. "The Supervigilantes: the Lebanese Kataeb Party as Builder, Surrogate and Defender of the State." *Middle Eastern Studies* 11 (October 1975): 215-36.

147

Suleiman, Michael W. *Political Parties in Lebanon: The Challenge of a Fragmented Political Culture*. Ithaca, N.Y.: Cornell University Press, 1967.

al-Sulh, 'Adil. *Hizb al-Istiqlal al-Jumhuri min al-Muqawama al-Wataniya Ayam al-Intidab al-Frnsi*. Beirut: Dar al-Tali'a, 1970.

Taqiy al-Din, Sulayman. *Al-Tatawwur al-Tarikhi lil-Mushkila al-Lubnaniyya (1920–1970)*. Beirut: Dar Ibn Khaldun, 1977.

Tuwayni, Ghassan. *Kitab al-Harb 1975–1976*. Beirut: Dar al-Nahar lil-Nashr, 1977.

Ziyada, Ma'n, et al. *Lubnan: Al-Hadara al-Wahida*. Beirut: Al-Nadi al-Thaqafi al-'Arabi Publications, 1977.

Zuwiya, Jalal. *The Parliamentary Election of Lebanon, 1968*. Leiden: E. J. Brill, 1972.

Zuwiyya, Yamak Labib. *Al-Hizb al-Qawmi al-Ijtima'i: Tahlil wa Taqyim*. Trans. by Joseph Shuwairi. Beirut: Dar Ibn Khaldun, 1973.

———. *The Syrian Social Nationalist Party: An Ideological Analysis*. Cambridge, Mass.: Harvard University Press, 1966.

PERIODICALS

Al-Anwar, Daily, Beirut, 1975–76.

Al-Nahar, Daily, Beirut, 1975–76.

Filastin al-Thawra, Weekly, Beirut, 1975–76.

Al-Hadaf, Weekly, Beirut, 1975–76.

Al-Hawadith, Weekly, Beirut, 1975–76.

Al-Sayyad, Weekly, Beirut, 1975–76.

Al-Watan al-'Arabi, Weekly, Paris, 1978.

INDEX

downplay fighting, 77–78; cabinet representation, demands for greater, 88; Central Political Council of, 13, 17, 67, 69, 93; major organizations in, 62–68; military offensive under Junblat, 90–91, 130; minor organizations in, 68–70; opposition to Syrian military intervention, 131; partial acceptance of Constitutional Document, 87–88; participation in National Dialogue Committee, 78–81; political reform program of (*al-Burnamij al-Marhali lil-Islah al-Siyasi*), 74–77, [seven parts, 75–77]; pro-Syrian elements, dissidence of, 81–83; Regional Political Council of, 69; Syrian attacks upon, 118

National Pact of 1943, 5–6, 16, 33, 35, 36–37, 40–41, 42, 47, 60, 142

National Socialist Front, 25, 64

National Union Front, 31, 93

National Woolen Products, 27

nationalism: Arab, 22, 26, 61, 64, 66, 68; Lebanese, 139

Nationalist Front (*al-Jabhat al-Qawmiya*), 68, 124

NDC (*see* National Dialogue Committee)

1958 Revolution, 22, 26

NLP (*see* National Liberal Party)

NM (*see* National Movement)

North African countries, 135

October War of 1973, 112, 122, 133

Organization of Communist Action (OCA; *Munazzamat al-'Amal al-Shuyu'i*), 66–67, 71, 82, 94

Organization of Lebanese Socialists (OLS), 62, 66

Organization of the Ba'th(ist) Party (OBP; *Munazzamat Hizb al-Ba'th*), 3, 18, 19, 38, 39, 67–68, 78, 81, 123, 124, 125

Palestine Liberation Army (PLA), 12, 43, 105, 110, 114, 126; Yarmuk Brigade, 84, 108

Palestine Liberation Front (*Jabhat al-Tahrir al-Filastini*), 100

Palestine Liberation Organization (PLO), 5, 13, 17, 18, 31, 39, 51, 55, 63, 74, 77, 80, 99, 104, 106, 107, 111, 113, 115, 116, 119, 123, 125, 128, 136, 137; establishment of, 99; Executive Committee of, 102, 105, 134

Palestine Resistance Movement (PRM; *Harakat al-Muqawama al-Filastiniya*), 1, 2, 3, 4, 9–19 passim, 31, 32, 33, 34, 37, 38, 39, 40, 43, 47, 48, 52, 53, 54, 55, 63, 65, 66, 67, 69, 70, 71, 72, 74, 79, 81, 82, 83, 84, 91–95 passim, 100, 101, 105–11 passim, 114–19 passim, 123–27 passim, 130, 132–36 passim, 139–40; Cairo Agreement signed, 102–03; disagreements with National Movement, 107; divergent views held by, 106–07; fighting with Lebanese Army, 103; foothold in Lebanon obtained by, 102–03; guerrilla forays by, 102; intentions of, toward Lebanon, 104; meetings with Phalangists, 115, 117; opposition to Syrian military intervention, 111–12, 131, [reasons for, 111–12]; participating organizations, 100, 101; peacekeeping role of, 109; and Phalangists, 104; support for National Movement, 109, 110, 111, 112; support from Arab countries for, 112–13; Syrian attacks upon, 118

Palestinian National Liberation Movement (*Harakat al-Tahrir al-Watani al-Filastini*) (*see* Fath)

Palestinian National unity, 100, 101

Palestinian Revolution (*al-Thawra al-Filastiniya*), 100

Palestinians, 1, 2, 13, 14, 15, 18, 24, 27, 29, 32, 33–34, 41–42, 47, 51–52, 53–55, 63, 69, 70, 71, 72, 73, 75, 79, 81, 82, 84, 85, 94, 109, 116; Communist alliance with, 12; concentrations of displaced, 102; continued linkage of, to Lebanon, 140; and National Dialogue Committee, 105–06; peacekeeping forces of, 105, 106; role of, in 1975–76 Civil War, 99–119; Syrian-Palestinian agreements, 13, 94, 110, 111, 115–16, 117, 135, 136

Parliament, Lebanese, 8, 40, 45–46, 48, 61, 80; Chamber of Deputies, 35, 36, 37, 40, 45, 71, 72, 76, 80, 86, 89, 90, 130, [makeup of, 6, 75, 85, 141]; Shihabist Nahjist Bloc, 61, 91; Upper House proposed, 76

Partisans' Forces (*Quwwat al-Ansar*), 66

Paul VI, Pope, 116

PDFLP (*see* Popular Democratic Front for the Liberation of Palestine)

155

PFLP (*see* Popular Front for the Liberation of Palestine)
PFLP-General Command (PFLP-GC), 101,
115
Phalangist Party (*Hizb al-Kata'ib al-Lubnaniya*), 1, 2, 3, 4, 6, 7, 8, 9, 12, 14,
16, 18, 19, 26, 27, 30–36 passim, 38–
50 passim, 53–54, 55, 62, 65, 70–75
passim, 77, 78, 79, 80, 82, 83, 84, 90,
91, 93, 103–04, 105, 107–08, 125,
127, 129, 130, 136, 141, 142; Central
Council, 42; history of, 21–25; manifesto of November 6, 1975, 34; meetings with PRM, 115, 117; Political
Bureau, 42
PLA (*see* Palestine Liberation Army)
PLO (*see* Palestine Liberation Organization)
political reform program of NM, 74–77,
112. 141; army reorganization, 76–77;
civil administration, 76; constituent
assembly to manage program, 77; individual rights, 77; popular representation, 76, 85–86; sectarianism, abolition of, 75–76; separation and balance
of powers, 76
Popular Democratic Front for the Liberation of Palestine (PDFLP), 14–15, 62,
71, 101, 104, 115; views of, 101
Popular Front for the Liberation of Palestine (PFLP), 62, 68, 71, 100, 101, 104,
105, 106, 107, 109, 111, 112; views
of, 101
Popular Liberation Forces, 13
Populist Nasirite Organization (PNO), 69
prime minister, weakness of, in Lebanese
system, 86–87
prime ministers, conferences of, 11, 12, 15
PRM (*see* Palestine Resistance Movement)
Progressive Socialist Party (PSP), 62, 63,
64, 67, 68, 70, 73, 82, 83, 87
Protein Company, 27
Protestants, 127
PSP (*see* Progressive Socialist Party)

Qaddumi, Faruq al-, 107, 111, 115
Qansu, 'Asim, 3, 18, 38, 39, 68, 78, 79,
123, 124, 125
Qassis, Father Sharbal, 29, 35, 40, 42, 47,
48, 88*n*, 90, 126
Qatar, 113
Qulailat, Ibrahim, 65, 70, 93

Qunaizih, Ilyas, 68, 113, 124
Qurnayil, 118

Rabbat, Edmond, 79
Rabbat, Raymond, 78
Ra'd, In'am, 67, 93
Rafi'i, Dr. 'Abd al-Majid al-, 64, 68, 93
Ra's al-Matn, 90
Rashaya citadel, 89
Rayfun, 29
Rejection Front, 15, 104, 105, 106, 107,
111, 112, 116, 117
"Revolution" of 1958, 61
Ribat summit, 112, 119
Rifa'i, Nur al-Din al-, 2, 72
Riyad, Secretary-General Mahmud, 52,
114, 115
Riyadh, 11, 12, 15, 17, 18, 53, 55, 119,
134, 137
Riyadh Conference, 134
Riyadh summit, 17, 18, 54, 55, 94, 119,
137; decisions of, ending Lebanese
Civil War, 137
Rizq, Fu'ad, 64
Rumania, 11, 134

Sa'ada, Antun, 22, 67
Sa'ada, George, 46
Sabah, Prince, 17, 94
Sabbagh, Hasib al-, 105
Sa'd, Ma'ruf, 61, 69, 70
Sa'd, Mustafa, 69
Sadat, President Anwar el-, 17, 94, 115,
116, 123, 136, 140
Sadiq, Pierre, 28
Sadr, Imam Musa al-, 68, 69–70, 71, 73,
81–82, 90, 91, 124, 129, 131
Sa'id, Brigadier Hanna, 3, 32, 34, 44, 77,
88, 89, 129
Sa'id, Nuhad, 62
Sa'id, Nuri al-, 26
Saida, 60, 61, 68, 69, 70, 102, 113, 114,
115
Salam, Sa'ib, 2, 3, 14, 15, 22, 27, 31, 35,
38, 39, 44, 54, 55, 61, 64, 72, 73, 79,
81, 85, 86, 87, 90, 92, 93, 94, 103,
129, 131
Salam family, 60
Salibi, Professor Kamal, 102
Salvation Cabinet (Inqadh), 1, 2
Sanin area, 114, 118
Saqr, Etienne, 16, 19, 29, 55

157

ABOUT THE AUTHOR

MARIUS K. DEEB is a Visiting Senior Fellow at Princeton University. He previously taught at Indiana University, Bloomington, Indiana. He also chaired the Middle East Program at Kent State University, and has taught at other American and Lebanese universities.

Dr. Deeb has published widely in the area of Middle Eastern politics and history. His articles and reviews have appeared in the *International Journal Of Middle East Studies, Middle Eastern Studies,* and the *Canadian Review Of Studies In Nationalism.* He is the author of *Party Politics In Egypt: The Wafd And Its Rivals 1919-1939*, St. Antony's Middle East Monographs Series, No. 9, London, 1979.

Dr. Deeb holds a B.A. and an M.A. from the American University of Beirut, Lebanon, and a Ph.D. from Oxford University, Oxford, England.